Understanding Intensive Interaction

by the same author

Using Intensive Interaction with a Person with a Social or Communicative Impairment
Graham Firth and Mark Barber
Forward by Dave Hewett
ISBN 978 1 84905 109 5

of related interest

Autism and Intensive Interaction DVD
Using Body Language to Reach Children on the Autistic Spectrum
Phoebe Caldwell
ISBN 978 1 84905ˑ088 3

Promoting Social Interaction for Individuals with Communicative Impairments
Making Contact
Edited by M. Suzanne Zeedyk
ISBN 978 1 84310 539 8

Using Intensive Interaction and Sensory Integration
A Handbook for Those who Support People with Severe Autistic Spectrum Disorder
Phoebe Caldwell with Jane Horwood
ISBN 978 1 84310 626 5

From Isolation to Intimacy
Making Friends without Words
Phoebe Caldwell with Jane Horwood
ISBN 978 1 84310 500 8

Understanding Intensive Interaction

Contexts and Concepts for Professionals and Families

- Graham Firth
- Ruth Berry
- Cath Irvine

Jessica Kingsley Publishers
London and Philadelphia

First published in 2010
by Jessica Kingsley Publishers
116 Pentonville Road
London N1 9JB, UK
and
400 Market Street, Suite 400
Philadelphia, PA 19106, USA

www.jkp.com

Copyright © Graham Firth, Ruth Berry and Cath Irvine 2010
Foreword copyright © Dave Hewett 2010
Printed digitally since 2011

Library of Congress Cataloging in Publication Data
A CIP catalog record for this book is available from the Library of Congress

British Library Cataloguing in Publication Data
A CIP catalogue record for this book is available from the British Library

ISBN 978 1 84310 982 2

'My first intentional communication using the approach [Intensive Interaction] was with a gentleman who was said to have no interest in people or communication. He had profound learning disabilities and a number of challenging behaviours. When I first met him he was lying on the floor, banging his head against the wall/floor joint, screaming and hitting his face with his hand and forearm. I lay down on the floor a short distance away and mirrored the arm movement. Within 10 minutes we were achieving eye contact and turn taking, the screaming had stopped, the head banging and hitting had stopped. We maintained our interaction for nearly half an hour. I was totally won over by this approach'.

Marion Crabbe, Speech and Language Therapist

Dedication

At the start of this book we have included a very powerful quote from Marion Crabbe who was an exceptional speech and language therapist, friend and colleague to myself and Ruth. Marion was an inspirational woman who had a uniquely quiet and yet forceful way of promoting Intensive Interaction and working for the benefit of many people with learning disabilities. She was also instrumental in the early development work for this book before her tragic and untimely death after a short illness. We still keenly miss her, and feel her absence in so many ways. We would like to dedicate this book to her memory.

Acknowledgements

As with many things in life, there are many people who contribute to our achievements by helping develop our skills and knowledge. Such people help by example and some by direct support and encouragement. We would especially like to thank the following people.

Graham's acknowledgements are to:
Dave Hewett, Melanie Nind, Gill Firth, Christine Smith, Debbie Evans, Bernie Kirwan, Pat Moody, Marjorie Howard, Peter Coia, Mark Barber, Helen Jeffries, Nick Guthrie.

Ruth's acknowledgements are to:
Pete Mullen, Jessica Berry-Mullen, George Berry, Helen Edmunds, Catherine Tighe, Louise Jones Barbour, MW and CW.

Cath's acknowledgements are to:
Juliette Goldbart, Dave Hewett, Melanie Nind, Penny Lacey, Jane Jones, Alison Matthews, Annie Irvine, Sue Carter.

Contents

Foreword

Intensive Interaction has come a long way. Indeed, the story of Intensive Interaction is the story of a journey undertaken by practitioners who care passionately *about* their work and *for* the people who are the focus of their work. Three such practitioners write for you here. I have the privilege of inviting you, the reader to connect with the passions of the authors.

One simple sentence in the introduction summarizes what you will find within: 'The aims of the book are to help to develop practitioners' thinking and practice beyond the "initial exposure" stage.' This book will tell you much about Intensive Interaction. Indeed, it will give you a further, deep understanding of what Intensive Interaction is, what it attempts to do, the brilliant, wonderful simplicity of its central structures. Clearly, one of the fascinations for Graham, Ruth and Cath is the beauty of this intellectual landscape. They wish to share this with you and convey both their fascination and the sense of fulfilment that arises from the way in which these deep understandings further inform practice and the outcomes from practice.

I hope the paragraph above makes crystal clear the sense in which the three authors' intellectual fascination is indeed a fascination, but this fascination is simply a servant of their main motivation. Namely, in this book you will also learn much about how Intensive Interaction works to transform the life experiences of people who have the most severe learning difficulties. In fact, I suspect that you, the reader, have also now discovered this central motivation and it is one of the reasons for picking up this book.

The story of the development of Intensive Interaction is chronicled here and is, I believe, an interesting issue in its own right and something of a lesson for all of us who care about our field and the development of our work. Intensive Interaction is a rare thing. It is a practitioner innovation and then dissemination. Way back in the 1970s and early 1980s, a clever psychologist did insightful work on the observations of teaching and learning processes within the natural model of human development and their application to teaching and learning with people who have severe learning difficulties or autism. He prompted some special school teachers to experiment with their communication teaching techniques. Those teachers started achieving results which, by comparison to all other attempts at teaching, were nothing short of spectacular. They continued their endeavours, developing and refining the approach, working at the inner understandings of the approach. Some of the teachers were also somewhat academic. They wrote articles describing their work for refereed journals. They took up the responsibility to carry out formal research. They wrote books on Intensive Interaction. Then, a few of them carried on the dissemination by giving workshops, many, many workshops.

The lesson for us all is that more than twenty-five years later, Intensive Interaction remains a dissemination in progress. The lesson is that it is first very, very difficult for practitioners to develop new techniques and approaches, and then also pretty difficult to get everybody else to know about it. The task is great, the obstacles many and the lines of communication, indeed the very culture required, do not really exist. We need to remember all this for the next innovation.

We must also remember, nonetheless, that through the sheer determination and hard work of your authors, amongst others, Intensive Interaction has now achieved something like mainstream status within the field of severe learning difficulty practice. It has achieved mention within the National Curriculum Learning Difficulty Guidelines and merits two whole pages within the 2009 government white paper for adult services, 'Valuing People'. It is starting to be recognized world-wide and there is an active organization, website and newsletter. Yet to this day, I can also visit a special school where no-one has heard of it.

So, I make no observation of despair here, merely one about the way the world works. These things take time, but with belief and persistence, you can get there. The present, healthy and vigorous state of our innovation is plain to see. However, this observation also emphasizes the need for a work such as this book. The content of this book contributes further, massively, to the general, current dissemination of Intensive Interaction by giving practitioners and services further tools for understanding it and talking about it.

Let's make the point again then. The dissemination of Intensive Interaction is still a work in progress. It is still the same journey that started more than twenty-five years ago. This book is one of the most recent milestones on the journey and it is a significant one. The three writers working here were not among the original innovators, those people are few now in our work. Graham, Ruth and Cath are among the present torch bearers for Intensive Interaction and have been for more than fifteen years. I know from much personal and professional experience of these three practitioners the extent to which they care about what they do and the extent of their fervent desire to share their knowledge and passion with you. Welcome to *Understanding Intensive Interaction: Context and Concepts for Professionals and Families.*

Dave Hewett
Malvern, November 2009

Introduction

This is a book for people who already have some knowledge about Intensive Interaction and, perhaps, some experience of using the approach. The aims of the book are to help to develop practitioners' thinking and practice beyond the 'initial exposure' stage.

We are three experienced professionals from complementary disciplines: Graham, with extensive experiences of the care and special education sectors; Cath, a highly experienced speech and language therapist and Intensive Interaction practitioner; and finally Ruth, a consultant clinical psychologist. We work mainly, although not entirely, in adult learning disability services. With our combined experiences, and our different (but complementary) professional perspectives, we thought that we could create a book that would look at the central conceptual definitions of Intensive Interaction, and then move out through some of the philosophical and theoretical issues associated with the approach. We also offer our views on some of the practical issues of actually using Intensive Interaction. Such a combination of viewpoints would, we thought, have an advantage in guarding against the book becoming overly reliant on the views of a single professional or personal perspective.

We are aware that Intensive Interaction is used by many different people. Some are being paid to support people with communicative impairments, others are family members. Some have professional qualifications, others have vocational qualifications and some have no qualifications. And some have a lot of experience of working in care settings whereas others are at the beginning of their careers. This book is intended to be accessible and useful to all these people. We believe that Intensive Interaction is not (and should not be) owned by any one individual or group of individuals and that no-one should feel excluded from being able to practise it and adding to what we know about it.

We decided to set out our ideas in a clearly focused and structured way that would enable the reader to access any subjects of interest most easily. The book layout is also designed to facilitate dipping in and out of the book – readers can take in as many or as few sections as they wish in a single sitting.

In some disciplines things can be categorized as right or wrong, but this is very often not the case in the human sciences. Intensive Interaction is a multi-faceted concept that can be understood and used in different ways (in this book we describe these as educational, therapeutic and companionship). One way of understanding Intensive Interaction is not more correct than any other – the different ways in which it can be conceptualized can be complementary and learning from within one domain (such as research in an educational setting) can have implications for another (such as the therapeutic potential of the approach). This illustrates our general belief that there are no right or wrong answers about issues connected with Intensive Interaction, just different perspectives. And it is our own perspectives that we present in this book – not the last word, but our reflections on various topics that we trust will stimulate the readers' own thinking.

We believe that Intensive Interaction will be developed most effectively and creatively (at the levels of both theory and practice) if its proponents can combine their expertise. This point is well made by M. Suzanne Zeedyk in the introduction to her edited book, *Promoting Social Interaction for Individuals with Communicative Impairments* (2008, pp.7–19). This book draws together material from writers with diverse backgrounds such as those who work directly with people with communicative impairments and researchers who have conducted empirical studies. In collecting this work into one volume, Zeedyk aims to illustrate that although there is great diversity in the range of people who are interested in understanding human interaction, the issues that are being addressed are 'not disconnected and separate. They have an underlying base that gives them more commonality than may at first be apparent. Recognizing this unity across domains can foster both theoretical and applied insights' (2008, p.7).

As authors of this book we have overlapping but distinct areas of knowledge and clinical experience which we have drawn on in our writing. This duality (overlapping but distinct expertise) is one of the overarching messages of this book – namely, that everyone has something unique to bring to Intensive Interaction, but that the approach will be taken forward most successfully though combining knowledge and insights from different individuals and different fields of study or practice. To be able to do this, everyone who is involved with the approach has to strive continually to develop their own expertise; be open to learning from others; be less fearful of revealing their individual areas of ignorance (none of us will ever know everything!), and be less protective of what they do know. This echoes some of the issues that practitioners have to face if they are to practise Intensive Interaction successfully. They have to seek continual self-development; be willing to learn from their interactive partner; manage fears about not knowing just how to interact with the person at the outset; and be willing to share what is learnt so as to create a community of interactors who can most effectively support the person's communication.

The authors of this book see their areas of particular expertise and relevant experience as follows:

Graham started working with people with a wide range of learning disabilities in the 1980s, initially on a voluntary basis and then as a paid carer (or Nursing Assistant as then titled) in a large residential 'hospital' for the 'mentally handicapped'. He qualified as a teacher and worked in mainstream primary schools for several years before commencing on a career in adult special education. After several years working in a unit that employed an 'asocial' teaching technique he became increasingly dissatisfied with his current practice and undertook some formal study and action research as a means of reflecting on how he should approach teaching people with severe learning difficulties and autism. During this period of study (with the Open University) he discovered a chapter on Intensive Interaction, and started to adopt more sociable aspects to his teaching style, formally adopting Intensive Interaction as central to his pedagogy. In 2003 he took on the role of Intensive Interaction Project Leader for Leeds Mental Health NHS Trust, and as well as training staff and undertaking research into the approach, he started to work towards creating a local self-sustaining 'community of Intensive Interaction practitioners' that would continue to disseminate and support the use of Intensive Interaction. With the creation of the Intensive Interaction Newsletter and the annual UK Intensive Interaction Conference, this work has taken on a more national aspect. Graham is one of the founding board members of the Intensive Interaction Institute.

Ruth qualified as a clinical psychologist in 1996. She had previously obtained a first degree in Psychology and worked as a direct-care worker supporting women with learning disabilities and challenging behaviour living in the community. This gave her direct experience of this incredibly demanding job and shaped her ideas about what helps people with a learning disability to achieve their potential (this is described in detail in Chapter 10, in the section *Being client-led or person-centred*). Since qualifying, her clinical work has been exclusively with adults with learning disabilities. The majority of her clients have had severe challenging behaviours; some have had associated mental health problems, and they have had a broad range of intellectual disabilities (from people with very mild levels of impairment to those with profound levels). She has therefore used Intensive Interaction with a select group of people – namely, adults who challenge. The majority of her clients would not be considered to be the 'classic' group for Intensive Interaction since they have tended to have some speech and more moderate levels of learning disability. None, however, would have been able to benefit from traditional talking therapies, and it was her wish to provide something on an individual therapeutic level that stimulated her interest in Intensive Interaction. In addition to this individual therapeutic work, she has done a lot of work with direct-care staff concerning their support of people with a learning disability. This has involved individual consultancy (inputting to the care of specific people) and providing training.

Cath qualified as a speech and language therapist in 1991 and became a specialist in learning disabilities in 1994. In 1995, Cath was given the added specialism of providing advice and training to staff working with people with profound and multiple learning disabilities. The search for meaningful, human approaches to working with this group of people led Cath to the discovery of Intensive Interaction. In 1996 Cath introduced the approach to Somerset, initially in a project within a day centre (Irvine, 1998) and thereafter by training Intensive Interaction coordinators around the whole county and negotiating supportive structures within services. Cath now works freelance, combining work in the UK in which she trains and supports Intensive Interaction coordinators in both child and adult services, and work in other countries working with children who have experienced serious deprivation in institutional establishments. Cath's Intensive Interaction work in developing countries is done in conjunction with UNICEF.

Cath has extensive experience in directly using Intensive Interaction, in training and supporting other people to use the approach and in negotiating structures within organizations to facilitate sustainable and systemic use of Intensive Interaction. Cath is also one of the founding board members of the Intensive Interaction Institute.

In the spirit of the aforementioned duality, this book is made up of some chapters where the authors have combined their thoughts (Chapters 1 and 12) and some where one author has taken the lead by writing the chapter individually. These latter chapters are not wholly solo efforts, however, as the other two authors shared their thoughts and insights with the leading author. In this way the authors have aimed to utilize their individual strengths as well as provide insights from a combined perspective.

We cannot think of any endeavour that is more worthwhile than trying to make a connection with somebody who is difficult-to-reach. We want to acknowledge the efforts of all who undertake this task and who have contributed to the well-being of individuals both directly and indirectly (through adding to the literature, sharing their experiences, inspiring colleagues and so on). This book is our contribution to this collective endeavour.

Graham, Ruth and Cath

A note about terminology

As authors we have not always been able to reach an agreement on certain issues. We spent a long time, for example, trying to decide how to refer to the 'target group' for Intensive Interaction – should it be people with a communicative impairment? People with a communicative and/or social impairment? People with profound and multiple disabilities and/or autism? Clients? Less-expert interactive partner? We all felt that it was important to get the terminology right so as not to show disrespect or cause offence. But in the end, it seemed that different language suited different contexts and that no one word was right in all contexts. So the reader will come across all these various terms, and perhaps a few more.

We also disagreed on using the term 'professional'. At a couple of points in the book, direct-care staff and professionals are referred to separately. Using this terminology is not, however, intended to convey the message that one group is seen as superior to or more professional than the other. Rather, one group have received a professional training and been assessed as meeting the standards for receipt of the relevant qualification. We recognize that in practice, such distinctions tend to set up groups which often criticize each other. Direct-care staff, for example, may dismiss the input from professionals on the basis that they do not know the individual well enough. And professionals may criticize direct-care staff for their lack of theoretical knowledge. This venting may help people to feel better in the short term, but will not move anyone forward one inch. Rather, what would be helpful would be for everyone (from whatever group) to adopt the same principles that underpin Intensive Interaction work – namely, an openness to learning from each other; an acknowledgment of the areas where we do not know; and a willingness to share what we learn. In addition, acknowledging and exploring differences can enable a resolution rather than a burying of unaired resentment. As the authors have found when writing this book, successful resolution may ultimately involve agreeing to disagree, but the process of getting there can leave everyone feeling satisfied that their view has been stated and heard.

Throughout the book there are references made to people we have worked with, and some are presented as short case studies. When we have done this we have changed the names of those involved to protect their right to confidentiality.

1

What is Intensive Interaction?

The greater part of instruction is being reminded of things you already know.

Plato

As a starting point for this book we thought that it might be useful to restate some of the fundamental aspects of Intensive Interaction, and also to look at some of the important background issues that might influence the contexts underlying the approach. To do this we thought that answering four broad questions might help give the reader a more rounded understanding of what Intensive Interaction is, and so that is what we have tried to do.

These broad questions look at what Intensive Interaction actually is, trying to define the essence of the approach; at the history of Intensive Interaction, trying to understand more about where it came from; at what Intensive Interaction is made up of, setting out its constituent techniques and practices; and finally at the specific aims of the approach, clarifying what is it for, and what can realistically be achieved.

Therefore by initially giving our answers to the questions set out below, we hope to provide a preliminary foundation upon which to build a broader knowledge base and a more profound understanding of the approach that is called Intensive Interaction.

What sort of thing is Intensive Interaction?

Ruth writes...

Definitions can seem tedious, but they are vitally important. Unless we share an understanding of what something means, we are going to run into difficulties pretty quickly. This applies to Intensive Interaction as much as any other concept. I do not say that everyone has to agree, but there has to be a starting point from which points of consensus and dispute can emerge. Just as you can't plait fog, you can hardly have an informed debate about something that means quite different things to different people. If the differences remain unconscious and unspoken, confusion and dissent will reign. If they are recognized and shared, you can then explore them.

Though we believe we should be clear about definitions, there is no perfect definition of Intensive Interaction. Any definition is going to be partial, conveying something of the meaning of what Intensive Interaction is, but missing other parts too. Definitions are not carved in stone – they should be expected to change and evolve over time as the concept develops. We have probably all been to conferences and workshops where people trot out the same definitions year after year. They become so familiar that people stop thinking about them. It is dangerous to assume that we *know* with certainty what something is (since others may have quite different definitions that they *know* are right too) and we should guard against giving definitions as the 'last word' or accepting them as such. If we stop thinking, we stop growing and developing.

Definitions can be the few lines that we read in books which often try to convey just the essence or gist of the concept being defined. At the other end of the length and complexity spectra, we each carry inside us our own definitions of things that will be partly conscious and partly unconscious and far richer than any book definition can hope to be. To improve our own practice, it is worth taking the time to really think about our own personal definition of what Intensive Interaction is and whether this is shared with colleagues or whether there may be differences that could be explored and used to enhance practice.

When we are talking about something as abstract as Intensive Interaction, definitions can get pretty complicated. Over-simplify and you lose the richness of what Intensive Interaction is. Over-complicate and you confuse with detail. Each of the authors independently wrote what they see as the essence of Intensive Interaction. Our thoughts follow and illustrate the previous points about there being no right definition and the partiality of any one definition.

- Cath wrote: Intensive Interaction is a conversation between two people, adjusted by the more competent communicator to enable an exchange that both parties can contribute to and be equal participants in.

- Ruth wrote: Intensive Interaction is an approach for trying to find a connection with someone who is difficult-to-reach.

- Graham wrote: Intensive Interaction is the process of promoting sociable interactivity between people (generally one of whom has a severe or profound learning disability and/or autism) where previously sociable interactivity was absent or difficult to maintain, thus enabling people to become participants in an inclusive sociable community.

Some of the differences in these statements make sense when you consider the professional backgrounds of the writers. Cath is a speech and language therapist and so she focuses on the communication aspects of Intensive Interaction and on the processes that takes place in dyads. I (Ruth) am a clinical psychologist and preferentially highlight the emotional and relational aspects. Graham, in contrast, particularly focuses on the problem that Intensive Interaction is seeking to solve (social isolation) and on inclusion in **communities** rather than the processes that occur in dyads. Graham has been involved in setting up large scale projects to get direct-care staff to use Intensive Interaction with clients and much reflection on the sustainability of these projects has led him to view **communities of practice** as key.

The literature also contains other definitions and descriptions which will repay some reflection. Some examples are:

…an approach to teaching and spending time with people with learning disabilities which is aimed specifically at the development of the most fundamental social and communication abilities. (Nind and Hewett, 2001, p.1)

Intensive Interaction uses our partner's own non-verbal body language to get in touch with them. (Caldwell, 2006, p.13)

> ...a practical approach to interacting with people with learning disabilities who do not find it easy communicating or being social. (British Institute of Learning Disabilities, Factsheet 2002)

The reader might like to consider the similarities and differences in these definitions and the meanings of some of the words used. For example, whereas Nind and Hewett describe Intensive Interaction as an approach aimed at **developing** people's skills, Caldwell talks about using the skills that people **already have** (their non-verbal body language) to make a connection with them. The Nind and Hewett definition talks of Intensive Interaction as an approach to **teaching** but also to **spending time with** people with a learning disability. Does Intensive Interaction always have to be about teaching or can it just be about spending time together? And can that time be therapeutic rather than educational? The British Institute of Learning Disabilities definition, written by Melanie Nind, talks about Intensive Interaction as a **practical** approach. Does this mean that it is only about practice or is there a supporting theory behind it? To give some brief answers to the above:

We consider Intensive Interaction to have a number of major uses, namely, educational, therapeutic and inclusive. The form that Intensive Interaction takes does not necessarily differ between these three, but the aims of the practitioner do. In educational Intensive Interaction, the practitioner has the aim of improving the learner's communication abilities. In therapeutic Intensive Interaction, the aim is to ameliorate the client's psychological distress (or promote their emotional well-being) and in inclusive Intensive Interaction the aim is to spend time with the person in a way that makes sense to them and which they enjoy. Perhaps the central feature of Intensive Interaction that permits these varying uses is that it is about the experience of **being with** someone. And by being with someone the formerly isolated person might, for example, learn how to communicate their intentions to other people and/or that they are valued by the other person and/or that they like spending time with other people. Most of us take these things for granted since we have been fortunate enough to learn the fundamentals of communication naturally through our infant relationship with our primary caregivers, have people around who value us, and converse easily with others around us. Intensive Interaction is for people who may not have been so fortunate, and giving them these commonplace things can require us to go to extraordinary lengths. Intensive Interaction helps us to get there.

Intensive Interaction is also about more than practice. It has a scientific basis with its roots in detailed observational studies of mother–infant interactional patterns. It has scientific support from some robust case series (e.g. Kellett, 2000, 2003, 2005; Nind, 1996) and has links to some major schools of psychological thought, particularly humanistic and positive psychology. It has a value base in which people are seen in their entirety (not broken up into 'bits' of behaviours-to-be-treated) and valued for who they are (not what they can do). The practice of Intensive Interaction is a skill which is (usually) refined by a practitioner over months or years of experience and reflection combined with knowledge of the theoretical underpinnings of the approach and its techniques. A unique feature of the approach, however, is that the practice of Intensive Interaction draws on abilities which most of us possess, since they are those that we use (automatically and unconsciously) when we interact with infants. The authors' clinical experience is that some direct-care staff intuitively use these skills to interact with the people they work with or care for, and so are doing something very like Intensive Interaction without knowing it and without needing any formal training.

Intensive Interaction, then, is a multi-faceted and complex concept. This makes it even more vital that we are clear about what we mean when we communicate about it. The potential for misunderstandings is huge. On the other hand, however, there is tremendous potential for collaboration and growth. Since Intensive Interaction is not one 'thing' that is 'owned' by any one group of experts, if the various parties interested in Intensive Interaction can speak to each other openly, they can bring a tremendous richness and diversity to our understanding of it. This will not necessarily be easy, since professionals like the clarity and certainty of owning an approach. But it is fitting that an approach that is about making connections will be best advanced through collaboration across professional boundaries.

What is the history of Intensive Interaction?

Cath writes...

Perhaps before discussing the beginnings of Intensive Interaction it would be useful to have a brief glimpse at what the world of learning disabilities looked like before the influential practitioners at Harperbury School began their experiments with the approach that became known as Intensive Interaction.

Carol Ouvry (1991) describes the historical approaches to working with children with profound and multiple learning disabilities (PMLD) within schools since 1971. These phases were also reflected in adult services for people with profound and multiple learning disabilities. Prior to 1970, children with severe and profound learning disabilities were deemed to be ineducable but with the Education (Handicapped Children) Act 1970 (HM Government, 1970) responsibility for the provision of this group of people transferred from Health to Education. For the first time in history all children were now entitled to an education. There was a paucity of knowledge about what to do with this group and activities veered towards a major focus on personal care. Ouvry calls this phase *Tender Loving Care*. For example, in 1968 Stevens wrote:

> There was an overall impression of sentimentality towards these children without much thought for their possible educational progress. Love was a word too frequently used (though now it seems we have swung too far away from the concept in this field I think) with little evidence, to me, at any rate as a newcomer that much was done about the 'love' in a way that could be described as professional. (p.4)

The next phase, *Stimulation*, aimed to challenge the passivity of tender loving care and introduced activities to stimulate, interest and entertain individuals. This was the heyday of multi-sensory rooms, bus rides and music groups amongst many other stimulating activities. These activities didn't, at this time, necessarily have any aims to 'teach' the individual anything specific and could, sometimes, result in the person being over-stimulated and confused. People were being asked to participate in activities that they had no control over, being given no choice and having no, or little, understanding of the activity.

The *Behavioural* phase came next and attempted to address the inadequacies of stimulation by structuring activities and predicting outcomes. Teaching was goal-centred rather than person-centred. Targets were decided for the individuals and programmes written and carried out by staff. Again, the individual had little control or understanding about what was being done to them. It was during this phase, when behaviourism was at its height, that various practitioners across the UK began to question what they were doing. (Despite the limitations of behaviourism, however, it is important to note that the approach challenged the existing view of people with a learning disability as ineducable.)

The aforementioned writings of Stevens were highly unfashionable when first published but the principles implicit in the book were similar to the principles that led to the development of Intensive Interaction. Roy McConkey (1981) challenged the ideas of focusing exclusively on outcomes and products rather than on process-based learning where the student was actively involved. In particular the staff at Harperbury School in Hertfordshire had recognized that communication was the key to learning but began to question why they were attempting to teach signing to students who did not have any apparent understanding of symbolic language. They were experts at shaping, reinforcing, prompting and rewarding but saw little point in what they were doing. The students were not making progress and they got little job satisfaction. In 1981 the Harperbury team began discussions and experiments with building relationships with the students. They recognized that what their students needed was for them to 'lighten up' and increase their playfulness. As a result of their experiments in playfulness and fun the students were making progress and were happier. The team, too, were happier in their work.

Thus Intensive Interaction is an approach that evolved as a result of practitioner experimentation. Rather than being driven from theory those initial practitioners began to look around for a theory to validate the playful, relaxed but successful work they were doing. In 1982 some of the staff began to look at the work of Geraint Ephraim. Ephraim (1986) was using what he called 'Augmented Mothering' and it looked similar to what was going on in the classrooms at Harperbury School. The main similarity was that both Melanie Nind and Dave Hewett along with their team at Harperbury and Geraint Ephraim had discovered that the natural and spontaneous teaching strategies that caregivers use with very young infants could also work with people with severe and profound learning disabilities. Unfortunately Ephraim published little, but his influence during this period of learning disability history is quoted by many interactive practitioners.

The Harperbury team continued to discuss, experiment and evaluate the work they were doing and by the end of 1986 they felt that they truly understood what it was they were doing. The value of teamwork is constantly emphasized by Nind and Hewett. Dave Hewett regularly reports that all the team at Harperbury was involved in the process of evolving the approach now known as Intensive Interaction. Melanie Nind reports that Dave and she weren't the best practitioners of Intensive Interaction at that time – but that they were the people who read the books, did the formal research, published articles and spoke at conferences. The name Intensive Interaction naturally evolved from the staff as the need for a label became apparent for their distinctive approach.

People involved in special education at this time report that it was a period where there was a great deal of collaborative working and sharing of information. This collaborative working was reflected in a conference held at Westhill College, Birmingham in 1987. The conference, 'Interactive Approaches to the Education of Children with Severe Learning Difficulties', is reflected upon by many people in the world of disabilities as being the beginnings of the Interactive phase. The education of children with profound learning disabilities was not the main focus of the conference. Sheila Glenn (1987) presented a paper giving an excellent overview of the theories as to why interactive approaches are feasible with people with profound learning disabilities. Mel Nind and Dave Hewett initially went to the conference as delegates, but following discussions in between sessions they were given a slot to present their work in Sheila Glenn's workshop. This was the first public airing of Intensive Interaction and was followed up by an article 'Interaction as curriculum' by Nind and Hewett in the *British Journal of Special Education* in June 1988. The *British Journal of Special Education* was widely read by teachers in special schools and the publication resulted in a great deal of interest. Harperbury became the place people wanted to visit to see the approach in action and invitations to share the work of the staff team began to pour in. Research projects were undertaken and written up in the PhD theses of Melanie Nind (1993) and Dave Hewett (1994).

Whilst the initial dissemination of Intensive Interaction was in educational settings, there was a growing interest in how it could be used in adult learning disability services, and at least in adult settings there was no National Curriculum to contend with. Other issues, however, did have an impact on the spread of Intensive Interaction in adult settings. As in educational settings, a lot of the work done within adult services was heavily based on behavioural techniques, programmes and strategies. The introduction of Intensive Interaction into environments where many staff had been trained in behavioural techniques was interesting. Where staff had been encouraged to take away people's 'twiddlies' (i.e. their personally chosen/favourite stimulatory thing) because they distracted from the person's learning and attentiveness, now staff were being asked not only to leave the person's twiddly alone – but to have one themselves and join in. Where staff had been told to give people time out or ignore behaviours that were not 'normal' (non-specific vocalizations – especially if loud, ritualistic behaviours, throwing objects), now staff were being asked to respond playfully to those behaviours. Some professionals saw responding as reinforcing unwanted behaviours rather than seeing behaviours as the only language a person had that we could join in with.

Another major barrier in the 1990s were the principles of 'Normalization'. Or perhaps to be more accurate, most of the blocks to using Intensive Interaction were not based on any of the core philosophies of Normalization, but on some of the misunderstandings of the original principles. Briefly, Normalization was a set of principles initially articulated in Scandinavia during the 1960s by Bengt Nirje (Nirje, 1969). For Nirje, Normalization meant giving people with disabilities the opportunities to have lives like everyone else. He noticed that the children who were cared for at home by their families may have had more profound disabilities, but had fewer developmental problems than the children with less profound disabilities being raised in institutions. He proposed that abnormal conditions led to abnormal outcomes. Thus, more normal conditions would lead to more normal outcomes. Few of us would argue with this. For Nirje, Normalization meant changing the environment and expectations of people with disabilities rather than forcing them to conform to someone else's view of what is normal. In many adult settings however, Normalization had evolved into a set of beliefs, amongst which was the belief that people, even with profound disabilities, should be interacted with in terms of their chronological age rather than at a level they could understand and join in with.

The introduction of Intensive Interaction into settings where Normalization had been misunderstood was (and continues to be) difficult at times. The thought of a member of staff getting at the right physical level and making noises with a person was a challenge indeed. In particular the issue of age appropriateness was raised regularly as an objection in the early days of Intensive Interaction in adult settings. During courses in the 1990s this would be discussed most avidly. Towards the early 2000s, the emergence of person-centred planning had put the issues of age appropriateness in the context of individual needs and it is rare now to have an organization that has not begun to re-examine these issues in a person-centred context.

In education, teaching staff were and continue to be the driving force behind using Intensive Interaction. In adult services the approach belongs to everyone. No one profession lays claim to it. Speech and language therapists, psychologists, occupational therapists and FE tutors have published articles on Intensive Interaction, but as was the case at Harperbury School, these are often the people whose professional roles have a built-in expectation that they will read the books, do the research and write the articles. Very often they are not the people doing Intensive Interaction on a daily basis. There are many unheard and excellent practitioners out there.

What is Intensive Interaction made up of?

Graham writes...

What a practitioner does, or thinks they do, when engaging in Intensive Interaction can be dependent on many things – it is very much influenced by the characteristics and history of the two people involved, their expectations of the process and their current context. So when reflecting on what Intensive Interaction is made up of, we could usefully look at the process from at least two different angles. We could ask what techniques are used in Intensive Interaction. We can also look for some insight into the way that the techniques are employed. Although generally employed as a holistic approach Intensive Interaction can at times be analysed by looking at individually identifiable techniques that are sometimes employed simultaneously, and sometimes even intuitively. Also, as mentioned earlier, the generally accepted techniques of Intensive Interaction are those associated with infant–caregiver interactions which were described in *Access to Communication* by Melanie Nind and Dave Hewett (1994). So, when looking to list the individual techniques of Intensive Interaction, we could and perhaps should include the following:

- **Sharing personal space** (Nind and Hewett, 1994, p.81) with someone, however wide or close their comfortable personal space might be. When thinking about using this most basic of techniques we might need to reflect on how close we get, and how we position ourselves with respect to the other person. We might also need to think about the best height to be, or at which side it might be best to sit, stand or lie. The aim is to provide people with positive experiences of mutual proximity.

- Engaging, or trying to engage someone using **eye contact** (Nind and Hewett, 1994, p.81) can be an important means for giving and receiving inclusive social signals (although we should remember that, for some people with autism, direct eye contact can be aversive and even potentially painful). Engaging directly in sustained eye-to-eye contact can be a bit unsettling, and so for most people it is often best to employ eye contacts intermittently, and sometimes even indirectly e.g. via a mirror.

- Engaging someone with **facial expressions** (Nind and Hewett, 1994, p81) is an important means of giving and receiving inclusive and positive social signals. The deliberate and sustained use of easily comprehensible facial expressions can create social exchanges that can be easily reciprocated. .

- **Vocal echoing** (Nind and Hewett, 2001, p.44–5) is, not surprisingly, the process of echoing someone's vocalizations. Such vocal echoing can and often does develop into conversation-like sequences, with both interactive partners taking turns to exchange vocal signals. Such vocal echoing may also include the sensitive use of dramatized or exaggerated intonation.

- **Imitation or mirroring** (Nind and Hewett, 1994, p.126): mirroring of another person's physical activity or behaviour is a very person-centred technique, as it can only be led by the person themselves. Such mirroring is not a mechanistic reproduction of what the person does. Rather, it is an attempt to reflect back something of what the person is doing and also feeling. However, if successful, this technique can also develop into turn-taking interactive sequences that involve both partners engaging in similar actions. Again, dramatized or exaggerated reflections of aspects of another person's activity or behaviour can be effectively employed, and this can then give a game-like or jovial characteristic to an interactive episode.

- We can use **physical contact** (Nind and Hewett, 1994, p.129) as a means of sociable communication, and this can be an effective means of promoting mutual trust and sociability. Giving and receiving physical contact can provide a powerful signal of inclusion, and equally the denial of it can provide a powerful signal of the opposite, social exclusion. The types of physical contact available to use can be firm or light, given via hands or other body parts, received via hands or other body parts, sustained or intermittent, continuous or rhythmical. But should always be under the control of the individual with a learning disability and/or autism.

- **Joint attention/joint-focus activities** (Nind and Hewett, 1994, p.111) are activities in which both people within an interaction focus their attention on the same activity or object, structuring their sociable engagement around that activity or object. This often means that the interactions occur through intermittent eye contact, sequenced actions, intermittent physical contact or vocal exchanges going on around some other shared experience. Such a joint-focus activity can have various degrees of structure in its nature, and various levels of relative activity or passivity (e.g. by jointly exploring a sensory object or just watching the world go by) .

- **Joint action** is similar to a joint-focus activity, but the essence of joint action is that it requires both interactive partners to act simultaneously on the same object, or simultaneously engage in the same physical activity. Joint actions can again possess varying degrees of structure, and can be simply 'doing things together'.

- **Burst–pause sequences** (Nind and Hewett, 1994, p.74) are generally seen in the types of activity that deliberately use pauses and timing to build up a 'game-like' or teasing sense of tension and expectancy.

- **Turn-taking** (Nind and Hewett, 1994, p.21) is a technique often deliberately aimed for within an Intensive Interaction episode or exchange. Such turn-taking is evident when both individuals within an interaction sequence their actions in some way, share and acknowledge an exchange, and are both aware of their turn within that exchange or interaction. Such turn-taking can take many forms, with varying levels of observable activity, from simple sequenced exchanges of eye contact, facial expression or vocalizations through to more structured sequences of physical actions or verbal exchanges.

- As well as these practical techniques used to engage people in Intensive Interaction, if we are looking to define the approach there is also an over-arching **Intensive Interaction methodology** that is employed. Central to this **methodology** are three procedural concepts that ideally should be in the minds of practitioners when they apply the approach:

  ○ First there is the idea of **establishing mutual pleasure** (Nind and Hewett, 1994, p.23) whilst engaging in Intensive Interaction. With this in mind practitioners should always endeavour to make every interactive episode a positive experience for both themselves and the person they are interacting with, and therefore rewarding for both parties to take part in.

○ Second, there is the issue of **ascribing of intentionality** (Nind and Hewett, 1994, p.21) to the actions of the person with a learning disability. Such ascribing of intentionality is done by practitioners deliberately imputing communicative intent into the actions of someone with a social or communicative impairment during an interaction, even if such intentionality is not obviously present.

○ Finally, there is the idea of **tasklessness** (Nind and Hewett, 1994, p.185). This is something which practitioners aim to achieve during an interaction by being deliberately unconcerned with concrete or predetermined outcomes. Instead, Intensive Interaction practitioners tend to concern themselves with the quality of an interaction, and the level of engagement of their interactive partner.

As sessions of Intensive Interaction can vary widely between participants and occasions, with the individual techniques often being employed in idiosyncratic and individualized ways, the intensity, form and pace of interactive episodes can vary widely between sessions and participants. Therefore it is perhaps the over-arching **Intensive Interaction methodology** that sets the approach apart from other, more superficial types of interactions. This Intensive Interaction methodology is perhaps best characterized as a combination of the following:

- A wish on the part of the practitioner to interact with someone with a learning disability in a way that is meaningful and significant to him or her, and through such interactions come to know the person better.

- A wish to develop a mutually respectful relationship through the use of Intensive Interaction.

- An intensity of focus on the part of the practitioner during an interactive episode.

- An ability to improvise, 'go with the flow' and creatively respond to the sociable communications of the learning disabled person.

- An overall empathic atmosphere manifest through acute sensitivity to the interactive partner's feedback, even if this is difficult to discern.

- A determined perseverance on the part of the practitioner to attune to the person and achieve the maximum level of engagement.

- A constant process of deliberation by the practitioner during an interactive episode on the appropriateness of its form, intensity and pace.

- An active process of reflection on the form, intensity and pace of an interactive episode, after that episode has finished, with a view to informing future interactive episodes. (This process of active reflection can take various forms, but it is generally enhanced by the systematic use of some structured recording format, with frequent video-recording and analysis being generally the most useful and informative.)

Such a combination of methodology and techniques might make Intensive Interaction seem potentially complex and thus difficult to achieve practically, but our experience of supporting others to use the approach has not borne this out. The application of the techniques of Intensive Interaction via the Intensive Interaction methodology can in fact be achieved by many people – after all, the types of interactions used are those naturally occurring during infant–caregiver interactions, which most people generally find simple, unproblematic and hugely enjoyable. Like most things in life, however, the skills of employing Intensive Interaction tend to develop and improve with repeated exposure and continued practice.

What is Intensive Interaction for?

Ruth writes...

In the most general terms, Intensive Interaction is used for making relationships with people who find it difficult to be with and relate to other people. In making relationships, we enable people to experience the benefits that most of us get from an ordinary conversation or shared experience – feelings of being connected to another person, acknowledged, valued and listened to, for example. The aim is that the person will want to relate to others (because interaction is now something pleasant) and, in so doing, will learn fundamental communication abilities. By this, we do not mean age-appropriate communication abilities. Intensive Interaction is not a way to teach people to say 'hello' and 'goodbye' for example. Rather, in the first instance, it is about learning how the person themselves communicates, and how this information can be used by the more expert interactor to make a connection with the person. The 'expert interactor' also benefits since when they are engaged in Intensive Interaction they are less likely to see their partner as someone who is an inferior version of the 'normal', and more likely to see an interesting person who they want to get to know better.

In more specific terms, different 'experts' may use Intensive Interaction for different things, as described in the section *What sort of thing is Intensive Interaction?* earlier in this chapter. To recap: teachers, educationalists and speech and language therapists are likely to use it for developing a person's fundamental communication skills. A psychologist is likely to use it to alleviate a person's emotional distress. Direct-care staff and parents may use it with either an inclusive or developmental aim in mind. This is an oversimplification, of course, as each of these people may well hold a number of aims in mind simultaneously.

Graham has developed the ideas of development versus inclusion in his 'dual aspect process model' (Firth, 2008) which proposes that when a relationship is first established with someone who has been difficult-to-reach they express their latent interactive skills within this relationship. An observer would see what may look like a very rapid development in their interactive abilities, but more plausibly, what happens is that the relationship gives the person a context in which they *want* to relate and to use skills that they already have. Further development *can* take place if the person is offered regular and sustained Intensive Interaction aimed at this. This development, however, is likely to be at a slower pace than seen previously since the person is now, it is hoped, learning new skills rather than expressing latent ones.

As to the recipients of Intensive Interaction, the 'classic' groups of people who have been offered the approach are those with severe or profound levels of intellectual disability and those with autistic spectrum disorder (ASD). In the case of people with profound levels of learning disability, their lack of speech and difficulty in any kind of learning typically makes them difficult-to-reach. Similarly, difficulties with being social are a requirement for the diagnosis of ASD. Clinicians working in learning disability services, however, are now regularly using the approach with a wider range of people. These include people who have challenging behaviour, serious mental health problems, and less severe psychological or psychiatric problems such as withdrawal, anxiety, depression, distress and self-injurious behaviour. My own clinical experience suggests that Intensive Interaction also has potential as a therapeutic approach for people with a range of levels of learning disability (that is, not just people who lack speech) and a variety of psychological/psychiatric problems, but further research is needed to substantiate this.

In clinical practice, I do not exclude people because they do not belong to the 'classic' groups and have used Intensive Interaction with people, for example, who do have some speech and who are in the moderate range of intellectual disability. What my clients have had in common is that they are all difficult-to-reach through standard means. This is not to say that being difficult-to-reach is necessarily a quality of the person. Rather, it can be seen as arising from a mismatch between what the person needs and can tolerate and what their environment provides. Thus, someone with ASD who feels overwhelmingly threatened by direct eye contact will retreat from people if they persist in trying to look them in the eye. Similarly, some environments for people with a learning disability remain impoverished in terms of the frequency and type of interactions and activities available. When levels of stimulation and contact are very low, people may retreat into stereotyped and self-injurious behaviours as forms of occupation. This may make them appear inwardly focused and so difficult-to-reach. This is not necessarily the case and can be tested out by using Intensive Interaction principles to offer appropriate forms and levels of contact and activity.

Intensive Interaction should not be seen as a cure-all or magic wand, and it can often be used alongside other approaches. The clients who I see, who have severe challenging behaviour and/or mental health problems, may have a management plan that has been developed on the basis of a functional analysis of their problematic behaviours as well as receiving Intensive Interaction. My clinical experience has also been that the approach has the potential to impact on the more expert interactor (be they parents, direct-care staff or professionals) to the ultimate benefit of the person who is difficult-to-reach. Using Intensive Interaction means that you understand someone better, not just in terms of their behaviours or problems, but as a person. This builds empathy which, in turn, can increase the likelihood of helping someone. Intensive Interaction also sees people as capable of progression, and this can foster optimism for change, one factor shown to increase the likelihood of helping (Sharrock et al., 1990). Similarly, Intensive Interaction focuses on what people can do rather than what they cannot do, which gives a more positive view of the person, and so may also engender optimism.

Many people have become disheartened by the behaviourally derived approaches which have come to dominate many services for people with a learning disability. In some cases, the emphasis on behaviour has been to the detriment of seeing the person with a learning disability as a person – rather they can come to be seen as a collection of 'maladaptive' behaviours that those 'in charge' seek to control through (largely) aversive consequences. I have worked in systems where staff seem to judge themselves by the success or otherwise of these controlling techniques, and sometimes they can come to blame the clients for not 'getting better' when the techniques fail. Intensive Interaction's emphasis on spending time with people is a radical shift from the emphasis on controlling their behaviours, and I believe that training in this approach (plus other supportive measures) has the potential to impact on staff attitudes towards their clients and their own role in supporting them.

Whereas some approaches can lead to the person with a learning disability being seen as an inferior version of normal (who needs to be changed), Intensive Interaction can help anyone who uses it to see someone who is interesting and enjoyable to be with. As a professional working in these systems, Intensive Interaction has given me hope that these changes are achievable.

2

Issues Associated with Personal Characteristics

Through Intensive Interaction we can shift our vision of our sons and daughters from impaired versions of us, to fulfilled versions of themselves.

Intensive Interaction trainee from Australia

Cath writes...

When we consider the people who actually participate in the practice of Intensive Interaction, we need to consider the qualities of both interactive partners. What makes Intensive Interaction appropriate for someone? Who might benefit from the approach? Who will be good at, and embrace, Intensive Interaction?

According to Nind and Hewett (1994), during the development of Intensive Interaction at Harperbury Hospital School the students who were engaged with Intensive Interaction:

...experienced profound and multiple difficulties in learning and in relating to others. Often their lifestyles were characterized by stereotyped, ritualistic behaviour, aggressive defence of their own isolation, and apparent self-absorption. (p.5)

Nind and Hewett did not advocate the use of Intensive Interaction for everyone. Yet with the most basic description of Intensive Interaction being a conversation at a level that both partners can understand and equally participate in, many more people now benefit from the use of the approach. I have seen videos of staff using the principles of Intensive Interaction with adults with learning disabilities who have some understanding and use of verbal language. However, a major joy of the approach is to be able to connect with the world of people with profound and multiple learning disabilities who have been communicatively neglected and overlooked for many years in traditional services. Using Intensive Interaction with people who experience severe autism can also provide some powerful moments of communicative and social connection that were previously thought to be unachievable.

This chapter examines the personal characteristics of the people who benefit from and support the use of Intensive Interaction and some associated issues. A recurring theme through this chapter is the need to relinquish requirements to know everything about the person and what they are experiencing before we begin interacting with them. Again, if we view Intensive Interaction as a conversation at a level that both partners can understand and equally participate in, then we accept that our conversational partner may have many issues that we are not fully aware of, but that does not necessarily get in the way of a good interaction. As with any conversation we may have in our day-to-day lives, it is unrealistic to expect that we can know everything about a person before we talk to them.

Motivating factors for an individual with learning disability and/or autism

One of the central aims of Intensive Interaction is to encourage a person with learning disabilities and/or autism to view other human beings as being pleasurable to be with. However, for many years other human beings may have spoken to them in a language they cannot understand, may have demanded that they do things they do not like, and may have delivered personal care in a way that disregards their dignity or their need for human warmth. Why would they suddenly now be motivated to be with us?

First and obviously, we need to stop doing the things which makes the person see us as unattractive and even threatening to be with. Second, a period of time just to observe the person can give some valuable insight into how they occupy their time, and thus what may motivate them to be with us. To overcome the directiveness of previous practices, we need to give signals of availability, acceptance, and interest in how the person chooses to spend their time. We need to validate their activities by joining in. Again, and this is a recurrent theme throughout this book, we need to analyse and reflect on videos of interactions.

One staff team I worked with had very strong feelings that a certain lady enjoyed interactions with music playing in the background. This was felt to be largely intuitive knowledge so we looked at a few videos, some with music and some without. Indeed, the lady showed more animation when the music was on – demonstrated by the movements of her eyebrows in time to the music. As this did not distract from the interaction and appeared to make her more alert, music was a regular feature of her interactions from that day forward. Interestingly, the staff had been unable to identify what was different about this lady's behaviour with or without the music until we reviewed the video. Despite that lack of recognition, every member of staff who was on those videos engaging in an interaction had been mirroring her eyebrow movements perfectly!

One of the central aspects of Intensive Interaction is to get your face in the right place. The reason for this is that your face will be the most interesting, flexible, motivating and engaging thing available to the person. Young children are born with what appears to be a pre-programmed desire to see the human face (Goren, Sarty and Wu, 1975, Johnson *et al.*, 1991, Johnson and Morton, 1991) and there is no reason to think that this changes as we get older – it is the focus of most direct human communications.

Autism

The National Autistic Society (www.nas.org.uk) summary of autism (or ASD – autistic spectrum disorder) tells us that 'the three main areas of difficulty which all people with autism share are sometimes known as the "triad of impairments"'. They are:

- difficulty with social communication

- difficulty with social interaction

- difficulty with social imagination.

There are a multitude of approaches for working with people on the autistic spectrum, although many of these do not address the central issues of what it means to experience autism. Although Intensive Interaction is not an approach which is specifically for people with autism, it can work powerfully in addressing these central issues. Intensive Interaction very gently and sensitively offers the opportunity to control an interactive sequence in which the fundamentals of communication are repetitively and enjoyably rehearsed and extended in a highly social context. Within an interaction, usually it is the person with autism who begins to experiment with their interactive partner by extending the activities they engage in – carefully watching their partner to ensure that their actions are being followed. These extending behaviours could be seen as a hypothesis, usually non-verbal: 'If I do this, will this happen?' This could be seen as social imaginative thinking.

Where some people with ASD struggle with sensory overload from various environments and approaches, the focus of Intensive Interaction is on two individuals exclusively experimenting with communications and social engagement – often having the effect that an over-stimulating environment becomes irrelevant as a result of the total absorption within an interaction.

Additionally, once interactive sequences are established some aspects of the interaction can be employed to help a person through other life challenges, for example:

Cilla is a young lady with learning disabilities and ASD who finds walking through doorways difficult. In the past this has seriously affected the quality of her life and that of her family. She suffered distress every time she needed to go to the bathroom and going out was even more problematic. During initial interactions Cilla really enjoyed taking turns in 'twiddling' pieces of string. Sometimes she initiated a string exchange. Now, if Cilla has her pieces of string to twiddle and someone walks beside her mirroring her actions with warm regard she has no problems with moving through doorways.

Depression, social withdrawal, isolation, distress

The emotional well-being of people with profound and multiple learning disabilities and/or autism has been a neglected area for many years. In reality we may not be able to know what has happened to someone that makes them withdraw to the extent that people believe 's/he prefers to be on their own'. This has sometimes been compounded by a belief that staff should not get emotionally attached to someone, and that we should respect an individual's preferences to be alone if apparently desired.

We could dwell endlessly on the reasons and symptoms of depression, social withdrawal, isolation and possible mental health issues, but in reality some people with a learning disability have had impoverished, boring, powerless lives where their dignity has been disregarded. They may also have been patronized, overlooked, neglected and, in some cases, over-scrutinized and assessed for diagnoses/conditions/limitations/problems.

The use of Intensive Interaction with people who are withdrawn, isolated and/or distressed needs to be done with sensitivity and respect, but it is a first step to understanding what the person is experiencing and giving them an opportunity to be 'listened to'. The person who appears to prefer his/her own company is often the person most in need of being with another human being who can relate at a level that does not demand too much of them, or confuse them.

There is an Intensive Interaction scenario that I have seen repeated many times with people who are withdrawn and isolated. I will use an example of one person to demonstrate what is commonly observed.

Mustafa is 42 years old and lives in a curled up, almost foetal position, quietly humming to himself, rocking and rubbing his forefinger against his thumb repeatedly. Michelle began Intensive Interaction by sitting near him, her body facing slightly towards him. She looks towards him with a warm look on her face (not too effusive – just warm). She mirrors his hum and moves in rhythm with him. For the first three minutes there appears to be no reaction (the video review later shows that he was glancing at her with increasing frequency). After a few moments he stops rocking and humming momentarily and appears to be thinking, then he begins his movements and sounds again. In the next four minutes he continues his movements without any sounds and looks at her more regularly and more directly. Then he stops his movements again, looks at her, makes a sound that isn't part of his humming repertoire, then looks away. She mirrors the sound. He looks at her again briefly, looks away and makes the sound again. She mirrors it. He puts his head down and begins the rocking again (the video review shows a brief smile on his face at this point). He is silent for a while but the rhythm of the rocking has changed and there are regular still moments as he appears to be testing her – he is watching her movements closely. Again, he puts his head down and smiles more obviously.

Perhaps for people like Mustafa, the first session of Intensive Interaction will be the first time someone has just sat with them without making any demands. Perhaps it is the first time someone has attempted to communicate with them on a level they can understand and participate in. No wonder one of Mustafa's first reactions appears to be puzzlement. In my experience of using and supporting the use of long-term Intensive Interaction with individuals like Mustafa, a gradual opening up of body posture and a greater awareness and interest in the environment and other people is a common development.

Learned helplessness

Learned helplessness (Seligman, 1975) is a term used to describe a condition into which a person may sink if they experience very little control in their lives. If a person consistently feels powerless to alleviate suffering, then the person gives up – even when opportunities arise that may bring release from negative circumstances. Learned helplessness provides a model for explaining depression: a state characterized by a lack of affect, motivation and feeling.

The man who first identified, described and labelled 'learned helplessness' conceded that there were examples of people who had experienced negative life experiences and a lack of control who did not become depressed, and this he explained by a person's 'explanatory style'. The more pessimistic the person's explanation for their circumstances, the more likely they were to become depressed. Conversely, if a person found a more optimistic reason for their circumstances, they were less likely to become depressed. Seligman (1998) developed work on changing pessimistic explanatory style to more optimistic thinking using cognitive therapy techniques.

So, how is this relevant to Intensive Interaction? Cognitive therapies are, on the whole, unavailable to many of the people for whom Intensive Interaction is appropriate so any attempt to move a pessimistic explanatory style towards a more optimistic style would need to be done non-verbally. Perhaps for a person with learning disabilities this could be done by having someone sit with them regularly with a positive 'I like being with you' look on their face, someone who joins them in their chosen activity and celebrates their behaviours no matter how idiosyncratic. This sounds remarkably like Intensive Interaction and may go some way towards explaining the opening up of body posture that I witness regularly in my work with staff using the approach.

Challenging behaviour

One of the most commonly used definitions for challenging behaviour is: 'behaviour of such intensity, frequency or duration that the physical safety of the person or others is likely to be placed in serious jeopardy, or behaviour which is likely to seriously limit or deny access to and use of ordinary community facilities' (Emerson *et al.*, 1988). I prefer Geraint Ephraim's rationale:

> ...there is no such thing as challenging behaviour. What we have is exotic communication... A punch in the face is an act of communication which is very difficult not to hear. Its effect may be heard but the message behind the punch may not have been listened to, let alone understood. (Ephraim, 1998, p.211–12)

There is common agreement that difficult behaviours usually have a reason: communicative, sensory, reaction to pain, occupation, frustration, disempowerment or habit. Ephraim referred to people who display challenging behaviour as 'the pained, the unheard and the unloved' (Ephraim, 1998, p.210). In day-to-day life, analysis of possible reasons for challenging behaviour takes up hours, and sometimes the reasons are never discovered. And yet, many of the possible reasons for challenging behaviour outlined above are resolved through the levels of attention and acknowledgement that Intensive Interaction brings to an individual.

Intensive Interaction is not primarily an approach aimed at working with people with challenging behaviour. It is, first and foremost, an approach for allowing people to learn about relationships and communication. However, from my own working experience it so happens that the focus on individual, respectful and equal interactions does often appear to have an effect on the levels and intensity of difficult behaviours displayed by some individuals.

There are behaviours in some people that we may struggle with but which don't necessarily constitute challenging behaviour. The behaviours can have an effect on the amount of interactions a person receives. People who spit, pick their nose, dribble, smear faeces, indulge in anal exploration, projectile vomit, blow raspberries...the list could be endless. Different staff appear to be able to stomach different things, and good teamwork should support one another through the difficulties of working with people who behave in such ways. There is little point in insisting that a member of staff interacts with someone who they struggle to be near as messages of availability and acceptance and the ensuing mutual enjoyment are likely to be affected in these circumstances. However, watching colleagues interact with someone perceived to be difficult to be with and seeing the mutual enjoyment emerge can sometimes be enough for a re-evaluation of the person rather than the behaviours.

Self-injurious behaviour

A frequently asked question about using Intensive Interaction is 'should we mirror behaviours that are self-injurious?' *There is no definitive answer to this question.* Mirroring, or not, is person and situation dependent. Obviously there is no expectation that interactive partners should be hurting themselves in mirroring self-injurious behaviours but rather, mirroring some of the actions and/or rhythms of the behaviours. In some interactive episodes there may be a variety of behaviours that could be mirrored in preference to any harmful actions and these safer behaviours could become the focus of the interaction whilst not responding to more painful activities. However, occasionally there may be circumstances where the self-injurious behaviour dominates a person's time to the extent that there is little else to join in with. I offer an example from my own work:

When I was very new to Intensive Interaction I worked, in conjunction with a staff team, with a young man who was in extreme distress and his only behaviours were self-injurious. Perhaps if we had stopped to think about it or seek advice we may have thought twice about what we did. We mirrored his screaming (but making our responses less distressed sounding) and we mirrored his behaviours when he thumped his head (by smacking some furniture, or our thighs if there was no furniture available). As it happened what we did was effective and he began to anticipate and wait for our responses. Our responses became gradually and subtly delayed to provide more time between thumps and they became softer. The success of this was that the young man in question moved very swiftly from thumping his head very hard to a gentle slap. The vocalizations which had initially been screaming also reduced in intensity and became more conversational and the main focus of subsequent interactions.

With hindsight I believe we did the right thing and I would probably do the same again today as a more experienced interactor.

Parents and carers

I sometimes hear Intensive Interaction referred to as an expert approach. We have certainly learned a lot from research and theory. The use of video has greatly enhanced our practice and observation skills. But does this make the professionals the experts? Personally I have a differing view. Numerous parents have related the stories of programmes they have been expected to participate in, programmes that discouraged natural caregiver–infant interactions and encouraged parents to become teachers rather than responsive and warm interactors. These programmes were usually introduced by 'experts' and the parents, desperate to do the best for their child, frequently embraced this advice. Parents who were tempted not to follow the expert advice were, and still are, accused of 'not fully engaging with services'. I squirm with embarrassment when I listen to many parents' stories, knowing that I, too, have been part of the systems that are supposed to be there for their support, but are often the cause of even more pressure and angst.

In the stories of some parents, the atmosphere of concern and uncertainty immediately following the birth of their child interferes and disrupts the joy, wonder, awe and celebration that usually surround a family on the arrival of a new child. Tense, negative reactions of medical staff to the birth of a child with obvious problems can often affect the parents whilst they are feeling vulnerable and confused. Parents who are vulnerable, confused, afraid and facing the inevitable increased isolation and helplessness can be excused for finding it difficult to give the joyful and warm responses their child needs.

With all this in mind, I believe the introduction of Intensive Interaction to parents and carers should be done with the utmost humility and cooperation. Had we listened to parents more thoroughly, had we not disempowered them in the face of our 'expertise', we may have been in a position to embrace what is now called Intensive Interaction many years ago.

Age/early intervention: children vs. adults

The presence of the lovely interactional dance that occurs with typically developing children and their caregivers very much depends on both partners in the interaction having the necessary skills, signals and incentive to ensure the mutual pleasure that is so important in motivating both partners to repeat the process regularly. Research has demonstrated how easily the parent–child interactions can be disrupted if a child is visually impaired and so cannot indulge in mutual gaze (Fraiberg, 1975). Likewise there is likely to be an effect if the child was born prematurely (Field, 1977). Although not specific to Intensive Interaction, research also demonstrates that interventions focused on improving patterns of interactions between parents and infants are beneficial and can have a long-term effect on cognitive and social development (Achenbach *et al.*, 1993).

If introduced in the first few years of life Intensive Interaction would be extending the natural learning that would occur in these early years and, it is hoped, prevent or delay the development of some of the more exotic behaviours that occur in individuals with little or inappropriate stimulation. If a child with PMLD and/or autism finds the only appropriate stimulation and interest is in fingers that wriggle in front of his eyes, this finger twiddling will become a regular occupation. However, if the child has an attentive and responsive interactive partner it is likely that this person will be more interesting than his fingers – leading to communication, social, emotional and cognitive development. Although there is no direct research evidence yet to support this position, common sense would suggest that the earlier this approach is used, the better the results for the child's life.

From my own clinical experience, for most parents the benefits from using Intensive Interaction is that they begin to have, or retrieve, a relationship and some communication with their child that they had begun to think wasn't possible. Further development of social, emotional, communication and cognitive skills are then possible through regular interactions.

Yet there is an ambiguity with using Intensive Interaction with young children in that it would be difficult to separate progress which can be attributed to implementation of the approach from the natural development which may occur with no intervention. If a child with a disability is being taught sign language, we know the programme is successful when the child first uses a sign that isn't a natural gesture. If the child is being taught to exchange a picture for an object or activity, the people around the child know the programme is having an impact since this behaviour is not part of the repertoire of a typically developing child. However, if Intensive Interaction is being used with a child, there is no knowing if the new extended eye contact or the expansion in vocal repertoire is due to the approach or natural maturation. Perhaps one of the challenges for introducing Intensive Interaction to young children is for professionals to forgo the expectation of measurable outcomes and concentrate instead on the improving quality of the relationships for and around the child.

Reassuringly, Intensive Interaction can be effective with people of any age.

Professional support

Intensive Interaction is often introduced into a service through speech and language therapists, psychologists, occupational therapists, creative therapists or teachers. These professionals often have a great deal of knowledge and experience in working with people with learning disabilities and/or autism and Intensive Interaction practice is promoted and championed by many such professionals. However, it must be acknowledged that many of these professionals are only able to work in a consultative/investigative/research role rather than having the time to be regularly involved in sessions of Intensive Interaction.

The people who are best placed to offer consistent and reflective interactive sessions are the people who work on a daily basis with those people who benefit from the approach. Professional support to improve skills of observation and analysis of progress can be important in the continuing use of Intensive Interaction, as can the intermediary role they can undertake in promoting and supporting the approach at a management level. This lack of direct experience can be frustrating for the professionals who passionately promote Intensive Interaction but rarely get the opportunity to be 'hands-on' themselves. I would advocate always protecting some time to participate in sessions alongside staff – particularly if professionals are involved in teaching Intensive Interaction to others.

Intensive Interaction is multi-faceted and rightly belongs to different professions. No single profession has become the dominant force in developing the approach, a fact which may be off-putting to some professionals. Fortunately, my experience is that there are few professionals now who are actively antagonistic towards Intensive Interaction. There is an increasing amount of evidence for the efficacy of the approach (see

Chapter 12) and support has been gathering momentum in the light of the general move within services towards person-centred approaches and the inclusion of Intensive Interaction in the government White Paper *Valuing People Now* (DoH, 2009).

Management characteristics

Managers who promote and support the use of Intensive Interaction within their organizations can make a huge difference to many people's lives – both the people who use the service, and those who work within it. However, they can have a difficult task since Intensive Interaction does not conform to services that are largely target driven. SMART targets (Specific, Measurable, Achievable, Realistic and Timed) do not apply to an approach where any developments that occur are in the control of the person receiving the service rather than the staff. We can predict vaguely what progress may be made (e.g. increased interest in being with other people, straightening of body posture, increased eye contact) but not specifically enough to become SMART targets.

Dr Penny Lacey (of Birmingham University) presented her version of Intensive Interaction targets at the 2006 Intensive Interaction Conference in Leeds. These tongue-in-cheek targets are SCRUFFY: Student-led, Creative, Relevant, Unspecified, Fun For Youngster (and young at heart).

It takes a brave manager to tolerate this type of floatiness within services. Whilst for most staff using Intensive Interaction the rewards are intrinsic, for managers there needs to be some extrinsic evidence to justify the use of the approach within their service. Consistent record keeping and progress updates can help managers to continue their support for the use of Intensive Interaction.

Many managers are keen on the approach but have little time to ensure the consistency and accuracy of practice. Because Intensive Interaction has been available for years and picked up by various groups of people, no-one really has the responsibility for monitoring standards of practice. A delicate task for anyone managing, promoting and supporting the use of Intensive Interaction within their organization is how to encourage and monitor staff's practice. This is not an approach that anyone can be forced to use; it's not an approach we can easily put targets on, and it's not an approach that will work with a management style that is directive. Staff using Intensive Interaction need an environment in which they can be relaxed enough to engage in one-to-one sessions. They need encouragement, positive feedback, enthusiasm and opportunities to celebrate progress.

Reflective practice and practitioners

One of the refreshing aspects of Intensive Interaction is that the approach refocuses us away from the constant assessment that many people with learning disabilities have been subject to and moves us towards self-assessment. Whilst Intensive Interaction is sometimes seen as a natural spontaneous activity, reflection can help us tidy the style we use with individuals.

When first using the approach some lengthy periods of video reflection are useful in helping us to see what we may have done that got a good response, and what we may have done that did not work – or got a negative response. It helps us to see signals that the person may have made that we did not spot during the interaction. Often first-time interactors see where they have tried to lead the person rather than allowing the person to lead. Or they see that their face is looking a little stern and not giving out an 'I like being with you' message. Frequently these video reflections help staff see that the person they thought did not communicate did, in fact, have clear signals that had not previously been observed.

In the initial stages of Intensive Interaction practice I have found that staff are very good at reflecting on what they could improve on and often very poor at identifying what they did well. Some gentle mentoring through the early reflections can help practitioners reflect realistically and positively.

Staff characteristics

> Those who know about Intensive Interaction* are not equal to those who love Intensive Interaction,* and those who love Intensive Interaction* are not equal to those who delight in Intensive Interaction*
>
> A paraphrase from Confucius. (*Truth)

The staff who regularly participate in Intensive Interaction have one thing in common – they had the courage to try it out in the first place. Even more courageous are the practitioners who have been videoed and spent time reflecting on their practice. Intensive Interaction is easy to talk about, read about and advocate for other people to adopt as a worthy approach, but actually participating in interactive sessions is a hurdle all regular practitioners have managed to jump. This first step is often the most difficult. This is particularly true for people who began to use the approach before the days when it became popular and relatively well accepted.

So, who are these practitioners? Are they male or female, introverts or extroverts, relaxed or tense and anxious, are they speech and language therapists, psychologists, occupational therapists, care staff, managers, teachers, parents? There are still a lot of unanswered questions about what makes a good Intensive Interaction practitioner. I have spent a great deal of time trying to identify what I now call the 'it' factor, and despite numerous personality tests administered with good and not-so-good practitioners I am no nearer a conclusion. Since 1996 I have trained and supported many fantastic people to use Intensive Interaction including men and women, introverts and extroverts, I've met speech and language therapists, psychologists, occupational therapists and creative therapists who have the skills at their fingertips. But I have also met therapists who struggle to give up their therapeutic agendas to enable an interaction of true equality. This was also a challenge for me in the early days, and is still something I need to be constantly aware of as an Intensive Interaction practitioner.

I have seen care staff and teaching assistants who have truly been doing Intensive Interaction for years without knowing it had a name. Sometimes these sessions have been done behind closed doors since there have been periods in services where managers and/or clinicians would have frowned on such practices.

However, one thing I have never seen is someone effectively using Intensive Interaction because their manager or a clinician has told them they must. Motivation for Intensive Interaction practitioners is largely intrinsic. People use the approach because they want to, they get job satisfaction from doing so and they see that it makes a difference to the lives of the people they are working with.

For many people the introduction of Intensive Interaction into the workplace comes as a relief. The approach chimes with their human behaviour and experience. Intensive Interaction is unlike approaches I have been involved in previously. It does not feel like work to me – and yet it can be exhausting. However, after the first attempt at using Intensive Interaction there is a tendency for practitioners initially to think, 'Is that it?', 'it can't possibly be that simple!', 'I must be doing something wrong' or 'surely something that simple and pleasurable can't be effective'. This, I believe, is the second hurdle that practitioners need to overcome. The very simplicity of the approach can lead to Intensive Interaction being devalued and more complicated approaches having more credence.

Gender issues

If we revisit the developmental model of infant–caregiver interaction there is some tentative evidence of gender differences in interactive styles, but these are not deemed to be better or worse – just different (Parke and Tinsley, 1987). Perhaps, as the slight differences in male/female interaction skills seem to serve a function for developing infants, they may also serve a function for other people who are yet to learn the fundamentals of communication.

There are some highly skilled interactors of both genders in all services. Andy Culham (2004) did some research and concluded that although it isn't always clear what difficulties relate specifically to maleness, and what difficulties exist for practitioners of either gender, there was a clear need for male practitioners to access specific support in the area of Interactive Interaction. Many services are haunted by the fear of physical and sexual abuse and this, as Culham discovered, can have an effect on men being willing to be involved in Intensive Interaction. Because of issues of touch in working with female clients, and fear of allegations of sexual abuse, some of the men in Culham's research thought being male was an obstacle to doing Intensive Interaction with females. Therefore Cullen felt that re-assurance through guidelines or policy statements about physical contact should be developed to help protect both staff and students. Having other people present and/or videoing interactions can also help in this area.

Underestimation/overestimation of capacity... 'they understand everything I say'

As a speech and language therapist I have often heard people say that the person with profound and multiple learning disabilities 'understands everything I say'. Likewise I have experienced assumptions that nothing is understood as the person is talked about in their presence as though they were in another room. In truth, assessing the comprehension of people with learning disabilities is difficult. Understanding of verbal language is a complex skill usually learned only after the easier communication skills have been acquired – the easier skills being features like listening, attending, looking at, eye contact, turn-taking and anticipating. Until a child looks repetitively at a toy and has the toy repetitively labelled (requiring listening and attention) they will not learn the word.

Thus, not only may the child's primary disability (e.g. visual impairment, hearing impairment, learning disability) affect the learning of these labels but the opportunities to learn these labels may not be given often enough, and for long enough, in the midst of the many other priorities parents have when they have a child with disabilities. Consider some of the typical early words of a child like 'more', 'up', 'Daddy'. A child may begin experimenting with the use of these words somewhere between eight and fourteen months. Even for the verbally advanced child, who begins at eight months, they have probably heard these words at least three times a day for those eight months – that is a minimum of 720 repetitions. They will have understood the word for some time before they used it, but the repetition is key to the understanding and expression – forming a definite link between a person/object/action and a set of seemingly random phonemes put together to form a word.

This is not to say that people with profound and multiple learning disabilities have not learned some language. I well remember one gentleman with cerebral palsy who would quietly smile at staff conversation – apparently at the appropriate humorous moments – but gave no response to any attempts to assess how much he understood.

Whilst not wishing to deny that some people with profound and multiple learning disability may understand some language, if we return briefly to a typically developing child we may get some insight into this belief for some people. A child of around four months old can distinguish between angry and playful voices – they have, at this tender age, learned to interpret tones of voice (rather than the meaning of the words spoken). It is thus likely that someone with profound and multiple learning disability has also learned this skill as well as many other interpretations of their environment that will take a great deal of observation to understand.

However, having a thorough picture of how much someone understands is not essential for the use of Intensive Interaction. Indeed the wish to know everything about the person before you begin can result in never beginning to interact. We will actually learn much more about all aspects of a person by using and reflecting on our interactive practices than we learn by any out of context assessments. If there is a strong belief that a person understands language then a feature of any interaction will probably include some use of words and phrases – the constant scanning and responding to a person's signals will indicate whether we are conversing at an appropriate level.

Individual staff resistance to Intensive Interaction

There are some people working in learning disability/autism services who will not be comfortable with the use of Intensive Interaction. Some resistance may be overcome when they see the results of regular sessions, and those still resistant may become more at ease once interactivity is an accepted aspect of a service.

However, some people may remain unable to participate in Intensive Interaction, and we need to ensure they at least understand and appreciate the approach despite this lack of participation. It would not be wise to attempt to force people to take part in Intensive Interaction if they are not willing to do so since they are unlikely to implement the approach effectively. There are often enough people in services who will embrace Intensive Interaction, and it is wise to pursue the enthusiastic rather than the antagonistic! The practitioner, however, should be mindful of possible attempts to sabotage Intensive Interaction interventions on the part of strongly antagonistic staff.

In my early days of Intensive Interaction use I was expressing some frustration about resistant staff to a colleague and was gently reminded about the nature of the approach. We enter an interactive session with an individual accepting that we must do so on their terms. We meet them on an emotional, psychological, communicative, physical and cognitive level that is comfortable and accessible for that particular person. We need to do the same with staff who are not quite ready to embrace Intensive Interaction.

3

Issues Associated with Social Inclusion (Being with Someone)

I have days when I go home happy after a hand squeeze is returned...
being involved in human communication, that thing which surely
brings us all the most happiness.

Christine Smith (teacher)

Graham writes...
In this chapter I offer some thoughts on issues concerned with the process
of social inclusion, and how I believe this process can directly involve
Intensive Interaction. It has certainly been my working experience that
the use of Intensive Interaction has proved successful at promoting much
more symmetrical sociable interactions for people with severe or profound
and multiple learning difficulties (and also for some people with autism)
than other strategies that I have used or seen used. However, making
judgements on the promotion of social inclusion will very much depend
on how you view social inclusion, and how you think it is evidenced.
How Intensive Interaction might address the issue of social inclusion
might well depend on your own view as to how the process of sociability
is defined, and what the process of social 'inclusion' actually entails.

Initially in this chapter I look at some of the historical context of attempts to address the issue of social inclusion of people with a learning disability, and then try to define my own view on what social inclusion might mean for some people with severe social or communicative impairment. From my own experiences of working in this field I also think it is important to look at the various terminologies used when people discuss this issue, and how such language might help inform or even define our interactive aims and practices. Finally I look briefly at some of the related sociological, emotional and psychological issues that might be important factors to consider as a context within which Intensive Interaction might be practised.

For the past 25 years there has been a widespread acceptance and adoption of 'Normalization' principles (Nirje, 1969; Wolfensburger, 1972) or Social Role Valorization (Wolfensburger, 1983) across UK learning disability services (as already noted by Cath in Chapter 1), and this has been seen as a major philosophical driver to an improved quality of life for people with learning disabilities. The Normalization rationale promoted the idea that people with a learning disability should have improved access to mainstream services and socially valued roles, and from this gain greater inclusion in mainstream community activity and more generally in society at large. Nirje advocated for people with learning disabilities to have 'patterns of life and conditions of everyday living which are as close as possible to the regular circumstances and ways of life of society' (Nirje, 1980). This philosophy has been a very powerful tool in improving services for, and the social acceptance of many people with a learning disability, but it has tended to work best for people who can, and also who wish to be included in mainstream social or societal activities, even if they require some level of support to do so.

However, if we define social inclusion as a process whereby a person with intellectual disabilities becomes an active and confident participant in sociable activity, as opposed to 'community integration' – a position of physical presence but not of equitable participation – then it is my belief that the Normalization philosophy has worked less well for some people with a severe social or communicative impairment. Normalization has not really improved the inclusion of people who, because of the severity of their intellectual disability or their level of autistic spectrum disorder, cannot realistically be expected to join in equitably with mainstream social or societal activities – no matter what the level of support that could be offered.

That is not to say that people with severe or profound and multiple learning difficulties or autism cannot genuinely be included, or be active participants, in equitable sociable activity. As a starting point the types of sociable activity have to be of the right kind and at the right level for the person. It should also be remembered that for genuine social inclusion to occur then the person with a learning disability or autism also has to *want* to be with other people – they have to be engaged and interested by the social experiences being offered to them, and I think that that sounds very much like Intensive Interaction!

Sociability and social inclusion

The word 'sociability' is used as a descriptive term indicative of someone's greater or lesser inclination to be sociable with other human beings. Our own levels of sociability seem to be associated with a number of personality traits such as shyness or openness, extroversion or introversion, communicativeness, passivity and others. Moreover, an individual's level of sociability doesn't appear to be absolutely set, it seems that for many people (certainly including myself) our level of sociability seems to be highly context dependent. For many people it would appear that we tend to be more or less sociable depending upon the sort of social scenarios we happen to find ourselves in. In familiar and affirming social scenarios we tend to be at ease and therefore more sociable, whilst in others, ones which are non-affirming, or very different from our usual social settings, we tend to be less comfortable, possibly even anxious, and therefore often less sociable. It therefore comes as no surprise that most of us actively organize our social lives, and the social scenarios we engage in, to be generally familiar and affirming.

Unfortunately this type of active social organization is something that is often outside of the control of the majority of people with severe or profound and multiple learning difficulties and autism. It is my contention that those of us who can influence services and policies should aim to help such people engage in social scenarios that are deliberately organized in a way to optimise their potential for sociability.

My understanding is that 'social inclusion' is seen generally as an active process of ameliorating or removing societal barriers that impose 'social exclusion' on certain individuals or groupings ('social exclusion' being a state of social disadvantage that stops people participating fully in the culturally valued activities of a society). If we accept that being part of a community is one of the good things in life, social exclusion can only diminish somebody's quality of life.

Historically people with severe or profound and multiple learning difficulties and autism have suffered, and in some cases continue to suffer extreme social exclusion, whether intentionally or inadvertently practised. Indeed *Valuing People* (DoH, 2001) states that:

> Despite the efforts of some highly committed staff, public services have failed to make consistent progress in overcoming the social exclusion of people with learning disabilities. (p.26)

Too often, for people with severe or profound and multiple learning difficulties social inclusion has been seen as a process of allowing 'them' access to mainstream social activities, rather than all 'our' needs, capabilities and motivations shaping these activities together. Intensive Interaction actively and deliberately removes barriers to sociable interactivity and so should be seen as an approach that purposely counters social exclusion. Gaining positive experiences of sociability by being included in (and contributing to) appropriate, meaningful and affirming sociable activity is one of the most obvious and primary outcomes of the approach, and this is perhaps the first step in a process of genuine social inclusion.

'Accepting' and 'acknowledging' the person

It is my view that people who support those who are withdrawn, isolated or have communication impairments have a responsibility to develop their sociability deliberately. They need to look much more actively for possible signs or 'accessing' points (Nind and Hewett, 2005, p.84) of potential sociability and actively acknowledge (respond to) these signs.

Even the most exotic or idiosyncratic means of communication are worthy of acknowledgement if those are the only communication means that someone can or does employ (although we will have to proceed very carefully and reflectively if such communications include challenging or self-injurious behaviour). We have to start with a realistic acceptance of who a person really is, and how they really are in the world (i.e. how they currently act), and then endeavour to create sociable occasions with them on that basis. Seeing people with severe or profound and multiple learning difficulties as inadequately developed versions of humanity at large, and then hoping that our mainstream communication means will suffice in some moderated form is not sufficient. The use of moderated symbolic language may be useful for simple and concrete functional communications, but is unlikely to facilitate free flowing, spontaneous, equalitarian and creative social interactivity.

Once we see a person as they actually are, we can then go on to acknowledge their communication or potential communicative means in some way. The aim is not to teach the person how to be sociable in a directive way – for example, the person's communications should not be corrected because we judge them to be 'inappropriate'. Rather, we should be attempting to give people frequent affirming messages of acceptance and acknowledgement. Although not always easy or straightforward, such an acceptance and acknowledgement can be a good first step in helping people come to see themselves as social communicators.

One man, Tony, who I have worked with over many years used to grab at any staff members' legs who sat or stood near to his wheelchair. When I started working with him I was told that this grabbing had some sexual overtones as it was directed at the legs of his staff, almost entirely female. However I found that he seemed fairly indiscriminate in whose legs he grabbed, and because this behaviour was self-directed, and something he seemed to find pleasure in (he would laugh when staff asked him to remove his hand) I actively encouraged it by standing or sitting near to him. Then, when he inevitably did grab at my legs, I would laugh as well and playfully push his hand away saying something like 'Tony, don't do that... Don't...' (in a good humoured and affirming tone of voice). This developed into a well-recognized and well-practised routine that made us both laugh and lasted over increasing times. This game then led to the development of other jovial 'don't do it' type activities, included picking up items placed in his lap and dropping them as we said 'Tony...don't drop it, Tony...don't drop it', or playfully pushing away balloons we held up in front of him in a teasing trial of strength (which we always let him win, eventually).

'Accessing' or 'getting in touch with' or 'finally meeting' someone

'Accessing' someone is the process and outcome of connecting with someone for the first time. Nind and Hewett describe the term 'accessing' as '...the sensation of getting through to a student [or person], establishing mutuality with a person who was formerly remote from social contact' (1994, p.84). As these authors acknowledge, this process of participatory social inclusion can range from being rapid to extended or even 'painstaking' (1994, p.85).

I have also heard the terms 'getting in touch with' or 'finally meeting' someone used to describe this same process. Again the meaning behind these terms is indicative of those early tentative and sometimes halting moments when someone opens up to us as a sociable person, thus demonstrating their acceptance of our attempts to include them socially.

'Accessing' someone is, I believe, a process or outcome that cannot be judged against standardized criteria. The sense of having accessed somebody is very much a subjective feeling that can come with differing levels of intensity. It is something that is experienced by the two people involved in an interaction – those people will know (feel) it when it happens, although it may not be obvious to an observer.

Novice practitioners who are in the early stages of using Intensive Interaction techniques may feel anxious and apprehensive about accessing someone. This can be especially so when the practitioner feels pressured for time, or they are attempting to demonstrate the appropriateness of Intensive Interaction techniques to an observer. Feelings of anxiety and apprehension can be counterproductive as they tend to make us strive even harder to *make* the moment come. Often, as with most social occasions, it is when we are at our most relaxed that the most sociable moments occur. On the other hand, a little bit of pressure and associated anxiety can help to focus our minds, and subsequently our observations of the other person's activity and potential feedback can become more acute and therefore more insightful and productive. It may also be useful for the practitioner to remember that 'accessing' cannot be forced upon a person – the person being accessed has to *want* this to happen and is more likely to respond positively to a calm, relaxed approach than an anxious one.

'Being with'

After this first time of accessing, the language used can become somewhat confusing, but repeated episodes of accessing individuals tend to be labelled with a variety of terms: 'Being with'; 'gaining mutuality'; 'tuning in with'; 'attuning to'; 'going with the flow'; 'just hanging out with'; 'chilling out with'; 'sharing quality time with'; and presumably numerous colloquial or individualized others.

Having initially 'accessed' someone we can move on. Terms like 'being with' someone, or 'being with someone in the moment' can be used to describe the simple activity of sharing time and space with someone in a mutually enjoyable way (it's that process of participatory social inclusion again). This kind of 'being with' as opposed to 'caring for', 'doing to', or 'helping or supporting them to…' should follow on from an acceptance of the person's behaviour and communication as they are. Just 'being with' someone can only happen if we put to one side any agenda of physical care, behaviour modification or educative development, enabling us to share moments with people in a way that is truly non-directive. This may sound simple and unproblematic, but in many service settings it is a process that needs careful and supportive management.

'Being with' should involve our 'going with the flow' with someone. From a personal perspective, it is at such moments that I have found myself at my most relaxed and thus receptive of taskless sociable interactivity. When attaining this sense of 'being with' someone it is then that I have felt at my most focused and attuned with the person I am interacting with.

Gaining a state of 'mutuality', 'tuning in' to someone, or 'attuning to' someone are also terms that I have heard used to describe being in a state of mutually pleasurable and symmetrical sociability with someone with severe or profound and multiple learning difficulties and autism (and there are many others, just some of which are listed above). I think these terms are often used by people in a prosaic sense (as opposed to an academic and tightly defined sense) to describe generally the times of the most successful Intensive Interaction – that is, when they *feel* that a session has gone particularly well. This feeling might involve a sense of social participation and inclusion, and an accompanying affective or emotional engagement. In Chapter 8, Ruth writes about attunement in more detail, including the way that it has been defined in the literature.

'Quality time' is a term that I have heard staff use to indicate a specially designated period of time spent one-to-one between people with severe or profound and multiple learning disabilities and/or autism and a more expert partner (I have also heard it used in exactly the same way to describe time spent between busy parents and their offspring!). Such a term brings to mind a sessional use of Intensive Interaction, but it is a term that makes me wonder about the motivation behind its use. There seems to me to be an underlying or implicit assumption that the rest of the time spent with the person has been less than 'quality', and in some way this quality time is meant to make up for that fact. Because of this, it is a term I do not use myself.

'Opening up' or 'sharing yourself' in Intensive Interaction exchanges

Another issue worthy of consideration by Intensive Interaction practitioners is the process of 'sharing yourself', or 'opening up' to the other person. This is generally what is seen to happen to the person with severe or profound and multiple learning disabilities and/or autism, as they reveal more of themselves within a progressive Intensive Interaction intervention. However, practitioners themselves are required to open up and share themselves in some way at the same time.

Generally, during our ordinary social interactions, we gradually reveal things about ourselves, such as our thoughts and personal preferences. Opening up is therefore a process of sharing personal information that others would not normally know or discover. We usually expect opening up to be a mutual or reciprocal process – if one person is not willing to open up, their partner is likely to hold back too, creating a barrier to sociable interactivity.

In Intensive Interaction there seems to be a big overlap between 'opening up' and 'being with' someone. However, 'opening up' is more than just 'being with'; it additionally suggests something to do with a practitioner's genuine willingness to give something of themselves during an intensive exchange. However, this kind of opening up is unlikely to occur via a symbolic verbal exchange such as relating personal narratives, insights and opinions (although not impossible). Opening up is much more likely to arise through a practitioner's actions, their behaviour and their body language. Opening up will be evident in the kinds of actions and behaviours someone is willing or able to take part in, or not take part in, and this will reveal something about them as a person – quite probably how relaxed and trusting they are within a situation or interaction, or how uneasy and inhibited they feel within the social/interactive environment as it currently stands. On a wider level, whenever we work with someone with communicative or social impairments, by the strategies that we use we constantly reveal just how socially inclusive, or not, we are willing to be.

Empowerment

Empowerment is concerned with having influence or control over various aspects of one's own life. For those people in society who are described as disempowered, and this includes people with severe or profound and multiple learning difficulties and/or autism, changing this situation will require them to be afforded *genuine* opportunities to control and influence the way that they live their life. This can be difficult to achieve in practice, but I believe that enhancing a person's communication abilities creates potential to expand such control and influence.

Intensive Interaction explicitly aims towards developing a person's competence and confidence in being communicative. It can give somebody real and repeated experiences of having influence over some aspect of the environment around them. Repeated experiences of exercising control over the social behaviour of other people can lead people to engage more in that process and this can have a beneficial effect on their self-esteem and their self-efficacy expectations, i.e. whether they come to expect to exercise influence on the environment around them.

Although a precise measurement of someone's self-esteem or self-efficacy expectations is not possible, especially for people with more severe or profound learning disabilities, I believe such an increase in a person's self-esteem has happened on many occasions with the sustained use of Intensive Interaction. This, I believe, has been evidenced in a number of people I have worked with who have increasingly initiated social interactions with the staff around them, where previously they were passive and initially required staff to initiate sociably with them: an example being Jim, a middle-aged man who would sit passively and somewhat timidly in 'his' chair in the corner of the lounge. This intervention started with an eye contact game that I would play with him from across the room, with Jim initially looking at me and then quickly (and a bit nervously) away when I looked back at him; this game developed with me doing the same when he looked at me, and then it progressed further with both of us doing it together. This would make us both smile, and wasn't too invasive of his personal space. As staff have continued to work with him interactively, he seems to have become increasingly empowered by the process, and his confidence in effecting the social behaviour of others has concurrently developed. He is now reported as regularly and actively seeking out staff in other rooms to interact socially with them.

Sharing control

Closely related to the issue of empowerment is the issue of sharing control. In Intensive Interaction the practitioner works towards shared control over the means, the form and the pace and timings of an interactive episode. This is often in stark contrast to most other scenarios people with severe or profound and multiple learning difficulties and autism find themselves involved in, when they often lack ultimate control over such features.

Rotter (1954) writes about a person's 'locus of control'. This is a personal and subjective sense of where control lies. This locus can be seen as being internal (meaning someone believes that they have control over themselves and their life in general) or it can be seen as being external (meaning someone believes that other people or some environmental factors control them, their behaviour and thus their life).

In some psychological literature the concept of 'locus of control' has been associated with the state or concept of 'learned helplessness' (Seligman, 1975; also see Chapters 2 and 7 of this book) where an individual perceives an absence of internal control over the outcome of a situation. The use of Intensive Interaction techniques can be seen as having the potential to affect somebody's locus of control to move it away from the external to be located more internally, with the person being more centrally involved in ordering the sociable world around them.

'Okay to proceed?'

When practising Intensive Interaction, we need to be constantly looking for signals from our communication partner that tell us it is okay to proceed, i.e. that they consent to the Intensive Interaction carrying on. Any such 'consent to proceed' can be evidenced in a variety of ways, but we always need to give very close attention for any signals that might be indicative of the person withdrawing that consent. Continuing with an interactive episode when consent to proceed has been withdrawn is unethical and will almost certainly prove counterproductive in the long run.

However, making judgements about 'consent to proceed' when observing someone's feedback is certainly not an exact science, and it is inevitable that different people will make different interpretations of a person's behaviour. Since these interpretations differ, different practitioners might continue unchanged, alter some aspect of their own behaviour or cease interacting altogether in response to a person's feedback.

Sometimes an interpretation of withdrawal of consent is more obvious than at other times, and as Geraint Ephraim wrote: 'A punch in the face is an act of communication which is very difficult not to hear' (in Hewett, 1998, p.212). Sometimes, therefore, very clear negative signals of withdrawal or dislike are given. However, there may be times when someone very subtly withdraws their attention, thus signalling that they have had enough of an interactive episode. Equally, there may be times when there is only a neutral type of feedback, a kind of grey area in-between an explicit 'consent' and a definite 'don't go on', and this type of 'in between' feedback could equally be interpreted as being either 'okay proceed' or 'not interested, please stop'. It is at such times that reflecting on experiences of similar scenarios, either with the individual or with other people, can help inform the practitioner as to whether consent cautiously remains, albeit somewhat in abeyance, or if it has been definitely withdrawn. Sometimes it is also a matter of individual confidence, as to whether to continue or not. If a practitioner is struggling to resolve such issues through personal reflection, seeking advice from a colleague or supervisor is essential.

Signals of consent to proceed may not *always* be overt. Sometimes the practitioner will have an intuitive feeling that 'consent' is no longer on offer, although it can be hard to say exactly why. It tends to be at such times that the feeling of mutuality has become strained or no longer present, or the pace or intensity of the interactivity has begun to wane or dissipate. One of the decisions to be made at this point is how to respond, with an all-out cessation or some change to the form, pace or intensity of the joint activity. If consent to proceed is no longer present for the current activity, can this be assumed to carry for all interactivity? Perhaps instead it indicates a need for a change rather than a need to cease completely. Making a change and carefully monitoring for an increase in our partner's interest can test this out.

In summary, a sensitive and cautious perseverance can pay off in establishing and maintaining a connection with people who are remote or withdrawn. However, overdoing an Intensive Interaction session can be detrimental to future chances of progression. Careful, reflective judgement is the best way to move forward, involving other people when necessary in this reflective process, specifically those who know the person well: care staff, colleagues, or someone who can offer objective yet supportive supervision.

In one case I worked with, a young man with autism and severe challenging behaviour, it took many weeks just to be allowed in his room without being assaulted. Very careful observation and collaborative discussion gave me the confidence to persevere and inch my way into his room (one chair leg at a time) trying never to go past the point of him being able to accept my presence. At the time he could not give clear affirmative consent to my presence, but equally any withdrawal of consent would have been very rapid, seriously assaultative and therefore quite obvious. But through a process of careful and reflective perseverance, I was able to move incrementally into his room and eventually engage him in some non-directive sociable activity, to which he slowly but positively responded. After many weeks of this process he started to smile in recognition and could then state a wish to continue, or not.

Intimacy (emotional): 'lack of...' and 'fear of...'

If people with severe or profound and multiple learning difficulties and/or autism have had early life experiences which are characterized by rejection or lack of emotional intimacy, then this is likely to have a long-term impact on their abilities to form secure attachments and also on their views of themselves as potential actors within relationships (Bowlby, 1988; see Chapter 5 for more on Bowlby). Given such a situation some people may subsequently find it difficult to form trusting and mutually meaningful relationships with other people and thus they may become socially isolated. Just such a situation has been clearly evidenced with institutionalized children whose early years were spent in state orphanages in Eastern Europe. Interestingly, Intensive Interaction has now been identified as a tool with which to address this issue, and it has been used to work with such children in Romania (reported on in Zeedyk et al., 2009), and also used with such children under the auspices of UNICEF in Montenegro.

However, an issue that can act against a rectification of this situation is a condition that Bender (1993) has called 'therapeutic disdain'. According to Bender 'therapeutic disdain' is an attitude held by mental health professionals (in particular it is ascribed to psychotherapists) towards someone with learning disabilities – namely, the person being perceived as in some way 'unattractive' for the purposes of therapy. Such disdain is attributed to the professional's perception of the person with an intellectual disability as generating added demands on them, demands which might make an intense therapeutic relationship potentially more challenging and thus difficult to sustain over the longer term. As a result such disdain can create a communicative and emotional barrier between the professional and client that makes rapport and therefore a therapeutic relationship difficult to construct.

Such a situation of disdain might be at play for some staff members who struggle to overcome feelings of discomfort, upset or even disgust and revulsion at some of the behaviours in which people with severe and profound and multiple learning disabilities engage. It could even be that such disdain is built on perceptions of the physical appearance or profound level of intellectual disability of the more severely disabled individuals. This disdain will make the formation of close and meaningful relationships less likely unless people are supported in this process. Without the correct support such distain can lead to emotional avoidance on the part of the staff, and subsequently neglect of the social and emotional dimension of care.

Feelings (emotional avoidance by practitioners)

A practitioner's own emotional state or current feelings, whilst engaging or attempting to engage with someone using Intensive Interaction, should be attended to as a matter of course. It is my belief that consistent and genuine support for people who do this kind of work, which can be emotionally demanding, is vital, both for the successful advancement of any Intensive Interaction intervention, and also to be protective of the practitioner's well-being. Consistent and genuine support for the practitioner, someone with whom they can acknowledge and gain insight into their emotional responses to individuals they work with, should always be made available.

Feelings of anxiety brought on by possible fear of failure, or even fear of ridicule, will be detrimental to an individual's capacity to engage successfully in Intensive Interaction. This can be especially so if people work without a supportive team around them to sustain and encourage them if things do not always go well. When working with people with challenging behaviour, fear of physical injury can also be present, and this should again be acknowledged.

It might also be that people working with someone who regularly masturbates, or who is incontinent, or who smears saliva or even faeces could hold deep-seated feelings of disgust or revulsion at some of these behaviours. If this person is also endeavouring to be engaging and socially inclusive with the person then there is a clear conflict within the person that will have adverse consequences for their attempts to work productively. A failure to acknowledge or even allow for such mixed feelings could lead to a situation where practitioners become increasing anxious or tense when working with particular individuals, and sometimes actions will need to be taken to avoid a situation where a practitioner becomes avoidant or increasingly distant from the client. As noted previously, Intensive Interaction works better when both parties are relaxed and can gain mutual pleasure from their interactivity. Negative feelings on the part of the practitioner need to be acknowledged and managed for this relaxed position to be possible.

'Mutually pleasurable'

In the first chapter, under the heading *What is Intensive Interaction made up of?* it was stated that one of the important issues that should be in the minds of practitioners is that of establishing **mutual pleasure** whilst engaging in Intensive Interaction (Nind and Hewett, 2005, p.15). The idea is that practitioners should endeavour to make every interactive episode enjoyable for both themselves and the person they are interacting with, and therefore equally rewarding for both parties to take a part in.

In one way this overlaps with the earlier section on consent to proceed, *Okay to proceed?* – if an interaction is mutually pleasurable, then observations of a client's pleasure gives a practitioner implicit consent to proceed. However, the mutual nature of the pleasure is important, because if an Intensive Interaction intervention is to be sustainable through the long term, then staff or family members also need to find the process affirmative and rewarding. Such positive reinforcement should ideally come from doing the Intensive Interaction, rather than someone doing it through a sense of duty or being externally rewarded – for example, with the praise or encouragement of a third party (although when first coming to do Intensive Interaction this can be a vital additional ingredient to ultimate success and practice development).

However, it should be acknowledged that doing Intensive Interaction can, and perhaps should be, emotionally and cognitively effortful. It can at times be difficult to achieve successfully, and can thus be frustrating even for the most experienced participants or practitioners. I personally know this feeling well. However, given time and effort (and sometimes extended practice) mutual pleasure does generally come.

One young woman whom I worked with initially seemed very reluctant to share any time and space with me, in fact for the first month or so of coming to an Intensive Interaction session she would remain standing by the door of the room in which we worked. She seemed anxious, and possibly also suspicious of our attempts to engage her in sociable activity. However, slowly but surely she did open up to us, and eventually was tremendous fun to work with. To start our Intensive Interaction we went and stood near to her without placing any demands on her to do anything, just share her personal space with us. We tried to make eye contact, and vocally echoed her sounds (which weren't really all that positive). She then started to explore the room, and would stand away from the door (next to a radiator), and again we would spend time standing near to her. Gradually, over the next weeks and months the young woman became more at ease and then responsive to our eye contact and vocal echoing, and gradually more extrovert, and overtly fun activities developed, including twirling around together, rhythmical physical contact and even a 'hide and appear' game from under a parachute.

It could well be argued that the creation of mutually pleasurable interactions, even without any other outcomes, is justification in itself for the continuation of the process. However, secondary outcomes from such mutually pleasurable interactions could well be seen in improved participatory social inclusion; enhanced relationship building between clients and staff (e.g. in Watson and Knight, 1991); potentially reduced levels of social withdrawal, self-involved or self-stimulatory behaviours; increased levels of externalized attention and engagement in sociable activities (see Chapter 12 for further details of Intensive Interaction research papers and evidence).

The establishment of mutual pleasure is a first step, and can be seen as an important achievement in itself. As Nind and Hewett (2001, p.3) state: '[With Intensive Interaction] we believe it is the most important area to work on to make a difference to someone's quality of life.'

Issues Associated with Human Communication

Without conversation there is a battle for control.

Geraint Ephraim (1998)

Graham writes...

In this chapter I will try to address issues of human communication in a way that might help Intensive Interaction practitioners usefully reflect on their own practice. Human communication can however seem both straightforward and at the same time highly complex, depending on how you look at it. On one level human communication can be seen as a simple transfer of information between two or more people through some kind of shared means. At another level we might look to analyse the potentially complex and varied means of communication, both intentional and unintentional, that inevitably transpire between any two human beings who come to share the same social space. Such an analysis might include what is meant to be said, what is thought to be said (which might be different from what was intended), and what is not said, or perceived not to be said.

Therefore, in this chapter I look at different descriptive models of communication that might be of interest to Intensive Interaction practitioners;

I look at some of the potential interpretations of the content of Intensive Interactions that might help aid an analysis of non-verbal exchanges; and I look at some of the terminology used to describe aspects of communication related to the use of Intensive Interaction.

So how should we, as Intensive Interaction practitioners, start to untangle the complexity of human communication processes, and thus, it is hoped, enhance our understanding of the issues related to Intensive Interaction? Well, we could start with a simple view and move on from there.

One-way communication: sender–receiver dyads (or communication partnerships)

So what is communication? At its simplest level, we can say that communication is the process of transferring or transmitting information between at least two people through some shared means. In the most straightforward situations we can look at one person somehow encoding and then transmitting some kind of information (a **sender** of information) to another person who receives it, the **receiver** of the information (Shannon and Weaver, 1949). In this scenario the receiver subsequently processes the information in some way (without necessarily fully understanding its intended meaning), and then may make some response to it.

In this 'transmission' model (Shannon and Weaver, 1948) of communication we might also look to categorize the kinds of information transferred during such a communication – that is, the overt 'content'. This could be some kind of concrete information about something. However, there are many other types of 'content' that we might wish to communicate, and we might communicate these for a range of different reasons. The aims we have when making communications with differing content might include making communications about our basic needs or wishes (this often being termed **functional communication**), or making communications that include something about our feelings or emotional state (this sometimes being called **affective communication**). We can and also probably will at times employ **directive communication** to get other people to do as we wish, or use some kind of **instructional** or **educative communications** to help people develop certain skills. We might also communicate purely to be sociable with someone else, because we think it is the right thing to do, and find enjoyment in **social interactivity**.

There is also a difference between the types of communications we can make intentionally, with this often taking some symbolic verbal form, and the types of unintentional communications we might let slip, often in our non-symbolic body language. We can at times unwittingly communicate something with others about our views on perceived social positioning or hierarchy. This unwitting communication can indicate to other people where we might place them in some abstract social 'pecking order' (either above us, below us or as our equals). We can communicate this both intentionally and unintentionally, through what we do and what we do not do.

This list of communicative categories is not meant to be an exhaustive one, but it is meant to illustrate the potential complexity of any communication. This complexity can be become especially evident if a number of these types of communications are perceived as being sent and received at any given time. If we are trying to engage someone with a social or communicative impairment in some kind of communication for social reasons, or as part of an educational intervention, then it might be useful to spend some time looking at the types of communications that they currently generally engage in. Are they generally a passive recipient of directive communications? Do they themselves tend to initiate mainly functional communications? Is much of their communication experience brief and in one direction, either as a sender or receiver, or are they engaged in more sustained communications where they can simultaneously play the part of both sender and receiver?

Time spent looking at these issues might show us that genuine and sustained sociable interactivity is relatively infrequent, or possibly entirely lacking, and once we have identified such a situation we might wish to do something to improve on it. Such an analysis will also give us some useful pointers about how to improve on the current situation, e.g. by observing a person's current communicative abilities that can be built on (see also Chapter 9, the section on strengths and needs analysis and planning, *Disseminating individual Intensive Interaction techniques – using the SNAP system*), and also noting the areas that currently do not appear to be employed, and so which may need to be curtailed or avoided in the early stages of an Intensive Interaction intervention.

Language: including symbolic language and pre-verbal communications

As well as looking at the possible content of a communication, we could also look to define the method or system of transferring information between people. In most circumstances this will be a recognizable system of symbolic communicative exchange or a language, although language itself can be further refined into various aspects. A language, when viewed in very simplistic terms, could be perceived as a system for transferring meaning through the use of some arrangement of symbolic or representational units. At a more complex level, a language can be viewed as any manner or means used to convey meaning between people, and thus can include pre-verbal or non-symbolic means including eye contacts, various aspects of body language, facial expressions, and other means, which have been labelled the **fundamentals of communication** (Nind and Hewett, 2001, p.7) – we will look at this in more detail later.

As noted above, the process of using language within communicative exchanges requires meaning to be encoded into some combination of representational units (usually words) by the sender of information. Such a message is then transferred to a receiver and subsequently decoded by the receiver back into some form that is meaningful to them. For all the different kinds of human communication to work successfully, we need to give some thought as to which forms of language are best suited to which types of information exchanges, and these might differ, say between communication for functional reasons or when communicating for purely sociable reasons (e.g. using a word, sign or symbol for 'toilet' is the most effective way of gaining necessary access to a toilet), however, sometimes quietly sitting down next to someone and smiling at them is a clearer statement of comfort in their presence than saying, 'hello, I am pleased to meet you' from somewhere across the room. When working with a person with a social or communicative impairment, we should be aware when the use of one type of communication is appropriate and likely to be successful, or when certain forms of communication are inappropriate and likely to fail, perhaps because they are potentially too ambiguous, abstract or complex.

A term I hear a lot to describe some people with severe or profound intellectual disabilities is 'pre-verbal'. This term tends to be used in learning disability services to describe a person who has not yet developed the ability to use or understand symbolic or representational speech, signs or gestures. In such cases an appropriate means of two-way communication will have to accommodate this fact. The over-use of symbolic language with such people, and this will include most people with a profound and multiple learning difficulty, will not engage them in a process in which they can be equal partners. Thus alternative communication means are required, and the challenge is for us to find means that are meaningful and engaging. Not surprisingly, it is my view that Intensive Interaction is a very effective method with which to meet this challenge.

Encoding and decoding of communications

For the process of communication to work effectively, it seems reasonable to suppose that there has to be some shared means of communication that can be encoded and decoded successfully by both participants. The sender of a communication will encode the content of any message into a form that serves their particular purpose, with their intended audience in mind, with the expectation that the receiver will then decode the message, i.e. take some meaning from the encoded communication. It is the sender's expectation that the receiver will decode and understand the expressed message in its original form, i.e. they will understand the message as it is understood by the sender – however, this will not necessarily always be the case.

In my own working experience of communications made within learning disability services, there has often been an excessive use of symbolic language for the purposes of encoding communication, i.e. an over-reliance on the use of symbolic verbal language, or representational signs or gestures, especially so with people with severe or profound and multiple learning difficulties. Some staff or carers may use words or even complex sentences with people who demonstrate little or no indication of being able to understand the language as it is understood by the staff or carers themselves. This can lead to a breakdown in the two-way nature of the communication.

In contrast, Intensive Interaction practitioners intentionally use other, mainly non-symbolic means to express or 'encode' meaning into their interactive communications. The encoded message or content is, or should be, almost entirely social or emotional in nature (see below in the section *The 'content' or information transferred during Intensive Interaction exchanges*), and the communication is intended to be understood by the receiver in the same way that it is understood by the sender. Therefore, in our role as a 'sender' during a period of Intensive Interaction, it is our responsibility to make our communications, and the content that they carry, as clear and unambiguous as possible. So, if we are giving affirmative facial signalling (for example via smiles and eye contact), we have to make our face easy to see, and the message it contains has to be easy to decode – for example, an affirmative signal of pleasure requires a smile to be generally broader and more sustained than is usually the rule in mainstream adult to adult communications. This is similarly the case for the use of eye contact, where eyes should be made larger and clearer, and in some cases employed much closer than in mainstream communications, so that the encoded affirmative message is easier to decode (very much like the naturalistic facial signalling we employ with our own very young infants). However, with both interactions employing eye contacts and exchanges of facial expressions practitioners will need to proceed carefully, as for some people getting too close could be anxiety causing or even very threatening, and for some people with autism direct eye contact can be very aversive, and so should be avoided.

It should always be acknowledged that, no matter what the content and complexity of any *intended* communication, there is always the potential for unintentional misunderstanding. For example, we may seek to make a connection with somebody by establishing eye contact. The receiver of our eye contact, however, may perceive this as a threat and respond accordingly. The practitioner therefore needs to consider not only their intention but also how their behaviour could potentially be perceived and (mis-)interpreted.

The 'content' or information transferred during Intensive Interaction exchanges

The content or information that is transferred between people during a communicative exchange is often quite basic and (generally, although not always) uncontentious: how healthy we currently are; comments about a period of inclement weather; news of mutual friends or acquaintances; comments about last night's TV or a sports contest; family or work related issues; where we would rather be at any precise moment, rather than where we are now! During such a seemingly mundane and commonplace communication there is an overt verbal exchange going on (e.g. the stuff about the weather), but also such an exchange can serve a more important 'covert' purpose – the most important thing not being the information conveyed about the weather, but is instead perhaps about feeling connected with someone, re-affirming our relationship with that person, and possibly feeling validated by the person's attention and response.

When engaged in a period of Intensive Interaction that is mainly or entirely non-symbolic, I often ask myself: 'what are we actually communicating to each other?', that is, what is the 'content' of such an interactive exchange? When I have asked this question, I have thought that, at various times during an Intensive Interaction, the content of such an exchange might be some combination of the following statements (although this is by no means an exhaustive list):

- 'I am listening to you – you have my full attention.'

- 'Your behaviour or activity is interesting/important/significant and/or fun.'

- 'You are interesting/important to be with.'

- 'You are fun to be with and I am enjoying doing this with you.'

- 'I want to be with you.'

- 'I want to know you better/find out more about you.'

- 'You can lead me, I will follow you during this interaction.'

- 'You know what you are doing and I would like to know what you are doing as well.'

I also think that during an interactive exchange you are also implicitly asking questions of the person with a social impairment. These questions might be some combination of the following (although again this is by no means an exhaustive list):

- 'What are you doing now?'

- 'Can I do that with you?'

- 'Do you want me to spend some time with you?'

- 'Would you like to spend some time with me?'

- 'Do you have something you wish to share with me/show me?'

- 'Do you like it when I do this, or when I do that?'

- 'What do you want me to do now?'

These questions will probably be asked in differing combinations at various points across an interactive episode, and in my opinion, they might well be viewed as the most significant content of the exchange.

'What is not said' to people

A related issue that is useful to reflect on is the possible lack of affirming and positive communications that a person with a social impairment might receive. It might be useful to ask at what other times, and during what other types of communicative exchanges, does someone with a social impairment have any affirming and positive things said to them, or asked of them, in a way that they can understand. Indeed, we could usefully ask ourselves how we would feel if these things were never said to, or asked of, us, in a way that we could understand.

Not having certain things regularly communicated to us can say something very clearly to us about how other people value and view us. A persistent lack of affirming communications would, I believe, have a negative effect on most people, and a similarly persistent absence of any meaningful and affirming communications might significantly contribute to how a person with a social impairment comes to see themselves. This is not just my view; John Bowlby (a leading figure in the development of attachment theory), for example, writes about the importance of having a 'lovingly responsive' parenting figure (1988, p.124) for the development of a secure attachment and positive self-view.

The reader may usefully reflect on how we might more often say affirming things to a person with a social impairment in a way that is meaningful to them. If, with the sustained use of Intensive Interaction, affirming and meaningful communications were presented more often, a person with a social impairment might have a better chance of constructing a more positive self-image. They may also come to see themselves as increasingly significant or appealing to be frequently engaged in sociable communications with, and also possibly come to see themselves as capable of initiating such communications.

The fundamentals of communication

If we want to pay more attention to positive and affirming communication that is expressed non-symbolically, then we need to look at models of communication that do this successfully. This kind of communication is seen to occur very regularly within infant–caregiver interactions (see Stern, 2000 for research summary), usually but not exclusively between an infant and its primary caregivers (usually mum, dad or immediate family or parental substitute(s)). The means of such exchanges are, according to Nind and Hewett (1994), the **fundamentals of communication**, these being those skills, or aspects of non-symbolic human communication that are exercised and developed in the very earliest stages of development. They are seen as the necessary precursors to all subsequent communication learning, leading eventually, in most people, to the use and understanding of highly complex symbolic language.

The fundamentals of communication have been summarized as being (Hewett, 2007):

- enjoying being with another person

- developing the ability to attend to that person

- concentration and attention span

- learning to do sequences of activity with the other person

- taking turns in exchanges of behaviour

- sharing personal space

- using and understanding eye contacts

- using and understanding facial expressions

- using and understanding physical contacts

- using and understanding non-verbal communication

- using vocalizations with meaning

- learning to regulate and control arousal level.

The above-listed fundamentals of communication are generally the shared means of communication during Intensive Interaction exchanges, and will be familiar to most Intensive Interaction practitioners. But a shared means of communication is not the only necessary ingredient for successful communication.

Means, reasons and opportunities for communication

The three main ingredients for a successful communication (Money and Thurman, 1994) could be seen simply as:

1. having a shared **Means** to communicate with

2. having a **Reason** or need to communicate, and finally

3. having a viable **Opportunity** in which to enact the communication, either by creating an opportunity or having one presented to you.

This short list of ingredients – **Means**, **Reason** and **Opportunities** (Money and Thurman, 1994) – can be used as a tool with which to analyse a situation where communication is problematic. It can lead us to consider whether all the necessary elements are present to enable successful communication to take place, especially when working with people with a significant social or communicative impairment.

Someone may have a wish to communicate something and may have the necessary time and space to do so, but may fail because they do not have a shared means available to get their message across. Equally, someone may have a wish to communicate something, and they may have a shared means available to get their message across, but they may never get sufficient time and space to do so – that is, they lack a viable opportunity. Perhaps for others, all previous attempts to communicate something have not received any meaningful response, and so they now no longer see any reason to communicate with others as they no longer hold any expectation of meaningful results. All these scenarios will be a barrier to successful communication.

Certainly with situations where we wish to employ Intensive Interaction, the **Reason** we have (and, it is hoped, come to share with the person with a social impairment) is that of mutually pleasurable social interactivity. But to do so we will need to find a common means to enact this, and we will need to create viable opportunities to do so. Once we have all three components, we can then start to create some form of meaningful and successful communication.

Functional communication vs. sociable interactivity

Functional communication is a term that is often used to differentiate a type of communication that people use to get their basic needs met, such as those associated directly with our basic physical requirements (or physical functioning). Thus functional communication is seen as a means for gaining access to such things as food, water, air, warmth or coolness, sleep or rest, the wish to use a toilet, and for adults, sexual activity (Maslow, 1943).

Functional communication is also seen to be employed when people try to achieve some basic sense of safety or security, such requirements being identified in the lower aspects of **Maslow's Hierarchy of Needs** (Maslow, 1943). Maslow identified our safety or security needs as those associated with our requirement for a consistent and predictable environment that is familiar, safe, and to some extent controllable. Satisfaction of Maslow's basic needs is associated with health and well-being, and protection from, or avoidance of apparent adverse events, or the anxiety associated with such adverse events (Maslow is discussed further by Ruth in Chapter 7). Functional communication, when it is used, is seen as being an attempt to influence the behaviour of the intended receiver to provide or allow access to a person's basic needs, and as such these communications are intended solely to meet the needs of the sender.

It has been my experience that in many learning disability services functional communication is often differentiated from and often prioritized over social interactivity, which does not have such concrete outcomes as its aim. Quite often great efforts are made to equip a person with a communicative impairment with a system of communication that enables them to have their more functional needs met. Systems such as signing (e.g. Makaton – www.makaton.org) or PECS (Picture Exchange Communication System – www.pecs.org.uk) include the use of recognizable signs or symbols that are mainly used, especially so in the earliest stages of use, to get other people to understand and thus respond appropriately to a person's functional requests.

However, these systems, and functional communication itself do not lend themselves to a sustained and sociable two-way conversation. Once a functional need is communicated and successfully responded to, then the reason to communicate is exhausted. Thus if we only focus on developing someone's functional communication, we will not be adequately addressing a person's need for social inclusion. Deliberate development of a person's social interactivity will be needed (alongside their functional communication development).

Directive/corrective/educative communication

For a person with a social or communicative impairment, a significant amount of the communication that comes their way can be directive, corrective or potentially educative in nature, rather than genuinely interactive. The rationale that seems to underpin such communications is generally to help the person do the right thing at the right time. This usually means that someone other than the person with a communicative impairment will take the role of a sender of information, very often in symbolic verbal form. That is, they will tell the person with social or communication impairment what to do, or how to do it, or when to do something, and often when not to do something (and so on).

The essential purpose of such communications is to change the behaviour of a person with a communicative impairment to a form that is seen as more acceptable or 'normal'. Such types of communications tend to be of the type that says: 'please do this' or 'please don't do that', or 'that is enough of that', or 'it's time to do this', or 'it's time to come here', or 'it's time go there', or 'this is the way you should do this', or 'that is not the way you should do that'.

The motivation behind such forms of communication is usually positive, and can certainly support people to develop new skills or employ their current skills in more socially acceptably ways. However there is a danger that such types of directive, corrective or educative communications come to dominate the communicative exchanges between a person with a communicative impairment and their carers or support staff.

These types of communication also tend to be similar to functional communication in that they tend to be brief, unidirectional and objective based. They do not generally create meaningful two-way communications and often leave little room for negotiation or interactivity. When the person with a social or communication impairment tries to make it a two-way exchange (for example, by resisting the demands made of them), there is a good chance that this will be seen as a challenging behaviour rather than a legitimate communication.

'Responsiveness' and feedback (positive and negative)

If we are to be socially inclusive with a person with a social impairment, and wish to sustain communication over a period of time, we will need to sequence our exchanges. This means being responsive or giving some kind of 'feedback' to the communicative or potentially communicative behaviour of a person with a social impairment. Interestingly, the word feedback generally appears to be used in two different although associated ways, depending on the context of its use.

In an educational or service management context providing feedback indicates a process of offering a critical assessment on some sort of process or activity that is intended to support or develop practice at some time in future. In this sense feedback is generally taken to be an external judgement communicated to the enactor of the process or activity, and this feedback can be affirmative, constructive and encouraging. Conversely feedback may be negative, disparaging or potentially disaffecting, and such feedback will usually be at a place and time outside of the activity.

In another, more technological or engineering context (e.g. in electronic circuit design), the word 'feedback' can be used to mean some kind of signal that is partially looped back into a system as the system or activity is in progress, and this feedback is intended to help inform and control the output of the same system during the progress of that activity (such as in some kinds of electronic amplifier). This use of the word also chimes with some of my own experiences of using Intensive Interaction (and some of those reported to me by Intensive Interaction practitioners and trainees), when echoed vocalizations or reflected behaviours have seemed to help some people gain increased control over their vocalizations or behaviour when it is used as a means of social interaction, rather than just engaged in as an individual and solitary activity.

A particular example of this was when working with a middle-aged non-verbal man who generally seemed highly anxious, and who would on occasions start to breathe very rapidly and start to sweat profusely as if in the throes of a full-blown panic attack (although he could not say if this was the case, nor if it was, what was the cause). The way that I would respond to this behaviour was to gain eye contact and breathe loudly and slowly very close up to him. This slowly and deliberately paced response to his rapid breathing seemed to help him calm his own breathing rate, and reduce his sweating and apparent anxiety. It was as if my similarly framed, yet slower paced feedback (through my deliberately slow mirroring of his breathing pattern) acknowledged some aspect of his emotional state and helped him gain control of his breathing. Quite quickly we would end up breathing in and out together at a more relaxed tempo, and our interactivity would then continue as normal, through eye contact, reflected facial expressions and physical contact through his hands.

Of course there may be many occasions when a person with a social impairment has received, and perhaps continues to receive no meaningful feedback to their actions or attempts at communication (i.e. any feedback that is meaningful to them!). This absence of feedback might be expected to have a powerful influence on a person's likelihood to continue attempts to engage in sociable actions or communications. So, if we set out wishing to engage a person with a social impairment in sustained sociable interactivity, we need to start by finding a means of responding that provides meaningful and encouraging feedback to the person themselves. However, we should also endeavour to keep the tempo and pace of our responsiveness at such a level that it does not over-stimulate or bombard the person with feedback or responses that they cannot successfully process.

So how should we do this in practice? It will come as no surprise to an Intensive Interaction practitioner that we should proceed with a combination of sensitivity, intensity and creativity. We can look at what the person is currently doing or what they are attending to, and somehow reflect back some aspect or join in with this activity, even if such activity looks essentially quite passive. This could be as simple as sitting near the person and attending to the people or things that they themselves are attending to, and doing this in such a way as to make this joint attention clearly observable to the person themselves: repeatedly looking at them and then at the thing they are looking at (and possibly slowly nodding and smiling as you do so).

Equally we might engage in some kind of recognizably parallel activity – that is, some kind of response that is directly associated to something that the person has just done themselves, e.g. rhythmically vocalizing in a way that matches the physical movements of someone who body rocks or repeatedly moves some part of their body. Also we could sensitively attempt to join in directly with someone's activity in some way, without taking over or attempting to lead the activity into some other form. We could also remain outside of the activity, but give clear signals of finding interest in and attending to the activity. We can do this by giving some signals, perhaps vocally or with our facial expressions and focus of our attention, of our interest and enjoyment or appreciation of the activity – for example, through some type of vocal or verbal commentary. Using a verbal commentary might be accomplished by saying something about the activity that *demonstrates* our interest in and focus on the activity (without giving the message that we wish to affect its course in some way). A vocal or non-verbal commentary might entail giving non-symbolic but positively intonated vocal signals or interest, perhaps using extended 'oohs', 'aahs', 'eehhs' or other sounds at timely points during the activity. These sounds could also carry a questioning intonation, with a rising pitch or end-tone to the sound, thus communicating an interest in what is about to happen, or where the activity might lead.

Developmental models of communication

It is interesting and informative to look at how communication naturally develops for all of us during our early months and years, and doing this can be useful when trying to build two-way communications with people who are still in the early stages of cognitive development. Indeed this is just what Nind and Hewett (1994) did when constructing the theoretical basis for Intensive Interaction.

A newborn human baby can communicate his or her needs and emotions through loud vocalizations (e.g. crying). It is now claimed that even at very early ages they can imitate the physical movements of those around them (Zeedyk, 2008). From birth onwards human infants learn to distinguish the vocal tones of familiar people (most usually their parents), and infants also quickly learn to impart differing tones into their vocalizations to communicate their basic needs e.g. being hungry, tired, wet, in pain etc. As their level of physical control develops infants will then learn to move their head and body so that they can focus their attention on the voices or actions of another human being, and will start to attempt to respond to such sounds with similar sounds of their own. They will also begin to differentiate meaning from the vocal tone of others, and then start to master some aspects of vocal pattern making themselves, so that their sounds become increasingly speech-like – for example, saying 'da-da-da', or 'bah-bah-bah' or 'mam-mam-mam'. They will also begin to use gesture to communicate wishes and needs (e.g. physically reaching out or moving to face or align themselves towards things) (www.child-development-guide.com).

At some point in the first year most infants will come to recognize their own name, and then come to recognize common words such as 'milk' or 'bottle', and start to use speech-like sounds to get attention. Eventually, and usually within the first two years, an infant will use a mixture of non-symbolic sounds with some aspects of symbolic speech, initially mainly concrete objects and names, and then increasingly a few verbs; next will generally come a few simple phrases, then more complex sentences associated with familiar people, objects and activities (www.child-development-guide.com). Eventually children will come to understand most things said to them, and also become understandable to others around them.

Looking to make an informed judgement on the approximate developmental level of someone with severe or profound and multiple learning disabilities can sometimes help us to make our communications fit with a level that is right for them. We should, however, be careful to differentiate a person's levels of expressive communication (their ability to use language expressively) from their level of receptive capabilities – that is, the level of their understanding of other people's communications. As these may be at different development levels, if we wish someone to be an active participant in an interaction rather than merely a recipient of a communication, then the interaction has to be framed so that their developmental level of expressive language is appropriately accommodated, as well as their understanding.

Based on the 'communication staircase' model of Dr Jim MacDonald (Emeritus Professor of Speech and Language Pathology and Developmental Disabilities at the Ohio State University) the following (very simplified) list of the developmental stages of language acquisition can help us in analysing, and then matching, someone's communicative level or stage (MacDonald 2003). The model starts at birth, when the assumption is we are not intentional communicators, and defines the broad developmental stages we all pass through as we eventually go on to develop complex patterns of symbolic speech. The stages are:

1. sounds and/or actions produced without communicative intent

2. non-symbolic sounds and/or actions deliberately produced with communicative intent

3. symbolic physical gestures (i.e. signs) produced with communicative intent e.g. pointing

4. symbolic sounds produced with communicative intent (e.g. 'bi-bi' for biscuit)

5. single words produced with communicative intent

6. simple phrases produced with communicative intent

7. whole sentences produced with communicative intent.

According to MacDonald all of us learn our communication skills and move up the communication staircase by building on the skills we currently have, by frequently repeating the same types of communication, either behavioural or vocal, and gradually developing more sophisticated means. We do this by observing other communicators, modelling our communication strategies on those that we see and experiencing interactions with them. As we become more sophisticated communicators, we are also then deliberately taught some aspects of communication directly by people wishing to educate or enculturate us.

This simplified model can sometimes be usefully employed to help staff or carers reflect on the communication styles or strategies that they use with the people they work with or care for. If their communications are at a level above that of the person with a social or communicative impairment then there is likely to be a 'communication gap' which will make communication difficult, and genuine two-way meaningful interactivity impossible. By communicating in a similar way (i.e. at the same developmental level), thus closing any 'communication gap', staff or carers can make meaningful interactivity possible, and might also support a person's eventual movement up the 'communication staircase'.

Infant–caregiver interaction models and Motherese (or Infant Directed Speech)

The extensive research and literature on naturalistic models of infant–caregiver interactions (including the works of Schaffer, Trevarthen and Stern amongst many others) was closely studied by Nind and Hewett (2001) as they constructed their ideas about Intensive Interaction. These identified strategies taken from the infant–caregiver interaction model were seen to create the conditions and experiences that allow us all to become highly sophisticated communicators. From the then current body of research on infant–caregiver interactions, Hewett and Nind identified parallels with their attempts to socially engage young adults with severe intellectual disabilities.

Nind (1996) identified five central features of Intensive Interaction which also paralleled the naturally occurring interactivity between infants and their caregivers, these being:

1. the creation of mutual pleasure and interactive games – being together with the purpose of enjoying each other

2. the staff member adjusts his/her interpersonal behaviours (e.g. gaze, voice, body posture, facial expression) in order to become more engaging and meaningful to the person with a learning disability

3. interactions flow naturally in time – with pauses, repetitions and blended rhythms

4. intentionality – crediting clients with thoughts, feelings and intentions, and thus responding to a client's behaviours as if they have intentional communicative significance

5. the use of contingent responding, following the client's lead and sharing control of the activity.

Among the techniques used within an infant-caregiver interaction, one particular method is that called **Motherese** this being a term used to label a particular form of language used with young infants which makes particular use of accentuated and tuneful vocal intonation. A form of Motherese is said to be used across all cultures by mothers to communicate with their babies, and some researchers believe it is a tool used to teach an infant the fundamental structure of verbal language. **Motherese** (Snow, 1972) or **infant directed speech** (de Boer, 2005) differs from the sort of vocal communication that happens generally between adults, and uses a vocal pattern characterized by ascending intonations used when repetitively delivering a range of simplified words or phrases, often in question form.

However, I feel that the conscious use of highly accentuated Motherese should be something that Intensive Interaction practitioners think carefully about when using it with people with social or communicative impairments. Unquestionably the use of Motherese type intonation can help carry meaning within vocal or verbal exchanges, but it should perhaps be used with some caution as the aim is not to 'infantilize' the recipient in any way. It may also be that an uninformed observer of a Motherese type exchange may misread the motives of the communication partner (with the exchange being seen as disrespectful to the person with a social impairment) and so care should be taken to inform other people of the motivations underlying the use of such a vocal exchange.

Integrationism

At the start of this chapter I suggested that human communication could be seen as a simple transfer of information between two or more human beings, and then went on to outline a basic sender–receiver type description to illustrate the process. However, human communication is not always modelled as being so straightforward. One school of thought has provided a relatively new theoretical perspective on the subject of communication, and that is the 'integrationist' view (Harris, 2006).

Integrationism does not accept the simple 'sender–receiver' transmission model of communication, and it also rejects the idea that communication occurs via separate 'channels' of communication – for example, via speech or signs or gesture. It even goes so far as to suggest that language, as a process, is not a simple transmission process bound by concrete symbolic representations and formal linguistic rules. Instead the integrationist view sees communication as a dynamic and creative process that requires 'the integration of activities' (Harris, 2008) of two people to communicate meaning between them, with such 'integrated activities' being simultaneously co-created by the participants to continuously share meaning, both verbally and non-verbally (Harris, 2006).

Additionally, from the integrationist viewpoint, any communication situation is defined by three distinct 'parameters', these being:

1. the individual capabilities of the individual participants

2. the cultural practices of the participant's community or social grouping

3. the specific circumstances of the communication setting or situation.

Also, according to the integrationist view, to understand a communication situation, we should simultaneously consider a participant's present capabilities, acknowledge the impact of their previous communications experiences, and also consider any expectations a person has of what will be the outcome of the communication situation. For more information on integrationsim see www.integrationists.com.

From our position as Intensive Interaction practitioners, acknowledging such a complex integrationist view of communication could help us accept the central role of context in defining the potential success or failure of a communication. The current context of a communication situation will include the environmental setting, as well as the social and the personal historical setting in which any interactivity is hoped for. Thus we may have to allow for the enduring influence of any previous problematic communication experiences encountered by a person with a social impairment – these influences will constantly be present for them in all subsequent communications, and thus will be important in defining the context for the current situation, and their expectations of what might come from it. Therefore equally we should also endeavour to understand and accommodate a person's expectations of any communication situation.

The expectations of a person with a social impairment of a given communication situation may well be neutral or negative, and so may lead them to feel indifferent or hostile towards any communicative 'intrusion'. Thus we may need to create many positive, or at least initially non-aversive, experiences of communication (for example, where minimal demands are made of the person) before we can realistically expect the person to become an active interactor. I have experienced just such a situation on a number of occasions when I have worked with some people with severe challenging behaviour. Some people have reacted very badly, and sometimes very aggressively, to communications they seem to perceive as directive or that carry a demand on them to alter their behaviour in some way. In such cases I have initially tried to give such people repeated experiences of me being present but essentially passive, to make the initial stages as demand-free as possible. If the person's expectations alter, and allow for potentially positive interactions, then they are more likely to become active participators in meaningful interactivity.

5

Relationship Building and Maintenance

You can't overstate the importance of communication, without it you can't interact, and without interactions you can't have a relationship, and without a relationship I don't think one can have a life of any real sort.

Clinical psychologist respondent in Intensive Interaction research project

Ruth writes...

What do we mean by a relationship for people with a learning disability? Most of us have many different types of relationship. To use myself as an example, at one extreme, I have a relationship with the young man who serves me in the Co-op. I see him once every week or so and he usually asks me how I am and whether I want a bag before he scans my items. When he asks me, 'Y'alright?' I do not have the feeling that he is genuinely interested in how I am. Rather, this seems to be a formality, a verbal habit performed for the sake of politeness. When my things have been scanned, there is a further formal exchange about payment and then to say, 'Goodbye'. My feelings about this young man are entirely neutral: he is pleasant enough, and we relate in a way that fits the rules for a customer and shop assistant and which gets the job done.

At the other extreme, there is the relationship that I have with my baby daughter. I am intensely interested in how she is: whether she is happy or bored or uncomfortable; wants me to give her something, or is hungry or tired. There are times when we have a communicative exchange that makes me feel utterly delighted, for example, my little girl will clap her hands, look at me and smile. I will then clap back and grin and she beams with apparent pleasure and might clap again.

There are also times when I want to get a job done – get my daughter fed and watered, changed and clean. But I see these tasks as opportunities for social exchanges – we 'chat' throughout my daughter's meals, with me naming what I am offering her and responding to her vocalizations. When I change her, I talk to her about what I am doing and at bath time we sing songs and play splashing games. Even when we are not actively talking or vocalizing, I am still attentive to her – for example, when she is independently exploring what's on our shelves, I am watching her to ensure that she is safe and listening to her to check that she is not getting bored or too frustrated by something out of her reach. And my daughter checks that I am attending to her – turning around every so often to see whether I am looking at her. If I am, she will usually return to whatever she had been doing. If I am not, she will either vocalize (I interpret this as her saying: 'Mum, look at me!') or crawl over to see what I am doing. In contrast with my feelings towards the man who serves me in the Co-op, my feelings towards my daughter are far from neutral – I love her intensely.

In Intensive Interaction, the aim is to establish a relationship where there is a sense of connection. If a carer or support worker is there just to get the job done, this is not a foundation for such a relationship. Making a relationship takes time – the carer or support worker has to be prepared (and supported) to share time and space with the person they support, getting to know them and how they prefer to communicate. They also need to be aware of their feelings about their role, about the person they care for or work with, and of the importance of relationship building and maintenance.

If we are to make, or help others to make, genuine connections with people with communicative and/or social impairments, we need to bear many issues in mind and we can draw on various theories to help us. Important issues that I write about in this chapter include the vulnerability of people with a learning disability to abuse – this has to inform the way that Intensive Interaction is practised and safeguards are vital. I also write about some concepts that are very well known in the 'standard' psychotherapy literature – empathy, congruence, positive regard (Rogers, 1957) and warmth within relationships – and outline how these should influence the way that Intensive Interaction is offered.

In terms of theories, I write in some detail about attachment theory. This is a major school of psychological thought and has many component concepts that can help the Intensive Interaction practitioner to reflect usefully on their relationships with people with a learning disability (it may prompt the practitioner to ask, for example, 'am I acting in ways that enable me to function as a secure base for my interactive partner?'). I argue that it also provides a theoretical basis for the therapeutic potential of Intensive Interaction and can help to guide our formulations of people who have complex histories. A second theoretical perspective that I describe is concerned with the roles that people take within relationships and I propose that Berne's (1964) ideas can help the practitioner to think about these.

A theme that appears in many of the sections that follow is that of openness to emotions (our own and those of our interactive partner). I argue that this openness is crucial to forming genuine connections with others.

Abuse

Research has shown that people with a learning disability are more likely to be sexually abused than those without a learning disability (Turk and Brown, 1993). Those who lack speech are particularly vulnerable since it is so much harder for them to tell what is happening to them in a way that other people understand. Intensive Interaction can involve touch and deliberately encourages proximity, spending time together and emotional closeness. It may therefore be misused by those who seek to abuse vulnerable people, and it may be experienced as abusive if not practised sensitively. Safeguards are therefore needed. Some safeguards should already be in place – for example, under the *No Secrets* (DoH and Home Office, 2000) guidance, organizations should have policies regarding the detection and reporting of abuse and staff should be trained in this.

More local guidance may also be useful, for example, within the NHS Learning Disability directorates may produce policies specifically about the use of Intensive Interaction and how touch is to be used within this. Such a policy might, for instance, include types of touch that are and are not acceptable and stipulate that people should only be touched as part of an agreed, written plan. At a yet more local level, managers of individual homes will need to oversee actively the implementation of such plans to protect the people living in that home. The manager will also need to ensure that the types of touch being used are at the right level to avoid causing any distress (some types of touch could well cause body memories of abuse for some people and so cause extreme distress – see, for example, Hall and Lloyd (1993, p.127). If there is any concern or doubt in this area then a suitable professional (such as a clinical psychologist) should be involved.

The practitioner may need to address other issues in order to minimize the potential for unintentional abuse when implementing Intensive Interaction. Carers or support staff should again seek guidance if they are unsure about the suitability of any aspect of an Intensive Interaction intervention – for example, people with autistic spectrum disorder may well have sensory hypersensitivities that could lead them to find particular types of touch extremely aversive and a sensory profile may be very valuable (such profiling is most often carried out by speech and language therapists and/or occupational therapists). Avoidance of unintentional abuse requires all staff to be vigilant in monitoring the effects of their actions on the person. Negative reactions may be obvious (for example, a person may hit out if you get too close to them), but can be far more subtle. A person may smile out of embarrassment, for example, rather than pleasure and somebody who feels abused may become less vocal rather than more so. The practitioner needs to tune in to the person's emotional state rather than just looking at their behaviour. If unsure, the practitioner should ask another person to observe them interacting to get another view.

Some people feel embarrassed when they do Intensive Interaction, particularly at the beginning when the techniques can feel very strange. This sometimes makes people want to do Intensive Interaction away from others and possibly behind closed doors. This should be avoided (unless there are client-centred reasons for doing so) and carers or support staff should be supported to carry out Intensive Interaction in the places where a client usually spends their time. There is far less likelihood of Intensive Interaction being misused if it is carried out in the client's usual environments with other people around. This open approach brings additional benefits – for example, it promotes the idea that Intensive Interaction can be part of a person's everyday care (rather than something that only happens once in a while when certain people are there to do it) and means that people can learn from each other's practice.

Attachment relationships

The two names that are probably best known in relation to attachment theory are John Bowlby (see also the later section in this chapter, *Deficits in parental care*) and Mary Ainsworth. Bowlby was trained as a psychologist, psychiatrist and psychoanalyst and he broke with the prevailing ideas in psychoanalytic thinking when he proposed that actual events in a child's life (such as separation from his or her parents) cause distress. The existing view was that **fantasies** in the child's mind were the cause of distress rather than anything that had actually happened to them. This had far-reaching consequences in that it meant that for many decades children and adults were not believed when they reported abusive experiences, and it is only in the last 20 to 30 years that the prevailing view has changed. Bowlby's contention that these events had a very significant impact may seem obvious today, but was very unorthodox at that time.

A much simplified overview of Bowlby's theory is that:

> We are born ready to make attachments because these relationships keep us close to our caregivers and so keep us safe from harm. (See, for example, Bowlby, 1988, p.120.)

A positive (secure) attachment relationship is made when the mother (or other primary caregiver) is sensitive to the needs of her child and she responds appropriately and consistently – for example, by comforting the child when he or she is distressed and by creating a dialogue in which the infant takes the lead. A sensitive mother can be described as being **attuned** to her child and I write about this concept in more detail in Chapter 8, in the section *Attunement and mis-attunement*. Bowlby (1988, p.7) describes the dialogue between mother and child as follows:

> [w]hereas an infant's initiation and withdrawal from interaction tend to follow their own autonomous rhythm, a sensitive mother regulates her behaviour so that it meshes with his. In addition, she modifies the form her behaviour takes to suit him: her voice is gentle but higher pitched than usual, her movements slowed, and each action adjusted in form and timing according to how her baby is performing. Thus she lets him call the tune and by a skilful interweaving of her own responses with his *creates a dialogue*. (italics added)

A positive attachment relationship leads to the primary attachment figure functioning as a **secure base** for the child (see, for example, Bowlby, 1988, p.11). As the child gets older, they will go off and explore the world, safe in the knowledge that they can rely on their caregiver to be there if needed. They will gradually move further away from their care-giver, coming back periodically for reassurance, then setting off again. When the child is frightened or unwell, they will stay closer to their caregiver.

A positive attachment relationship is vital for emotional and social development and for the child to have a positive view of him- or herself. Without such a relationship, the child is likely to experience a negative self-view and social and emotional problems in later life. Bowlby (1988, p.132) describes how avoidant infants have been observed to *not* commu-nicate with their mothers when they are distressed:

> already by the age of 12 months there are children who no longer express to their mothers one of their deepest emotions or the equally deep-seated desire for comfort and reassurance that accompanies it. [...] because a child's self-model is profoundly influenced by how his mother sees and treats him, whatever she fails to recognize in him he is likely to fail to recognize in himself.

Bowlby later (1988, p.143) hypothesizes that such children will subse-quently strive to 'be emotionally self-contained and insulated against intimate contacts with other people'. As we grow older, we form other at-tachment relationships – for example, with friends and romantic partners – but it is very difficult to 'escape' from the pattern that was established in our primary attachment relationship.

Ainsworth (e.g. 1967) was one of Bowlby's students who made some major contributions to our understanding of attachment. She is best known for the 'Strange Situation Test' (see, for example, Ainsworth and Wittig, 1969) which is used to study attachment patterns. This is the re-search which first identified the different patterns of attachment – *secure, anxious resistant, anxious avoidant* and *disorganized* (the interested reader is referred to Bowlby (1988, pp.123–126) for a concise description of these different patterns).

As described in more detail in the section *Deficits in parental care,* adults with a learning disability are likely to have experienced life events that will have predisposed them to having anxious attachment patterns. If we think about somebody with an anxious avoidant pattern, one fea-ture of this pattern is avoidance of negative emotions such as distress and anger. Emotions that are avoided, however, do not just go away, but can build up outside of the person's awareness until they can no longer be contained and may then be expressed explosively – a person might there-fore react very violently to a loss, but give very few signs that this is about to happen. Alternatively, a person might be so anxious that they feel unable to attempt anything without the help of others (since they have no secure base to venture out from) or feel utterly helpless and stop trying to interact with the world and other people (in other worlds, become very withdrawn).

So, can attachment patterns that are formed in infancy be changed later in life? Research with ordinary (intellectually average) adults indicates that they can. Bowlby (1988, p.127) cites a review carried out by Sroufe (1985) which showed that when parents treated their children (of up to three years old) differently, the pattern of attachment changes accordingly. Main, Kaplan and Cassidy (1985) similarly found that some mothers were able to overcome the poor parenting that they themselves had received and establish a secure attachment with their own children.

Bowlby (1988) proposes that therapy should specifically aim to provide a 'corrective' (positive) experience of a close relationship and notes that:

> [a]lthough the capacity for developmental change diminishes with age, change continues throughout the life cycle so that changes for better or worse are always possible. [...] at no time in life is a person impermeable to favourable influence. It is this persisting potential for change that gives opportunity for effective therapy. (Bowlby, 1988, p.136)

It would be extremely beneficial to be able to look at attachment patterns in adults with a learning disability and assess whether any approach can help those with insecure attachment patterns to achieve a more secure pattern. Such a process, however, would be incredibly difficult. Just measuring attachment patterns is a major hurdle in itself. So at present we have to rely on educated clinical hypotheses (guesses, you might say) about people's attachment patterns and what affects those patterns and how.

My best guess about Intensive Interaction is that it has the potential to enable secure attachments to be developed with some people with a learning disability. This will not be a surprise to readers who know about the origins of Intensive Interaction – namely, its roots in Ephraim's (1982) description of 'Augmented Mothering', derived from how sensitive mothers interact with their infants. And it is these very same interactions which (as described above) are held to lead to secure attachments. Of course, we have no body of evidence as to whether the attachment patterns of people with a learning disability are plastic (that is, whether they are capable of change) and so we have to extrapolate from theory and other empirical evidence. On the other hand, we have no evidence to suggest that they are not plastic nor that they will be less plastic than those of ordinary adults. The available evidence therefore favours the hypothesis that Intensive Interaction can help to establish secure attachment relationships with people who are anxiously attached, but there is a pressing need for research (at the case study level) to test this explicitly.

Avoidance

My experience has been that many services need to do more to support direct-care workers with relationship building and maintenance, and with their feelings towards their role and the people that they support. Supporting people who are disabled in profound ways necessarily raises powerful emotions and if staff are not given permission to discuss these feelings they will be repressed and avoided (see, for example, Whittington and Burns, 2005). Focusing on the tasks of the job – getting people bathed, dressed, fed and so on – can function as an avoidance strategy. Covert avoidance may also happen when the carer or support worker is thinking about something else rather than the person they are supporting. I write about avoidance in a lot more detail in Chapter 8 (in the section on *Avoidance*) and the reader may wish to refer to this section now.

Deficits in parental care

Bowlby was particularly concerned with the effects of deficits in parental care on children (for example, Bowlby, 1953). In 1950 he was appointed consultant in mental health to the World Health Organization, and in 1951 he published a report for them entitled *Maternal Care and Mental Health*. He based his later book, *Child Care and the Growth of Love* (1953), on this report. His central argument was that 'the quality of the parental care which a child receives in his earliest years is of vital importance for his future mental health' (Bowlby, 1953, p.11). He describes how this care is usually provided by the mother, but that a child may experience either **'partial deprivation'** or **'complete deprivation'** of maternal care (1953, p.12). Partial deprivation occurs, for example, when a child is temporarily removed from his or her mother and complete deprivation when the child is removed from his/her mother and no-one cares for him/her in a personal, warm way. Bowlby continues, 'The ill-effects of deprivation vary with its degree. Partial deprivation brings in its train anxiety, excessive need for love...[and so on]. Complete deprivation [...] may entirely cripple the capacity to make relationships with other people' (1953, p.12).

Any child – with or without a learning disability – can be subject to deficits in parental care, including repeated abandonments and what Bowlby would term 'complete deprivation'. A child with a learning disability is, however, at greater risk. O'Connor (2001, p.298) describes this succinctly: 'The reaction of parents to the birth of a disabled child can be devastating and it may take a long time for the parents to grieve the loss of the longed-for perfect child. In the grieving process, the attachment with the disabled child can be severely affected. The emotional availability of parents during the first years of a learning disabled child's life may be limited (Bicknell, 1983)'.

In the 1990s I worked at one of the old learning disability hospitals and was told that many of the adults who lived there had been placed in hospital as children. This was awful enough, but I was told that the hospital policy had been to advise parents not to visit for several weeks after admission to allow the child to 'settle in'. Bowlby (1953) gives us an insight into what the experience of these children was like when he describes the effects of maternal abandonment on a boy of 24 months. He had previously been a 'well-developed easy child with a good relation to his mother' (p.26). When she stopped visiting him, however:

> He became listless, often sat in a corner sucking and dreaming, at other times he was very aggressive. He almost completely stopped talking. He was dirty and wet continually [...]. He was [...] always in trouble and in need of help and comfort. (p. 27)

There is no reason to think that the reaction of a child with a learning disability would have been any different, but I suspect that their understandable grief and protest would have been labelled as 'maladaptive' or 'challenging' behaviour or seen as part of their learning disability and so not responded to empathically. These children would then have faced multiple abandonments as those around them would come and go – staff and professionals moving on to other jobs and peers moving to other placements. And the effects of these abandonments could be magnified by inadequate preparation. Many times, staff who are about to leave their post have said to me, 'I haven't told Susan [the person most attached to them] because I don't want to upset her.' So not only is Susan subject to the loss of this person, the abandonment comes suddenly and unexpectedly. In trying to protect people with a learning disability, we can end up by hurting them more.

As described in the opening paragraph of this section, Bowlby argues that deficits in maternal care will have profound effects on a person. In his 1953 work he describes the central effect as being 'the child's inability to make relationships' (p.35) and he sees other negative effects as springing from this. In his 1988 work (pp.123–126), other research (especially that of Ainsworth (e.g. Ainsworth, 1967); see the earlier section, *Attachment relationships*) meant that Bowlby was able to describe the different **patterns of attachment** that result from different shortcomings in parental care. A parent who is accessible and responsive is likely to have a securely attached child – such a child, for example, is confident to go off and explore the world, returning to the parent when feeling anxious or uncertain. This child is likely to experience positive mental health. Deficits in parenting, however, can give rise to different patterns of **anxious attachment** – these are anxious resistant, anxious avoidant and disorganized. To give one example – in an anxious resistant attachment 'the individual is uncertain whether his parent will be available or responsive or helpful when called upon. Because of this uncertainty he is always prone to separation anxiety, tends to be clinging and is anxious about exploring the world' (Bowlby, 1988, p.124).

The way in which these patterns are responded to later on can serve to perpetuate and strengthen them. People who want lots of contact, for example, are often labelled as 'attention seeking' (especially, I think, if they have a learning disability). At first carers or support workers may go along with this need and spend lots of time with the person until they feel overwhelmed because they sense that they can never give enough, and they may then try to deliberately limit their interactions with the person in the belief that this alone will solve the problem. In fact, my experience has been that this strategy tends to make the problem worse as the person works even harder to try to recapture the closeness that they have lost.

At the other end of the spectrum are people who withdraw from others and may acquire labels such as 'autistic' or a 'loner'. These labels can then be seen as a justification for not *trying* to interact with them – they are described as being 'happy in their own worlds' and as not wanting to be with people. Similarly, people who behave in extreme ways (which we can describe as exotic or challenging) quickly acquire reputations as being 'difficult' and carers or support workers may try to keep out of their way.

I am not advocating Intensive Interaction as a cure for the problems associated with deficits in parental care. Rather, it may be one part of a package that may help, but this needs to be guided by a detailed psychological formulation. Rushing in to make a relationship with somebody who has a complex history can make matters worse – for example, if the practitioner feels unable to continue with the work should the person become very challenging, and ends the input abruptly. This constitutes yet another abandonment. With a formulation in place, however, Intensive Interaction has the potential to offer people a positive experience of a relationship since the approach is about finding what works for the person – it is implicit in this that the relationship will develop at a pace that is comfortable for the person and involve detailed observation for any negative effect on them. Sustainability of the input will ideally be considered from the outset (for all clients) since depending solely on one practitioner builds in a high likelihood of the input ceasing when the worker moves on. This is one major reason why promoting the idea of a 'community of practice' (see Chapter 6, the section *Legitimate Peripheral Participation*) is important. Developing a community of people who can interact with somebody gives a far better chance of sustained input (see also Chapter 12, the section *Sustainability and 'initiative decay'*).

Empathy, congruence and positive regard

Rogers (1957) wrote about the conditions that he saw as necessary for therapeutic change in a person seeking help from a counsellor (for an overview, see Merry, 2002, pp.49–52). Rogers listed six conditions of which three have subsequently received the most attention and become known as the 'core conditions':

- empathy

- congruence

- unconditional positive regard.

Empathy is about being able to understand the world from another person's point of view. When we are working with a client with autism, for example, we have to be able to understand that the way in which they see and experience the world is very different from how we see and understand the world. Something which might seem insignificant to us – an ornament having been moved on a shelf, say – may trigger an extreme reaction in the person with autism. If we are going to understand this person, then, we have to try to look at things as they would look at them. (I write about this concept in more detail in Chapter 8, in the section *Empathy*).

Congruence is about being authentic or real. In her book, *Mental Handicap and the Human Condition*, Sinason (1992, pp.17–38) describes how difficult it is for us to be real with people with a learning disability. Rather than accept the difficult feelings that go along with a disability – frustration, anger, sadness, despair, shame and so on – we try to pretend that everything is all right and we cover up the negative feelings with false brightness. We also expect people with a learning disability to help us out and cover up their feelings of sadness or anger with a big smile – what Sinason terms the 'handicapped smile': 'some handicapped people behave like smiling pets for fear of offending those they are dependent on' (Sinason, 1992, p.21).

Unconditional positive regard is about valuing and accepting some-body *just as they are*, no conditions attached. This is such an important concept that it has its own section later in this chapter.

If we are going to be real with our clients, we have to start tuning in to *our* feelings *and* those of our clients. This can be incredibly painful. This was brought home to me some years ago when I did a file review for a client, Mary, who has been in hospital since early childhood. She has experienced neglect, abandonment and abuse of all kinds. I was pro-foundly angry and sad for months and cried many times for her. I was only able to bear these feelings with the help of a close colleague and my partner. Whenever I think of this lady and the life that she has endured these feelings return and remain powerful. I wanted to make everything all right for her and had to accept the frustration that I was not powerful enough to do this. With a colleague, we offered her sessions of Intensive Interaction with the intention that this would provide her with some pleasant experiences of human interaction. I believe that we were success-ful in this and in providing her with an opportunity to make safe choices and so have some sense of control in her life.

Fulfilling relationships and positive psychology

Dr Nick Baylis is a well-being scientist and was Britain's first lecturer in positive psychology. Positive psychology looks at things from a different direction than traditional psychology. A traditional psychologist would ask, 'what's going wrong?' and 'how can I fix that?' In this vein a psychotherapist would look at a person's childhood to identify the 'what's gone wrong' and would (if appropriate) offer therapy to help correct it. In contrast, a positive psychologist asks, 'what's going right?' and 'how can I build on that?'

In his book *Learning from Wonderful Lives* (Baylis, 2005), Baylis looks at what is known about people who have lives that are going well, people who have lasting happiness and accomplishments. The first chapter describes the importance of close relationships for good psychological health (which includes happiness) and he cites some big American studies that support this link (see pp.5–6). Such evidence is not new, however – a seminal study published 30 years ago (Brown and Harris, 1978) identified the importance of a confiding relationship in protecting women from depression.

Baylis (2005) talks about the qualities of relationships that matter, which include:

- closeness or intimacy, 'something deeply shared' (pp.6 and 7)

- seeking continually to develop intimacy (p.19)

- 'a union of equals' (p.17), and

- 'sharing enjoyable activities' (p.18).

Although Baylis is talking about 'ordinary' friendships and partnerships, these qualities are also features of the relationships that should be formed when using Intensive Interaction and should therefore mean that these relationships have the same life-enhancing qualities for people with a learning disability as they do for everyone else. That is not to say that forming such relationships will be easy. Developing a real intimacy or closeness, for example, requires the practitioner to identify any negative feelings towards the person with a learning disability rather than just cover these feelings up with false brightness (see the earlier section, *Empathy, congruence and positive regard*).

We can only be truly close to a person with a learning disability if we accept the profound sadness and negative impact of their disability as well as being open to seeing them as who they are and mindful of our own emotions. We need to be emotionally aware and responsive since, as Sinason (1992, p.74) writes: 'However crippled someone's external functional intelligence may be, there still can be intact a complex emotional structure and capacity. To reach and explore this emotional intelligence a great deal of guilt must be dealt with, guilt of the patient for his handicap and guilt of the worker for being normal.'

Similarly, it is not enough for carers or support staff to say 'I see you as my equal' – since this may cover all manner of negative assumptions about people with a learning disability (for example, that they are inferior or child-like or fundamentally *different* in some way). Again, these assumptions need to be identified and examined rather than hidden away.

The *sharing* of enjoyable activities also requires that the practitioner is present emotionally as well as physically. They need to observe closely and tune in to their interactive partner to ensure that they are reading their emotional state and responding accordingly at the level of feelings as well as action.

The relationships that we have with people with a learning disability deserve this level of attention since close relationships do not just protect us from sadness and make us happier but 'can imbue our whole lifetime with purpose and meaning' (Baylis, 2005, p.7).

Relationships: who with?

Baylis (2005, pp.5–6) summarizes a large scale American research project which found that the breadth and depth of personal relationships are crucial to our well-being. Ideally, then, we would like such relationships for people with a learning disability – namely, a handful of intimate companions and friendly neighbours, and a wider network of supportive folk. Indeed *Valuing People* (DoH, 2001), the UK government's strategy for learning disability in the 21st Century', clearly stated that the objective for learning disability services is to enable people, even with the most profound and complex learning disabilities, to '...develop a range of activities including leisure, interests, friendships and relationships' (DoH, 2001, p.7).

I see this as a laudable aim. The people that this book focuses on (those who might benefit from Intensive Interaction), however, often have quite superficial relationships with the people who are paid to care for them. I therefore think that change has to start with people in the person's immediate environment (carers, parents, advocates, professionals) through helping them to establish closer and more fulfilling relationships with the person. Using Intensive Interaction can be the route that enables this to happen.

Roles within relationships

One of the most famous books about the roles that people take in relationships is Eric Berne's (1964) *Games People Play*. Berne writes from a psychoanalytical perspective (see description of this term in Chapter 7, in the section *Psychoanalytic therapies*) and, in essence, he identifies three positions that people can occupy – Parent, Adult and Child. He then describes the **transactions** that occur between people which involve these different positions – he gives the following examples of Adult–Adult transactions (p.29):

> Person 1: 'Maybe we should find out why you have been drinking more lately'. Person 2: 'Maybe we should. I would certainly like to know!'

> Person 1: 'Do you know where my cufflinks are?' Person 2: 'On the desk'.

In these examples, Person 1 speaks from an Adult position to Person 2's Adult position and Person 2 replies from their Adult position to Person 1's Adult position. But things are not always this simple. Person 2 – in replying to the same words from Person 1 – could reply as follows:

'You're always criticizing me, just like my father did' or 'You always blame me for everything' which are both Child–Parent responses. Such responses effectively end the Adult–Adult transaction until things can be 'put right'. Putting things right will involve either Person 1 taking up the Parental position (to respond to Person 2's Child) or Person 2's Adult being reactivated to respond to Person 1's Adult.

We are most likely to respond from the position that we are addressed in. So if I say from the Parent position, 'for goodness sake, will you clean your office', I am addressing my partner's Child position and so they are likely to respond from this position (although they do not *have* to).

These ideas can help us to think about our relationships with other people, including people with a learning disability. My own experience has been that adults with a learning disability are often forced into responding from the Child position by virtue of the way that they are addressed (for example, being *told* to do something which draws an angry refusal). I have also found that Child–Child interactions are often not used at all. These could be used deliberately – for example, to create playful, fun exchanges. Intensive Interaction can be thought of as a vehicle for stimulating such exchanges.

A common misunderstanding of Intensive Interaction is that it treats people as children since interactions are often non-verbal. The intent, however, is to treat the person as an equal not as an infant – to 'talk' with them in their language and so enable them to have social exchanges that are commonplace for most of us. In the terms of transactional analysis, the aim is to have an Adult–Adult or Child–Child transaction. If we talk to people in a language that they cannot understand we disempower and alienate them. If we try to find ways of communicating that are meaningful, however, we open up the possibility of the person having an effect on their environment, enjoying the company of others and being seen as a person (rather than a collection of needs or deficits). If we see somebody with a learning disability as who they really are, there is a better chance that we will genuinely value and respect them and be less likely to patronize or disregard them.

Unconditional positive regard

We all make judgements of others (pretty much all the time) and so we have to learn to be non-judgemental (for more detail about this issue, see Chapter 8, the section *Assumptions*). When we think that somebody has done something because they are lazy or bloody-minded or out to provoke us, we are judging them. As Merry (2002, pp.80–81) describes, we show unconditional positive regard when we are attentive to somebody and show that we care for them and prize them as somebody unique, worthwhile and valuable. The **unconditional** part refers to a 'no strings' acceptance of the person – we accept them good and bad and do not expect them to live up to a particular standard to gain our approval. In my clinical practice I try to *understand* rather than judge, and I have found that if we understand, we can usually do something that will help a situation.

As described in the earlier section *Empathy, congruence and positive regard*, our approval of people with a learning disability is often dependent on their behaving in a particular way – we will be full of smiles ourselves when the person with a learning disability smiles at us, but we find it troubling if the person is sad, angry or distressed. We may therefore tend to make our approval dependent on the person showing only positive emotions (happiness) and withdraw our approval when any negative emotions are shown. I worked with one client who was praised for not being sad after his mother died – as it was put to me, 'he's done ever so well – not cried once'.

Sinason (1992, p.27) argues that such things happen since, as we cannot bear the pain of the disability itself, we certainly cannot bear to see any additional pain. This also links to issues covered in the section on *Attachment* – if we cannot help the person with a learning disability to be with their own negative emotions, they will have no choice but to cut off from them. Intensive Interaction offers the possibility of responding to all the emotional communications of our partner, be they positive or negative, and so has the potential to help the person to learn to accept and (later) modulate their own feelings. I see this focus on emotions as a core feature of 'therapeutic Intensive Interaction' and its potential is very exciting (although not yet directly tested).

Warmth within relationships

My experience has been that most staff come to a caring or support role *wanting* to make relationships with the people that they care for and support. Some of these relationships have all the characteristics that we would want. Some staff, however, can be very warm towards the person that they support, but see their role as being that of always developing the skills of the person, rather than just *being with* the person at times. At a negative extreme I have also worked with staff who show very little warmth towards the people whom they support and seem to see their role as being one of containment and control. Such staff seem to have become entrenched in avoidance strategies (for avoiding negative emotions) which have resulted in burnout (Whittington and Burns, 2005).

In addressing these difficulties, recruitment of care or support staff into learning disability services should ideally favour those candidates who can demonstrate a genuine warmth towards and desire to get to know the people they will be supporting. Attention also needs to be given to the relationship between direct-care staff and their immediate and senior managers. If direct-care workers feel that they are not valued and that managers have little interest in them, it should not be surprising that they do not value and show interest in the people that they support. Managers at all levels within organizations need to demonstrate the characteristics that they would like to see their staff display. Training in Intensive Interaction for people who support those with communication and social impairments should also specifically address quality-of-relationship issues.

6

Issues Associated with Human Learning (Developmental Issues)

Learning, whatever else it may be, is an interactive process in which people learn from each other.

Jerome Bruner (1999a, p.162)

Graham writes...

In this chapter I will discuss some issues that the reader might usefully reflect on when considering how Intensive Interaction can promote communicative skill and cognitive development. I will also briefly characterize some theoretical models of learning that might be used to analyse Intensive Interaction, and thus throw some light on the learning processes taking place during Intensive Interaction activity. However, these learning processes are not always simple or straightforward, and it should be acknowledged that theoretical claims can sometimes be contentious, with different people taking different positions on issues.

In the first instance it might be useful to acknowledge that learning and teaching are separate issues or processes, although obviously closely interrelated. For the purpose of analysis it might be useful to differentiate the two, and even think about who does the teaching and how things are taught, and who does the learning, and how learning accrues.

Learning can be viewed and analysed from a number of perspectives and, as Intensive Interaction practitioners, it might be advantageous not to look at learning as something that an individual person does. It may be more useful to perceive and conceptualize learning as a more diffuse interactional or social process that involves a number of people. As Jerome Bruner, the famed educational theoretician, said: 'Learning, whatever else it may be, is an interactive process in which people learn from each other' (1999a, p.162). This interactive process is perhaps particularly pertinent in the earliest forms of communicative learning, where at least two participants are always required for communication to arise.

When we reflect on the processes of learning, we can also think about the nature of the skills or knowledge created by the process of Intensive Interaction for both the 'learner' and the practitioner. We may also see some value in reflecting on how different kinds or levels of knowledge are expressed or utilized, and how some insight into these might be useful to us in different aspects of our Intensive Interaction practice, and in framing our expectations of our interactive partners.

In this chapter I attempt to identify and shed some light on these issues. The reader is encouraged to see the material as a stimulus for their own reflection. The ideas will also, it is hoped, provide compelling theoretical arguments to support practitioners if they are required to explain their practice in educational settings.

'Dual aspect process model of intensive interaction' and plateauing

In a paper published in the *British Journal of Learning Disabilities* (Firth, 2008) I proposed a view that Intensive Interaction can be seen to be an approach employed in two different, although closely related, ways. First I suggested that there is a 'social inclusion process model' of Intensive Interaction, when practitioners use the approach with the primary aim of inclusively responding to the communication of a person with learning disability, however it is expressed. I also proposed that there was a 'developmental process model', and this could be seen to be evident when practitioners have identifiably educative or developmental goals for the person with learning disabilities, rather than the approach being viewed simply as a means of contemporaneous social inclusion. I termed this duality the 'dual aspect process model' of Intensive Interaction.

I presented my view that different practitioners use the approach with different aims in mind. Moreover I argued that early on, quite dramatic or rapid improvement in the fundamental communication and sociability a person with a learning disability might well arise as they express or employ latent communicative skills. I see this as due to the truly inclusive nature of the approach that allows a person with a communicative or social impairment to employ latent but previously unexpressed communication skills, and was thus evidence of the 'social inclusion process model' of Intensive Interaction. I also said that, when Intensive Interaction is employed as an educational tool over the longer term, then developmental progression can ensue, but at a slower pace than during the social inclusion aspect, and that this provides evidence for the 'developmental process model' of Intensive Interaction.

I also stated that a point would arise when any initial rapid change would segue into less discernible developmental progression, and that this process was described by the term 'plateauing' (Nind and Hewett, 2005, p.134). This 'plateauing' is, I argued, potentially an important time for providing practitioners with support, as the previous, easily discernible interactive growth levels off into a phase of less rapid development. At this point of 'plateauing' practitioners might need help, for example, to reflect on their continued practice and the expectations that they hold for future development.

Pedagogy and learning

Pedagogy is the term used to describe the art or science of teaching. A particular pedagogy is the way a teacher goes about instructing learners or facilitating learning, and it can be influenced by a number of practical as well as philosophical issues. Pedagogical analysis is focused on the actions and intentions of a teacher (a teacher being defined here as a person aiming to impart knowledge to someone), and it does not tend to focus on the role or activities of the person doing the learning. As such, pedagogy is teacher-focused, looking at what is being taught, how it is taught, and who it is taught to. Not surprisingly, when looking at Intensive Interaction as an educative intervention, the pedagogy of the teacher can best be described as 'interactional' and learner-centred.

Although learning can be defined in a number of different ways, perhaps a common-sense view of learning is that it is a process in which someone acquires new skills, knowledge or understanding (and also possibly new preferences, values or beliefs). Learning accrues through personal participation in activities or experiences that allow for the acquisition or construction of different types of skills, knowledge and understanding. Such learning activities or experiences can range in duration and complexity, they can be entered into alone or collaboratively, and they can be self-directed or led by someone else. Learning can be contextualized within real life events or purposeful tasks, or it can be decontextualized and abstracted from real life situations. It can also be either a conscious or unconscious process.

When Intensive Interaction is analysed from the perspective of the identified learner (usually, but not exclusively, the person with a learning disability) then the learning they are engaged in is perhaps best described as socially supported acquisition and development of fundamental communication skills and sociability. Put more simply, they are learning the skills to relate to, and communicate with, other people by actively engaging in that very process.

Active learning vs. acquisition models of learning (passive learning)

Learning itself can be variously analysed, defined and categorized. The comparison between 'active learning' processes and passive or 'transmission' models of learning is probably a good place to start when we want to compare learning models.

An 'acquisition of know-how' (Bruner, 1999b) model is a learning model that sees knowledge almost as an item for consumption that can be presented or transmitted to learners. The acquisition of knowledge tends to occur via didactic or formally instructional teaching methods such as showing and telling, and the learner is seen as a passive recipient of knowledge. The leaner is not seen to be involved in any exploration or questioning of the material, and is simply required to accept the knowledge unmodified. In such a model the teacher decides what is important to be taught, how and at what pace it should be taught, and who is allowed to learn it. A good example of this is rote learning of facts, such as historical dates or mathematical algorithms.

In 'active learning' scenarios the learner is engaged in a process of actively constructing their own understanding of a concept, issue or experience. In such scenarios, it is the learner who interprets the learning experiences made available to them by a process of active exploration, and who, according to learning theorist Jean Piaget, accommodates or assimilates any knowledge with their current understanding (Piaget, 1955). The process of assimilation is seen as a cognitive process which involves a person coming to an understanding of an experience by somehow fitting that experience into, or aligning it with their existing understanding (even if that understanding is incomplete or inaccurate). Accommodation, however, is seen as a process in which a person changes their understanding of an experience, in light of involvement in that experience. It is in such a scenario that learning takes place.

In active learning scenarios, it is the learner who decides the particular focus, method and pace of learning, and brings their own motivation to bear on their engagement in the process. Intensive Interaction can be understood as an active learning scenario.

Development and developmentalism

Going back as far as the 18th century the educational philosopher Jean-Jacques Rousseau proposed that there was a single developmental process common to all humans, and that specific stages of education should be differentiated to address the different developmental phases of a child (*Émile, or On Education*, and *The Social Contract*, Rousseau, 1762a, b). This developmental process was seen as an intrinsic, natural process, and subsequently proposed theories of 'developmentalism' (Stone, 1996) presume that there is a best possible developmental trajectory that developmentally appropriate teaching will optimally support.

More recently the pioneering educational theorist Jean Piaget proposed his own theory of developmental stages, and as part of his theory of 'genetic epistemology' he identified four particular 'cognitive' stages that he suggested all naturally developing humans pass through before reaching their full cognitive capacity: (1) a Sensorimotor period; (2) a Preoperational period; (3) a Concrete Operational period; and (4) a Formal Operational period (Piaget, 1955). These stages have been used by educationalists and teachers to create distinct learning or teaching programmes that provide learning suited to these cognitive stages, and for some years Piaget's views were extremely influential in educational circles. Such strict developmental views are not, however, universally accepted.

However, in broader and perhaps less clearly differentiated developmental terms, seeing development as a progression from a novice state, with early levels of skill and knowledge development, to a more advanced state can be a useful analytic tool. If we see fundamental skills as a pre-requisite for the development of more advanced skills, then any educational experiences should look to provide someone with developmentally appropriate learning opportunities to practise, and thus develop their current skills (fundamental communication and sociability skills in the case of Intensive Interaction).

Thus, from a developmental perspective, it should be individualized and developmentally appropriate learning opportunities that Intensive Interaction practitioners endeavour to create, rather than imposing an externally devised and universally applicable curriculum model (although obviously a curriculum can be drafted in ways that account for an individual and their preferred means of interactivity). We can only teach people, or perhaps more accurately, support people to learn skills that are at an accessible developmental level, and an accessible developmental level will be at or only just in advance of their current developmental level. This accessible developmental level, the level ideally suited to learning, is described by learning theorist Lev Vygotsky as the 'Zone of Proximal Development' (Vygotsky, 1978), with 'proximal' in this term meaning the next level at which a learner can successfully engage in an activity (if supported by a more expert practitioner). Learning activities designed to take advantage of this conceptual Zone of Proximal Development (ZDP) are characterized by having an appropriate balance between aspects that are reassuringly familiar and aspects that are acceptably challenging (Rogoff, 1999).

Greater efforts and time spent looking to more accurately assess and identify the true nature of someone's developmental level can help educational services construct a more appropriate curriculum model and thus support more successful learning.

Different views of knowledge and skills

It might be useful at this point to give some thought as to the actual nature of what we call skills and knowledge. If we can try to define or characterize the types of skills and knowledge required to engage in fundamental communication or sociable activity, then we might better be able to make a judgement as to how it is best taught or learned. Of course, not all the learning takes place on the part of the person with a social or communicative impairment. Within interactive social engagement both parties act, perceive and learn at the same time.

Looking generally, from a theoretical point of view, there are a number of competing interpretations as to the forms which knowledge or skills can take, and generally knowledge and skills can be differentiated by how they are acquired and how they are exhibited. If we were to look at the engagement of a person with a social or communicative impairment in the processes of Intensive Interaction, we would want them to develop the necessary knowledge and skills to effectively employ and exercise fundamental communication and sociability practices (rather than acquiring abstract or declarative knowledge about its constituent aspects). These kinds of practice-based knowledge or skills, those that are learned and expressed in actions or behaviours, are sometimes referred to as 'procedural knowledge' (Bruner, 1999b), that is, the knowledge required to carry out procedures or practical actions successfully. Such knowledge or skill is seen to be expressed and employed without higher level cognitive processing, and has been termed as just 'knowing' (von Glasersfeld, 1996), i.e. knowing how to do something, rather than possessing knowledge or dry facts about something.

Most often, knowledge or skills tend to be viewed and are therefore often assessed in individualistic terms, with people being seen to acquire knowledge individually, and then subsequently recall and apply such knowledge without any support from others. It is this kind of knowledge that is most often prioritized in traditional teaching curricula (and therefore in most school classrooms), and it is easier to assess or test for, in terms of individual attainment. In contrast, we can see some knowledge in more active 'participatory' terms. In contrast to individualized forms of knowledge, this is a broader conceptualization of knowledge that is seen to be created through, and concurrently exhibited in, participation in collaborative activities. Learning theorists Lave and Wenger see knowledge construction as a process that is shared between co-participants, not a 'one person act' where 'learning is a process that takes place in a participation framework, not in an individual mind' (1991, p.15). Such participatory knowledge is therefore viewed as socially distributed and contextualized, with the necessary knowledge for the successful completion of a particular activity being held collectively by all the participants in a given activity. This is one way of modelling the knowledge in Intensive Interaction. As we will see later, this view of contextualized participatory knowledge fits very well with 'situated' views of learning and cognition, where individual task performance is seen as less important than collaborative engagement in socially constructed activity.

Applying this model to Intensive Interaction, instead of individual participants being viewed as acquiring decontextualized 'knowledge' of communication skills, the interactional processes instead allow for the concurrent socially supported expression and development of fundamental communication skills. Therefore, when looking to record and describe the skills developed as a result of Intensive Interaction, traditional individualistic conceptions of knowledge and skills seem insufficient. We need to be aware that Intensive Interaction is jointly constructed, collaboratively expressed and specifically socially contextualized. Therefore any attempts to decontextualize and individualistically assess communicative development from Intensive Interaction will not be an accurate reflection of a person's true attainment.

Participation frameworks

The concept of 'participation frameworks' was put forward by the distinguished sociologist Erving Goffman (1981) who recognized the complexity of the linguistic structures that regulate and direct verbal interactions. In Goffman's view conversations were more than just people taking turns to pass information between each other; he recognized that issues such as purpose, social context, identity and each participant's perceived role were also important.

Although developed through a process of 'Conversational Analysis' (Sacks, 1992) of symbolic interchanges, the concept of a 'participation framework' is, I believe, a useful tool to bring to bear in arranging and supporting Intensive Interaction activity for people with a social or communicative impairment, even if they are non-verbal. Although Intensive Interaction can be intuitive and 'in the moment', such a framework can and should be actively created to best facilitate Intensive Interaction from them individually. If we want to work successfully with people who find sociable interaction difficult or unrewarding, we can use such a participation framework idea to structure our thinking about how we create an encouraging and engaging physical and social environment that is supportive of the person's social participation.

Developing a 'participation framework' for an individual can be done by reflecting on a series of questions, and then writing them down for others to see and possibly follow. If we want to define the most ideal framework, we could usefully ask what environmental characteristics this 'framework' might require:

- Will the framework require the presence of certain people? (And possibly the absence of certain other potentially distracting people?)

- Will the framework require the defining of certain physical characteristics in terms of the space made available? (And possibly the absence of some other potentially distracting physical characteristics?)

- Will the framework require the inclusion of certain resources or sensory items, which could be made freely available during the whole, or periods of a session of Intensive Interaction? (And possibly the absence of other potentially distracting resources and items?)

- What context is in place to give meaning or purpose to an interaction?

- Are there certain times of the day, or particular places in a person's daily schedule that will make Intensive Interaction more likely to succeed?

- How active or passive will the person be, at what points might they be initiating or at what points might they be responding, and how will they be encouraged and supported to engage in the interactivity?

We could look at the classrooms or residential spaces that we find ourselves working in. Are these the best places for Intensive Interaction to occur for the identified individuals? If not, how do we create a 'participation framework' that is more contextually suited to the creation of successful Intensive Interaction? Reflection on these issues could well be time well spent and any clear framework created can then be shared with others who might also wish to create the most suitable environment for Intensive Interaction.

Apprenticeship models of learning

'Apprenticeship' models of learning have perhaps traditionally been associated with the dissemination of skills and knowledge from an expert or master of some industrial-type craft, to a young novice or apprentice.

According to some learning theorists, however, such 'Apprenticeships' can be seen to be at play when we all learn the most commonplace yet highly complex and important skills of human communication and social interaction. Thus language and social skills (and even cognition i.e. our thinking processes) are taught and/or learned in early life through the mostly unconscious application of apprenticeship-like methods, generally by our parents and primary caregivers (Rogoff, 1990). These methods generally employ non-didactic or non-direct teaching methods, such as supported joint engagement and concurrent commentary on or explanation of activities by the adult 'expert', with concurrent observation, exploratory participation and behavioural approximation on the part of the learner.

Further defining features of Apprenticeship models are that they arise during active participation in a joint endeavour, but with the recognizably asymmetric roles of novice and expert. As the novice increases in mastery of the requisite skills, then the supportive role, or the 'scaffolding' as the distinguished educational philosopher Jerome Bruner called it (Bruner, 1975), of the expert diminishes until the apprentice becomes an independent practitioner of the required skills.

Building on her analysis of such Apprenticeship models, Rogoff (1990) proposed an interesting concept termed 'guided participation' (a concept similar to scaffolding) which allows children (the learners in her studies) to be supported or actively guided through culturally valued activity that would be beyond them as individuals. Involvement in such guided participation was identified as both encouraging and supportive of a child's cognitive, social and cultural development. Guided participation was also seen to recognize the important role of tacit, as opposed to explicit forms of verbal and non-verbal communication implicit in the nature of an activity, and also identified the various roles and relationships between participants as significant issues that make up a part of the learning.

When analysing Intensive Interaction between a practitioner and a person with severe or profound learning disabilities, certain aspects of an 'Apprenticeship model' or 'guided participation' seem to be clearly evident at times. The sense of joint purpose, active participation, and the non-didactic teaching methods are all evident. Also the roles of relationship development and tacit forms of communication are seen to be important, not just the acquisition of skills and knowledge.

However there are also certain important differences to consider. The Intensive Interaction methodology is built around mutual enjoyment and tasklessness (Nind and Hewett, 1994), for example, rather than having the purpose of task completion. Relatedly, the aim in Intensive Interaction is not to turn a novice into an 'independent practitioner' of communication skills – as discussed above, these skills are seen to be dependent on a supportive social context, not something to be owned wholly by an individual.

In educational settings, the 'Apprenticeship model' or 'guided participation' is perhaps a useful analogy to employ when explaining Intensive Interaction to other people who need a clear conceptual framework on which to build their understanding of the approach.

Radical and Social Constructivist views of learning

Constructivist theories of learning are a set of theoretical models that, in their various forms, generally set out to describe the processes of acquiring or developing understanding. Such theories put the actions of the learner at the centre of their analytic framework, and they look to explain how learners develop or construct their own understanding of issues and events directly from their own experiences. Constructivism takes two generally recognized forms – Radical Constructivism (an elaboration of Jean Piaget's ideas of **Genetic Epistemology** and most often associated with psychologist Ernst von Glasersfeld) and Social Constructivism (most often associated with the Russian psychologist L.S. Vygotsky).

These two forms of Constructivist theory take different views of learning, and also take different analytic standpoints. Radical Constructivism (like Piaget's Genetic Epistemology) analyses learning from an individualistic perspective, and sees learning as an individual act, carried out by an individual in their exploration of, and interaction with, their environment (Roth, 1999). Social Constructivism, however, sees learning as bound up with, occurring within and contextualized by the prevailing culture and social relationships. These relationships are generally between a person with more mastery of a given discipline or issue (usually an adult) and a less experienced person (usually a child) who is learning the important aspects of that discipline or issue (Rogoff, 1990) – there are obvious overlaps here with 'Apprenticeship' models of learning and the distinction between individualistic and active/participatory forms of learning.

Both schools of Constructivism share some central tenets. Perhaps of most importance to the Intensive Interaction practitioner is the Constructivist perspective on the active role of the learner. Not only is the learner active in the processes of learning, but they are equally the main player in constructing their own understanding of the knowledge that is acquired. This is an important issue as it advances the view that the active engagement of the learner is central to the process of them constructing their own understanding, and that knowledge or understanding can only be constructed by the learner, from their own subjective viewpoint. We cannot tell the learner what to think about or take from a given learning scenario, instead we have to create appropriately individualized and meaningful learning scenarios from which they can learn.

Although Radical Constructivists would look to analyse the learning from the standpoint of the actions and thoughts of the individual learner, and Social Constructivists would look to analyse the activity in terms of the relationship and interaction between learner and the more expert practitioner, in the end they both view the knowledge constructed as belonging to, and lying within the individual mind of the learner. As we shall see in the next section, however, this is not the only view of knowledge available to us.

'Situated' or 'socio-cultural' views of learning

There is yet another set or school of learning or cognitive theories that propound a different and more all-embracing perspective on learning. Advocates of 'situated' or 'socio-cultural' learning theories look at, and attempt to describe, the processes at work when learning occurs in complex everyday social scenarios. The 'situated' view of learning is that learning is a social or cultural process within which learning and action are inextricably interlinked (Roth, 1999), because what people perceive in a scenario and how they behave within that scenario happen together, and the learning simultaneously accrues from concurrent action on and perception of the current scenario.

Thus, a 'situated' view would be that our knowledge of the world around us, and especially of the behaviour of other human beings, is constructed from our own experiences in, and interactions with, the world around us (and especially with other human beings). Knowledge and action are seen to lead, and be led by each other in a social encounter, and the knowledge and actions that make up an experience are socially shared between all those involved in that social encounter or experience. From this perspective, the combined knowledge and skills of a group or collective is seen to be held jointly by all the members of that group or collective, within what is sometimes called a 'community of practice' (Lave and Wenger, 1991).

Situated learning theory tends not to concern itself with what goes on inside an individual learner's head. For example, Lave and Wenger (1991), radical situated theorists, advanced the view that learning is essentially a social process that is shared between co-participants, not a 'one person act'. Indeed they explicitly conceive of learning as 'a process that takes place in a participation framework, not in an individual mind' (Franks, in Lave and Wenger, 1991, p.15). 'Situated' learning is therefore learning that accrues in the same circumstances to those in which it is applied, and the educational philosopher Eric Bredo identified one of the central tenets of a situated approach as 'the practical inseparability of individual task performance from social relationships' (Bredo, 1999, p.38).

Thus learning happens as people interact with the world around them, and part of that learning is a person developing a view as to their own social position and the potential roles that they might fulfil within the world and social nexus that surrounds them. From a 'situated' perspective learning is much more than just the acquisition of decontextualized skills and knowledge, and this could certainly be said to include any learning that accrues from engagement in Intensive Interaction. Learning during Intensive Interaction is not solely about acquiring and developing communicative techniques, but it is equally about the learner constructing a conception of themselves as a communicator and a socially active and significant member of a social group or community.

When applying this type of 'situated' thinking to Intensive Interaction situations, there are potentially several issues or implications that arise for practitioners. Initially it might well be important that Intensive Interaction practitioners share their rationale and aims with those other significant people involved in the care or service provision for the people with whom they are working. This way of thinking about learning should lead us to view an Intensive Interaction intervention as a means of altering a person's whole social context, rather than it just being about working with a person at an individual level. Even if Intensive Interaction is carried out in a classroom with one teacher, it should not be a one-off intervention that can be individually supported, and then finished with as someone leaves the classroom or school. Instead the teaching or learning aims will need to be cast much more broadly, and the regular engagement in Intensive Interaction outside of a classroom or learning environment is the ultimate ideal for the person with a social or communicative impairment. We may need to reflect this ultimate aim in the way we work, and the way we record and share information about a person's preferred means of inter-activity and their attainments in this area, and perhaps we should even be prepared to engage in a wider debate about the nature of the learning that takes place during Intensive Interaction intervention.

Legitimate Peripheral Participation

If we are looking to build a clear theoretical description of the processes through which engagement in Intensive Interaction activities might produce skill acquisition or progression, Lave and Wenger's (1991) situated learning theory of 'Legitimate Peripheral Participation' (see Figure 6.1) can possibly help.

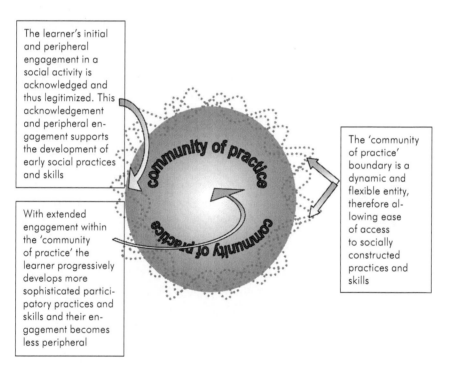

The learner's initial and peripheral engagement in a social activity is acknowledged and thus legitimized. This acknowledgement and peripheral engagement supports the development of early social practices and skills

With extended engagement within the 'community of practice' the learner progressively develops more sophisticated participatory practices and skills and their engagement becomes less peripheral

The 'community of practice' boundary is a dynamic and flexible entity, therefore allowing ease of access to socially constructed practices and skills

Figure 6.1: Legitimate Peripheral Participation: a visual representation of learning developing through engagement in a 'community of practice'

This model of 'Legitimate Peripheral Participation' (LPP) can, I believe, help us to visualize how learning accrues or develops from, and is made evident in, the learner's increasing participation in socially organized events or activity (in our case Intensive Interaction). In this LPP model there is no linear aspect to skill acquisition; we look instead at the gradual development of the practices and skills associated with, and collectively held and developed by the participants within a particular 'community of practice'.

The model illustrates how a learner gradually, but often inconsistently, becomes part of a 'community of practice' although in the case of Intensive Interaction it might be accurate to call it a 'community of social interactors'. For this to happen, a person's nascent or emergent communicative and sociable behaviour has to be legitimized through sensitive and affirmative acknowledgement, and the learner then being given some kind of meaningful response that encourages and allows for active participation. Initially the learner's engagement in such a 'community of social interactors' might well be tentative and exploratory. However, through repeated experiences of social interaction the learner can develop more sophisticated participatory practices and skills (see the developmental aspect of the Dual Process model described earlier), and in the case of Intensive Interaction that will be made manifest in communicative exchanges that may show greater levels of sophistication or are sustained for longer periods.

Thus, active inclusion promotes learning. Within such a learning scenario, instead of the individual acquiring skills, progression is more diffuse, as the learner increasingly becomes a member of the 'community of social interactors'. As this process of social inclusion continues, the learner moves (together with their communication partners) towards the centre of the 'community of social interactors' through increased joint mastery of the skills found within this particular community.

For people with severe or profound and multiple intellectual disabilities, or for those who are socially withdrawn and remote, the boundaries of a 'community of social interactors' will need to be flexible to accommodate the learner's active engagement. As Barber (2000) notes:

> It is not the flexibility of the learner's skills that enables interaction to occur, but the flexibility of the situation that allows the inclusion of the learner.

If we are to use such an LPP model to inform our Intensive Interaction practice, we should perhaps pay more explicit regard to the process of 'community of practice' generation. From this perspective, if we wish to facilitate learners in joining a 'community of practice' based on Intensive Interaction principles and techniques, then they will require easy and legitimized access to the social activities included in any 'community of social interactors'.

The traditional interpretation of LPP is such that 'communities of practice' are already in existence for newcomers to join in with and learn from. This is often not the case for our learners with the most profound intellectual disabilities, or those who are socially withdrawn and remote. For such learners action will be needed to create such 'communities of social interactors' around them for them to join in with and learn from. This will therefore require the adoption by carers or staff of behaviours and responses uniquely attuned to the learner's current behavioural repertoire, their personal motivating factors, and their communicative strengths – namely, the skills, knowledge and attitudes for using Intensive Interaction. Only then can the process of LPP begin.

7

Some Psychological Theories of Human Behaviour

Life's most persistent and urgent question is – what are you doing for others?

Rev. Martin Luther King, Jr.

Ruth writes...

In this chapter, I write about some of the major schools of psychological thought which I think have the most relevance for Intensive Interaction: behaviourism, cognitive behavioural, humanistic and psychoanalytic. This is a select group, there being some majors schools that are not included (such as narrative therapies and systemic approaches). Behaviourism had to be included because it is the dominant school of thought that has shaped approaches to people with a learning disability for decades and (in my experience) it is the approach that most workers in the field claim to use. My own clinical training in working with people with a learning disability was largely based on behaviourism, but I have become increasingly dissatisfied with its limitations and biases. These are described in detail below since I believe that behaviourism's deficiencies help to highlight just what Intensive Interaction has to offer.

Cognitive and cognitive behavioural therapies are those that are routinely offered to non-learning disabled people with emotional problems. They are therefore the approaches that are most familiar to most psychologists. In what follows I talk a lot about the overlap between these therapies and Intensive Interaction. In so doing, I aim to highlight the psychotherapeutic potential of Intensive Interaction.

Rogers' person-centred therapy is covered in some detail since I am increasingly struck by the overlap between the principles and processes of this approach and what I think should be the principles and processes of Intensive Interaction. Other therapies, approaches and theories are covered in less detail. This is not intended to diminish their importance as schools of thought, but signifies their lesser overlap with Intensive Interaction.

In clinical practice, I think that the differences between practitioners from different theoretical positions are (on the whole) diminishing. Whilst some dyed-in-the-wool behaviourists remain, for example, the majority practice some variation of positive behaviour support which has a value base about the rights of people with a learning disability and their quality of life. Differences in practice are therefore largely about the degree of emphasis placed on particular concepts and processes and different approaches can be combined to complement each other and enhance the quality of care that is delivered (see the section, *Positive behaviour support* later in this chapter).

This chapter is followed by one which covers some major psychological concepts – some of these concepts are associated with particular schools of thought (for example, ABCs are associated with behaviourism) whereas others are pan-theoretical. The division into theories and concepts seemed to allow for the greatest clarity of presentation.

Behaviourism

Anderson and Freeman (2000) write that:

> Perhaps no other sub-discipline of psychology has had such a dramatic impact on the types and quality of services provided to people with developmental disabilities and challenging behavior as applied behavior analysis. For example, until the 1950s, a widely held assumption was that people with severe and profound intellectual deficits were unable to benefit from teaching opportunities; that is, they were unable to learn. Using principles established through basic research conducted in the laboratory,

however, behavior analysts demonstrated that the behavioral repertoires of people with developmental disabilities could be shaped and maintained by rearranging environmental contingencies (e.g. Fuller, 1949; Williams, 1959; Wolf, Risley, and Mees, 1964). These early studies resulted in a gradual shift away from providing custodial care services to the development and implementation of active programming for people with developmental disabilities. (p.85)

In clinical practice, a behavioural analysis of a client's challenging behaviour will involve (as a bare minimum) identification of antecedents to the behaviour of interest and consequences that follow it – hence the acronym, ABCs (for Antecedents, Behaviour and Consequences). There is much basic research (carried out with animals such as rats and pigeons) which underpins this approach (e.g.Schwartz, 1989, p.34). In very simple terms, the idea is that all behaviours are learnt through a process of reinforcement – we learn to do those things that are followed by pleasant consequences – and undesirable behaviours can therefore be 'unlearnt' (for example, by presenting a punishing stimulus after the undesirable behaviour has occurred). It can be described as a reductionist approach – its core tenet is that you only need to look at what is observable to be able to understand someone and this understanding is achieved by the person being 'broken down' into 'bits'. This contrasts with holistic approaches such as humanism (see the later section in this chapter, *Humanistic theories*).

My clinical experience has been that a lot of direct-care staff who work with people with a learning disability misunderstand behaviourism. On a number of occasions, clients have been referred to me with the rationale that 'we think it's behavioural'. What the referrer actually seemed to mean by this is that the person is 'doing it on purpose'. There has tended to be some associated impatience in wanting the client 'fixed' of their undesirable behaviours. This contrasts with the attitude that I think that we should all be working towards, which is one of compassionate understanding.

I do not think that behaviourism has created negative attitudes towards people with a learning disability, but I think that in its most reduced form it allows such attitudes to persist. If we take the identification of ABCs (e.g. Iwata *et al.* 1994) as behaviourism at its most reductionist, I think that it is easy to see how this can lead staff to see clients in very narrow terms – namely, in terms of undesirable behaviours. This in itself is unhelpful since it distracts workers from considering more important issues – namely, the person's quality of life and how this can be enhanced

– and it hinders them from seeing the person with a learning disability as a person with unique feelings, desires, preferences and aspirations. (A reductionist behavioural approach would say that all these things are unobservable and therefore unworthy of scientific consideration.)

My experience in some services has been that an exclusively behaviourist approach can lead to staff becoming overly controlling of their clients. I believe that this can happen because of the focus on negative behaviours and their management. It is well known that challenging behaviours tend to be chronic (for some people, they may be lifelong patterns of behaviour (Royal College of Psychiatrists, British Psychological Society and Royal College of Speech and Language Therapists, 2007, p.44) and that although major changes (such as the move to community care) have improved people's quality of life, there has not been a corresponding reduction in challenging behaviour (Emerson and Hatton, 1994). I think that behaviourism gives the message 'you can control these negative behaviours' to staff who then find themselves dealing with difficult behaviours that can sometimes change little or not at all.

Direct-care staff who work in services that are explicitly for people who challenge are at a particular risk of defining their worth in terms of how well they manage (stop) challenging behaviours and my experience is that this can lead to feelings of hopelessness and sometimes even anger towards their clients. I believe very strongly that we need an approach that balances or complements what is missing from behaviourism. For me, it is an approach that (in its most radical form) is missing a value base which is vital if people with a learning disability are to be treated fairly and decently. I believe that everyone who supports people with a learning disability should have this value base presented to them from day one of their job, and that it should subsequently be supported through various means and at all levels of an organization, such as training sessions, supervision and peer support. Organizations need to have a strong value base at the core of everything that they do and demonstrate this from the top down.

I think that Intensive Interaction has an important role in complementing behavioural approaches because it has a strong value base and it is about putting this value base into action. I think that fine words often get lost in translation – talk about philosophies of care and person-centred care are important, but it is not always clear how to move from the words to the doing. In Intensive Interaction, it is clear what needs to be done (spending time with somebody in a way that they like and can make sense of) and the value base is implicit in this. By spending this time with somebody we are valuing them: respecting them and meeting their basic human need to make meaningful and satisfying relationships, which is central for a decent quality of life.

Intensive Interaction is also about emotions – to do it successfully we have to be attuned to the other person's emotions and aware of our own emotional responses. Whereas behaviourism (again, in its radical forms) pushes emotions out of sight, Intensive Interaction facilitates discussion of client and staff emotions both specifically in relation to Intensive Interaction sessions and more generally. All too often, I have seen direct-care staff struggling on under very difficult circumstances with little or no support or guidance. My belief is that showing workers a compassionate understanding is important in itself and that it will also filter down to how they interact with clients to the clients' ultimate benefit. Embedding a compassionate approach within an organization's culture, however, is a massive undertaking that will require staff at all levels to become less fearful of emotions and more genuinely person focused.

Cognitive and cognitive behavioural theories

The difference between cognitive and cognitive behavioural therapies is one of emphasis. In the former, only cognitions are focused on with the rationale that our thoughts and beliefs underlie everything else and so a change in cognitions will influence all other systems such as behaviour and feelings. In the latter, behaviours can also be a direct target of therapy – the rationale being that cognitions and behaviours are mutually influential, so a change in either one influences the other. For the sake of simplicity, hereafter I use 'cognitive' to refer to both cognitive and cognitive behavioural therapies. Aaron T. Beck (e.g. Beck, 1963) is seen as the founder of cognitive and cognitive behavioural theories and when I use the term 'cognitive therapy' I am referring to the Beckian school.

'Cognitive' refers to thoughts, beliefs and attitudes and a common misunderstanding about these therapies is that they are about changing how people think. In fact, they are about trying to give people more **flexibility** in how they think. To illustrate the difference, think about somebody you know passing you on the street and not saying 'hello'. What would you think? Quite often, somebody who is depressed will think something like, 'they didn't want to say hello – they don't like me'. If cognitive therapy were about changing how this person thinks, the therapist would point out the errors in this way of thinking (such as the complete lack of evidence for such a thought) and suggest a more helpful alternative (such as, 'Don't you think you'd feel better if you thought that perhaps they had just got some really bad news and were so preoccupied that they didn't see you?'). One of the reasons that therapy is not like this is because a client might go along with (but not believe) what a therapist tells them to think, but we are all more likely really to *believe* something that we find out for ourselves.

One of the guiding principles of Beckian therapies is therefore **collaborative empiricism** which means working together to test things out (the interested reader is referred to *Collaborative Case Conceptualisation* (Kuyken, Padesky and Dudley, 2009) where this concept is discussed extensively in relation to cognitive therapy). This means that the therapist does not set themselves up as the expert. Rather, the therapist brings their knowledge of cognitive/cognitive behavioural techniques and uses these to work with the client who is the expert in him/herself. The therapist does not presume that they know the way the client *should* think, but guides the client to find ways of opening up alternatives in their thinking. In the example above, a client might learn to question their first interpretation of being ignored and transfer this questioning to negative thoughts that occur in their daily life. If we really believe that someone ignored us because they do not like us we are likely to feel low and demotivated, but if we can question this and look at alternatives (such as, 'maybe they just didn't see me') our mood is likely to improve.

A second misunderstanding about cognitive therapy is that it is all about thoughts and behaviour and nothing about feelings. This is completely untrue. One of the maxims that I was taught in cognitive training was 'follow the feeling' (for a recent discussion about the importance of feelings in exposure therapies, see Brady and Raines, 2009). The thoughts that are really causing difficulties for clients are the ones that are associated with the strongest negative feelings. The skilful therapist guides the client towards awareness of these thoughts at a pace that the client can tolerate.

So what's all this got to do with Intensive Interaction? I think it is useful to ask this question, not because Intensive Interaction can be equated with any other psychological therapy, but because making such comparisons deepens our understanding of the approach. Second, I believe that Intensive Interaction has the potential to be used as a psychotherapeutic intervention and making links with established therapies adds some weight to this position. I also want therapists to get interested in the approach so we can explore and develop its psychotherapeutic potential and I hope that examining and establishing its relationship to existing therapies will legitimize Intensive Interaction as an approach that therapists *should* be interested in.

At first glance it may seem that cognitive therapy has nothing to do with Intensive Interaction, but they actually share the principle of collaborative empiricism. The Intensive Interaction practitioner does not presume that they know how the client *should* interact, but sets out to *discover* how they can make a connection with the person. This expert/ non-expert distinction is important because it is linked with the value base that we bring to our work with people and therefore underlies all our dealings with them. In an expert model, one person has greater power than the other and can exert that power over the less powerful person. However, the value base in non-expert therapies is that therapist and client are equal and so they find things out together (see the related discussion in Chapter 5, in the section *Roles within relationships*).

My experience has been that very often people with a learning disability are put in an inferior, less powerful position in everyday life. Often people talk to people with a learning disability using overly complex language that makes little or no allowances for the person's disability. And if the person with a learning disability gets professional help, this is most likely to be from a behavioural approach in which the therapist may assume that they know best and can devise a treatment schedule without even talking to the person about their preferences, life experiences, aspirations and so on. When this is the interpersonal context that somebody usually experiences, I think that being treated as an equal will be something pretty special. But it *should* be something that is commonplace.

For the practitioner to go into an interaction as a non-expert takes some courage. It feels much safer to be the expert behaviour analyst with checklists and monitoring forms and a sense of certainty that things can be understood in a relatively straightforward framework or to be the direct-care worker who gets tasks done. Being a non-expert means that we have to accept uncertainty – we do not know how the interaction is going to go; we do not know what we are going to be required to respond to; and we have to let go of our control of the situation and go with the flow. For professionals who have worked from an expert stance or care staff who have had their roles defined as 'getting jobs done' this requires a big shift in thinking and being, but it is only by letting go of control and allowing the person with a learning disability to take the lead that we create the conditions in which the person can be themselves and we can get to know them (see Shainberg (1993) for a related discussion).

I have written much elsewhere about the importance of feelings in Intensive Interaction work (for example, in the section *Empathy, congruence and positive regard* in Chapter 5) and in noting the overlap with cognitive therapies I explore the issue of both approaches being guided by the client's emotional responses. For example, with regards to physical proximity, the Intensive Interaction practitioner will observe for an emotional response as they get closer to their partner. If this causes anxiety, the practitioner will back off to a distance that is comfortable and will test out getting closer at a future time when they judges the time to be right (for example, when they feel that they have gained more of the person's trust). In cognitive therapy the therapist gets closer to the client's core (deep or most painful) emotional issues at a pace that they judge the client can tolerate. As with Intensive Interaction, this pace will partly be determined by the strength and direction of a client's reactions to emotional probes. The form is different – probing by increasing physical proximity (Intensive Interaction) or by a questioning/verbal reflection targeting core emotional issues (cognitive therapy) – but the therapist is actually doing the same task of checking out how much of a change (challenge) the client can tolerate and adapting the pace of change accordingly. And in both cases the therapist is helping to manage the client's negative emotions so that the client can master these emotions rather than be overwhelmed by them. A client who feels threatened and anxious when people get too close (whether physically or emotionally) can be exposed to tolerable levels of these emotions by a skilful therapist and learn to cope with increasing levels of closeness and associated feelings if the rate of change is right for him/her. The alternative would be to get very close very quickly. This would most likely cause intolerable levels of negative emotion and so cause the client to shut down completely or become angry and assaultive to make the unwelcome and frightening person go away. In the first case (skilful therapist), the client learns that emotions can feel unpleasant but that they can be lived with and do not have to be frightening. The client in the second case (therapist who pushes forward too quickly) learns that negative emotions can be overwhelming and frightening and lead to out-of-control experiences. As well as being an overlap with cognitive therapies, this aspect of Intensive Interaction is one of the features that suggests its psychotherapeutic potential.

Humanistic theories

In Chapter 5 I wrote extensively about Carl Rogers – see, for example, the section *Empathy, congruence and positive regard*. Rogers is considered to be one of the founding fathers of humanistic psychology along with Fritz Perls, founder of Gestalt therapy. McLeod (1996, pp.133–137) provides a concise overview of the philosophical basis of humanistic psychology, a selected summary of which follows.

Humanistic psychology developed in the early 1950s at a time when a growing number of psychologists were increasingly dissatisfied with the paradigms that dominated the field (psychoanalysis and behaviourism, especially in North America). It differs from psychodynamic (defined below) and behaviourist approaches in terms of its 'root metaphor' which is that of **growth** – '[t]he person is seen as striving to achieve, create or become' (McLeod, 1996, p.135).

In psychodynamic theory, the root metaphor is conflict resolution and in behaviourism it is problem management. This represents a fundamental difference in therapeutic aims – in humanistic approaches the aim is to promote growth or optimal functioning. In contrast, in psychodynamic and behaviourist approaches the aim is to fix what has gone wrong (that is, psychopathology). In the humanistic paradigm, emphasis is placed on the concept of **process** rather than on the end point to be achieved – therapy is a journey to be experienced. Change is seen as an inherent feature of people and changes that may occur in therapy are therefore *not* seen as a resulting from the actions or expertise of the therapist. In simple terms, the therapist does not fix the person. Rather, the therapist creates the conditions that help the person to move forward themselves. It is an anti-reductionist approach in which a core concept is that of **experiencing** – '[b]eing a person is not reduced either to cognition or emotion... life is apprehended through experiencing, which always involves an interplay of thought and feeling (Bohart, 1993)' (McLeod, 1996, p.137).

I argue that Intensive Interaction is consistent with these core concepts. First, its aim is to develop fundamental social and communication abilities and it is therefore very much concerned with growth and optimal functioning. Second, in its use as a therapeutic intervention (see, for example, the case of Lorraine in the section *Formulation* in the following chapter) it is most concerned with a process rather than an end point. When working with Lorraine, for instance, my aim was to see whether she could be engaged in enjoyable, non-controlling interaction and *not* to fix her self-injury. Third, Intensive Interaction can be non-reductionist

– it can be about being with and relating to the whole person, not breaking them down into bits. In this regard, I propose that when the Intensive Interaction practitioner is assessing/observing, they are adopting a more reductionist stance – for example, they may want to understand what sort of approach leads to a person hitting out and what sort is better tolerated and what feelings might underlie the behaviour. When engaged in an Intensive Interaction session, however, the practitioner is adopting a more holistic stance, attending to all of their partner's experiencing.

Maslow's hierarchy of needs

Maslow is a well-known member of the humanistic school of thought. He studied highly successful people (such as Albert Einstein), epitomizing the humanistic concern with optimal functioning rather than psychopathology. In 1943 he published his paper 'A theory of human motivation' which includes his hierarchy of needs. He proposed that human needs have a predetermined order of importance as follows (most important given first): physiological (such as food, water and sex); safety (such as personal and financial security and health and well-being); love/belonging (friendship, intimacy, having a supportive and communicative family); esteem (such as self-esteem, confidence, respect of others) and self-actualization (realizing one's own full potential). If needs at the lower levels are not met, Maslow's theory states that a person cannot attend to needs at higher levels. In order that s/he can attend to the higher level needs, lower level deficits must be met. If we think about this in terms of therapy, it means that therapy should only be offered when a person's other needs are being met – we should not expect them to be able to work on issues connected to their self-esteem, for example, if they do not feel safe at home. Once they are in a place where they do feel safe, they may then be in a position to look at their self-esteem.

If we relate Intensive Interaction to this hierarchy, it can be seen to span the safety, love/belonging, esteem and self-actualizing sets of needs. My experience has been that lots of people working in services for people with a learning disability have heard of Maslow's hierarchy of needs and that it has some credibility with them. I have therefore used it in training as a useful tool to help people to think about the needs of the people that they are supporting, what they are doing that meet these various needs, what might be lacking, and how these deficits may be met. Unsurprisingly, training participants often bring up lack of close relationships and this is a point which can be used to reinforce the rationale for offering Intensive Interaction.

Positive behaviour support

Anderson and Freeman (2000) describe the main features of **positive behaviour support (PBS)**. They note that the theoretical and technological basis of PBS is behaviour analysis. In practice, a professional using a PBS approach would carry out a comprehensive assessment based on functional assessment (this term is defined in the following chapter). In addition, PBS specifically involves 'a set of values regarding quality of life and the rights of persons with disabilities' (Anderson and Freeman, 2000, p.86). These are described as operating from a person-centred value base; recognizing the individuality of each person, and working toward and achieving meaningful outcomes. The primary goal of PBS is described as improving a person's overall quality of life (Koegel, Koegel and Dunlap, 1996) through interventions which may target their living environment; social relationships; access to meaningful activities; and/or participation in the community. The value base of PBS, then, is consistent with that which underpins Intensive Interaction.

So can the two approaches work together? I propose that they can since I integrate them in my own working practice. Most often when I work with a client I carry out a functional assessment. This will result in identification of factors that make somebody more likely to behave in a challenging way – such as their lack of a close relationship, difficulty being understood by others, or lack of meaningful engagement. Assuming that the challenging behaviour is impacting negatively on the person's life (for example, their relationships are impoverished as a consequence of it or they cannot access some services because of it), I would then draw up a plan describing proactive and reactive strategies. Reactive strategies are those which occur in response to a behaviour (for example, staff stepping out of the person's reach if they are hitting out) whereas proactive strategies are those which aim to increase a person's quality of life and/or reduce the likelihood of the challenging behaviour occurring. Intensive Interaction is one such proactive strategy that I might recommend.

Alternatively, I may offer Intensive Interaction in parallel with a behavioural intervention. To give an example of this, a former client, Sam, needed a very detailed behaviour support plan to help to manage his high intensity, high frequency aggression. He seemed to suffer from psychotic symptoms which appeared to dominate his attention and therefore meant that he was very isolated (his focus was almost exclusively on his internal world). I therefore offered Intensive Interaction in conjunction with a colleague to see whether we could establish a connection with Sam and draw his attention towards us and away from his internal world. This proved successful and Intensive Interaction is now offered regularly by his direct-care workers.

In Sam's case, the functional assessment also shaped the form in which we offered Intensive Interaction. When we first met him he reacted to *any* approach from other people by becoming highly assaultive. We spoke to his parents and reviewed his extensive case notes. This led to a formulation that included the specific hypothesis that Sam experienced others' requests as intolerable demands on him. This hypothesis about demands shaped the form of our intervention – specifically, we started off by reading to him (on subjects that his parents identified as being of interest to him) so that the interaction was as demand-free as possible. We wanted to see whether we could provide interaction that Sam enjoyed and we were largely successful in this. Over the course of some months he showed increasingly frequent signs of enjoyment (by smiling) and interactivity (for example, saying goodbye to us). As noted above, he is now regularly offered this interaction and he continues to respond positively.

Positive psychology

Wikipedia (www.wikipedia.org) describes the background to positive psychology as follows:

> Positive psychology began as a new area of psychology in 1998 when Martin Seligman, considered the father of the modern positive psychology movement, chose it as the theme for his term as the president of the American Psychological Association, though the term originates with Maslow, in his 1954 book *Motivation and Personality*.

Just as Maslow studied optimal functioning, so positive psychology focuses on the study of human strengths and how life can be made more fulfilling (rather than the more traditional approach of 'curing' what has gone wrong – that is, psychopathology). Its practical applications are seen to be in helping people and organizations to realize their strengths and to use these to increase and sustain their levels of well-being.

Intensive Interaction can be seen to be consistent with such approaches. As described above, it is concerned with promoting growth rather than fixing problems. Looking at the specifics of the approach, a practitioner may observe or assess a person in terms of their interactive (or potentially interactive) capabilities or 'strengths' and use such an assessment to produce a 'Strengths and Needs Plan' (SNAP; see Chapter 9, the section *Disseminating individual Intensive Interaction techniques – using the SNAP system*). This is explicitly concerned with building on a client's existing repertoire of skills as well as looking to develop areas where their skills are less evident but are potentially available if given an appropriately responsive social environment. This positive approach can help to counter the tendency to see people with a learning disability only in terms of deficits.

Positive psychologists have also written about the importance of relationships in promoting optimal functioning as described in Chapter 5 (the section *Fulfilling relationships and positive psychology*).

Psychoanalytic therapies

A number of terms are used in the literature to refer to these types of therapies – these include psychodynamic, psychoanalytic and dynamic psychotherapy. There are many variants of such approaches, the two best-known names in the field being Freud and Jung. Commonalities in the approaches are that the therapist takes an expert stance and the focus is usually on unconscious material (such as unconscious conflicts). As expert, the therapist makes interpretations of the material that a client brings to them – usually interpreting hidden (unconscious) meanings with the aim of helping the client to resolve the underlying conflict. The philosophy and process involved in psychoanalytic therapy and Intensive Interaction are therefore very different. Psychoanalytic ideas can, however, be very useful when thinking about the interpersonal context within which Intensive Interaction takes place.

Daniel Stern is a psychiatrist who is psychoanalytically trained and his work *The Interpersonal World of the Infant* (Stern, 2000) is often cited when authors describe the theoretical underpinnings of Intensive Interaction. This work is not purely psychoanalytic since Stern's aim was to marry the findings from observational work in developmental psychology with psychoanalytic theory to produce a (necessarily hypothetical) picture of the infant's inner world (see Stern, 2000, pp.4–5). I have therefore devoted a separate section to describing this unique perspective.

Stern, Daniel

Daniel Stern (2000) marries findings from observational work in developmental psychology with psychoanalytic theory to produce a unique picture of an infant's inner world (necessarily hypothetical since an infant cannot say if he has got it right or not!). Stern's ideas are highly complex – anyone who has read a psychoanalytic text is likely to have quickly realized that the ideas and language that are used can be pretty impenetrable to the lay person. I found Stern's book more accessible than other psychoanalytic texts that I have attempted to read, and he builds up a detailed, multi-faceted picture that is difficult to do justice to in summary. I attempt such a summary here, but the interested reader is referred to the original text which certainly repays careful reading.

Stern is particularly concerned with the infant's sense of self: 'the sense of self and its counterpart, the sense of other, are universal phenomena that profoundly influence all our social experiences' (2000, p.5). He notes that there are various senses of ourselves and that we are not usually aware of most of them (although, like breathing, we can bring them into our consciousness). He continues:

> I am mostly concerned with those senses of self that are essential to daily social interactions... Such senses of self include the sense of agency (without which there can be paralysis, the sense of non-ownership of self-action, the experience of loss of control to external agents); the sense of physical cohesion (without which there can be fragmentation of bodily experience, depersonalization, out-of-body experiences, derealization); the sense of continuity (without which there can be temporal disassociation, fugue states, amnesias [...]; the sense of affectivity (without which there can be anhedonia, dissociated states); the sense of a subjective self that can achieve intersubjectivity with another (without which there is cosmic loneliness or, at the other extreme, psychic transparency); the sense of creating organization (without which there can be psychic chaos); the sense of transmitting meaning (without which there can be exclusion from culture, little socialization, and no validation of personal knowledge). (2000, p.7)

Whilst most readers may not understand all the terms in this quote, I include it to make the reader aware that the issues that Stern writes about are profound and fundamental to our experience of ourselves as people, and that disruption in the development of these senses of self can have disastrously damaging consequences for the person (this is also a fundamental postulate of Bowlby's attachment theory – see Chapter 5, the sections *Attachment relationships* and *Deficits in parental care*). One of the areas that Stern (2000) covers in detail is that of **intersubjectivity** – the experience of sharing your inner world with another person which is based on the realization that you have a mind and feelings and that other people have a mind and feelings too. He describes how infants make this realization at around nine months of age and that they then:

> become relatively less interested in external acts and more interested in the mental states that go on 'behind' and give rise to the acts. The sharing of subjective experience becomes possible [...]. For example, without using any words, the infant can now communicate something like 'Mommy, I want you to look over here (alter your focus of attention to match my focus of attention), so that you too will see how exciting and delightful this toy is (so that you can share my experience of excitement and pleasure).' (2000, p.9)

He describes the parent's role as being that of setting limits around the child's intersubjectivity, so that the child learns such things as what types of subjective experience can be shared and how much:

> What is ultimately at stake is nothing less than discovering what part of the private world of inner experience is shareable and what part falls outside the pale of commonly recognized human experiences. At one end is psychic human membership, at the other psychic alienation. (Stern, 2000, p.126)

Stern sees interpersonal relationships as vital for the development of the various senses of self (not just the intersubjective self). He describes the infant as 'predesigned to be selectively responsive to external social events' (2000, p.10), and posits an interplay between development in the infant and changes in the way that s/he is responded to by his/her primary caregivers:

> any change in the infant may come about partly by virtue of the adult interpreting the infant differently and acting accordingly. [...] Most probably, it works both ways. Organizational change from within the infant and its interpretation by the parents are mutually facilitative. (2000, p.9)

To give just one example from the many possible areas of development, Stern (2000, p.43) writes about how parents attribute intentionality to their children when this is a quality-coming-into-being rather than fully developed:

Parents immediately attribute their infants with intentions ('Oh, you want to see that'), motives ('You're doing that so mummy will hurry up with the bottle'), and authorship of action ('You threw that away on purpose, huh?'). It is almost impossible to conduct social interaction with infants without attributing these human qualities to them. These qualities make human behaviour understandable, and parents invariably treat their infants as understandable beings, that is, as the people *they are about to become.* (italics added)

It is partly this treating-the-infant-as-the-person-they-are-about-to-become that enables the development to happen.

The processes that occur naturally and spontaneously in parent–infant interaction (such as attributing intentionality and attunement) are used deliberately and consciously in Intensive Interaction.

This section on Stern's work is intended to illustrate the potential for such work to have profound consequences for our interactive partners. For example, it has the potential to facilitate the development of intentionality and so enable people to communicate their desires, motives and so on deliberately to another person. And at the intersubjective level, it creates the potential for somebody who has been totally cut off from the world of others to feel connected with/to another person – to achieve 'psychic human membership' in Stern's words.

Rogers' person-centred therapy

As described in the section *Humanistic theories* (this chapter) Carl Rogers is one of the founding fathers of humanistic psychology. Merry (2002, p.12–13) notes that it is a 'democratic, non-authoritarian and non-directive approach to people that emphasizes constructive human relationships as the key to the change process'. It therefore shares some features with the cognitive therapies that were described above (in being democratic and non-authoritarian) and has some differences (the cognitive therapies are directive in the sense that the therapist guides (directs) the client to think and talk about particular things). A major difference lies in what is seen to lead to change – for Rogers, the quality of the therapist–client relationship is key, rather than particular interventions/techniques (as advocated in cognitive therapies).

Putting into words what a client-centred therapist actually offers is difficult, but Merry (2002, pp.12–13) gives a very evocative description:

The counsellor attends to the whole person of his client, listening to and responding empathically to the client's experiencing process as it is lived in the therapeutic hour. He has no goals for his client, only for himself. He sensitively and progressively becomes more familiar with his client's frame of reference [...] without judgement but with respect and authenticity. The counsellor extends himself towards his client as a person, and allows his client to affect him, each making a difference to the other. He neither absorbs the client's experiencing into himself, taking ownership of it for himself, nor does he direct it. Rather, he participates in it without losing his own sense of himself as both a separate person and as someone who, however temporarily, shares in this existential moment, this hour of cooperative living. He is an alert companion and, simultaneously, an empathic and non-judgemental observer.

For me, this describes how the Intensive Interaction practitioner should aim to be with their client. They need to attend to the whole of the person and demonstrate empathy. They need to be fully present and share in their partner's experience but also be separate from it. The practitioner has to be present so that their partner can feel their sharing of their experience, but they have to be simultaneously separate so that they can reflect on what is happening for their partner and think about the best way of responding. The lack of goals described here also has a clear echo in the notion of tasklessness in Intensive Interaction.

There are other ways in which person-centred therapy is very different from Intensive Interaction (at the most fundamental level, Rogers' therapy is a *talking* therapy despite the therapist attending to all the client's experiencing), but I think that there is much overlap in process and philosophy and that Intensive Interaction practitioners could benefit greatly from integrating person-centred ideas into their practice.

Some Psychological Concepts

The difference between participation and compliance is at the very core of the Intensive Interaction approach...

Adrian Kennedy (2001, p.17)

Ruth writes...

In this chapter I write about some of the big psychological concepts, and I have included the ones that I use most often in my day-to-day work with people with learning disabilities. For example, many people in learning disability services know about ABC charts – but my experience has been that only a few people fully understand the terminology and the underlying rationale for keeping these charts. I write in some detail about these because they are so widely misunderstood. Other concepts that I have included (such as assumptions, attributions, avoidance, empathy, explanations) are those that are (or should be) core to all psychological work and some are core to the process of intervening – such as making a formulation.

Antecedents, behaviour and consequences (ABCs)

When direct-care staff or parents seek help with a person's challenging behaviour, they are often asked to fill in 'ABC charts'. ABC refers to antecedent, behaviour and consequences and this way of understanding behaviour is particularly associated with the behaviourist school of thought, the ideas going back to the early animal experiments carried out by Pavlov and Skinner (see, for example, Schwartz, 1989, and the section *Behaviourism* in the preceding chapter).

The term **'antecedent'** refers to what was seen to be happening *immediately* prior to the target (challenging) behaviour occurring. The term **'behaviour'** refers to the behaviour that is of interest – also called the **'target behaviour'**. This should be defined precisely, in concrete (observable) terms. The term **'consequences'** refers to what happens in response to the behaviour.

The person with the task of interpreting the recordings will attempt to analyse what is **reinforcing** the behaviour, or what is making the behaviour more likely to occur again in the future. In the field of behaviour analysis, behaviour that increases can be either **positively** or **negatively reinforced**. There is, however, much confusion surrounding the use of the labels positive and negative when referring to reinforcement. In behaviour analysis, positive and negative does not refer to something being good or bad, it simply means that something is being added (positive) or something is being removed/terminated (negative).

When something is presented following the occurrence of the target behaviour and the likelihood that the behaviour will happen again in the future is increased, it is labelled as **positive reinforcement**. The 'thing' being presented can be reprimands, toys, food items, time-outs, activities, or anything that acts to make the behaviour more likely to occur in the future. Consider a group home where a resident is eating dinner and spills his drink on the floor. The direct-care worker reprimands the resident and the behaviour of spilling his drink happens again and again. This is considered to be positive reinforcement. The addition of the reprimand increased the occurrence of the drink spilling.

When something is removed or terminated following the occurrence of the target behaviour and the behaviour is likely to occur more in the future, it is labelled as **negative reinforcement**. As with 'positive reinforcement', the 'thing' does not have to be something unpleasant. Negative simply means something removed or terminated. Let's say a child stops attending school. This follows her being bullied at school and she eventually tells her mum about it who rings the school. This ultimately results in the bullies being suspended. The child is then more likely to go to school (behaviour) because the bullying has been removed.

Punishment can also be positive or negative. If I present a stimulus that makes a behaviour less likely to occur in the future, this is '**positive punishment**' (positive in the sense that I am adding something to the situation). If I take away something that the person likes and this reduces the likelihood of a particular behaviour in the future, this is '**negative punishment**' (negative in the sense that I am taking something away from the situation). If Fred hits a staff member, Joy, and Joy later says, 'I'm not taking you out today because you hit me', this could be an example of negative punishment. (It is also an unacceptable breach of Fred's human rights.) If Joan injures herself and I give her an electric shock (a 'treatment' that has actually been applied for self-injurious behaviour), this can be positive punishment. As with reinforcement, the technical definition of punishment concerns its effect on behaviour (a punisher being something that weakens a behaviour, making it less likely to occur in the future). In everyday usage, however, it tends to be used in a non-technical sense – that is, as something that the person finds aversive (unpleasant).

As a clinical psychologist, I get asked a lot of questions about **consequences** – staff want to know how they should respond to a behaviour once it has started and they are very concerned about not reinforcing behaviours. They often ask, for example, 'should we ignore it?' in the hope that this will make the behaviour go away.

So what's all this got to do with Intensive Interaction?

At the level of fundamental skills, both Intensive Interaction and a behavioural approach crucially depend on good observation skills and an ability to suspend interpretations whilst observing. Relatedly, both depend on a scientific approach of hypothesis generation and hypothesis testing. My clinical experience is that people who support those with a learning disability often jump to conclusions about the causes of challenging behaviour, attributing it to particular causes without any substantiating evidence. If a behavioural or Intensive Interaction approach are to be implemented competently, it is necessary to hold back on drawing conclusions until objective observations have been made (see also the following section, *Assumptions*).

My view is that neither Intensive Interaction nor a behavioural approach is 'better' for understanding challenging behaviour. Rather, their different strengths make them complementary. Behaviourism's insistence that we focus on concrete behaviour opens up the possibility of understanding it differently and Intensive Interaction's focus on preferred ways of communicating sensitizes staff to ask about the meaning of the behaviour and whether it can be understood as a communication.

In relation to **antecedents** and **consequences**, I have become increasingly convinced that the most important questions are not about consequences but are 'What can I do to make this (challenging) behaviour less likely to happen?' and 'What can I do to make alternative (positive) behaviours more likely to happen?' This is not just my view but is one that is consistent with approaches such as functional communication training (for example, Carr and Durand, 1985) and positive behaviour Support (for example, see Anderson and Freeman, 2000 and the section *Positive behaviour support* in the preceding chapter). The former is an approach based on applied behaviour analysis in which the communicative function of a challenging behaviour is established and the client is then taught a functionally equivalent way to achieve the same end. For example, if a child's behaviour becomes challenging when they have finished a piece of work and they start to get bored, they could be taught to ask for more work. If their asking for work reliably results in their being given more work, their asking serves the same **function** as their challenging behaviour and (under certain conditions) will come to replace it.

Positive behaviour support is a much broader concept than functional communication training. One aspect of the approach is a focus on multifaceted intervention strategies that aim to improve a person's quality of life as well as reducing the occurrence of challenging behaviours. These strategies include preventative measures such as teaching new skills that are functionally equivalent to challenging behaviours (cf. functional communication training described in the preceding paragraph) and finding opportunities for people that are meaningful, stimulating and enjoyable. If we consider the paucity of the relationships between people with a learning disability and others (see, for example, Arthur, 2003) then Intensive Interaction can be seen as wholly consistent with these preventative/life enhancing approaches.

Assumptions

I think that a key question that practitioners need to ask themselves to develop their practice is, 'What assumptions am I making?' These are usually hidden from our consciousness and, as Coia and Handley (2008, pp.108–109) note, they are applied to observations very quickly. This results in our arriving at explanations for what we see without being aware that we have made any assumptions in the process. Regular professional supervision can be vital to bring assumptions into awareness.

Particularly in expert-based approaches, the practitioner is making assumptions that they know best – for example, a behaviourist will assume that they know which behaviour should be targeted for change, what the functional relationships are, and what intervention plan should be followed. They are assuming that their assessment means that they know the person well enough to make these decisions. A single professional, of course, may make erroneous assumptions and the dangers of this can be mitigated by involving a team in making assessments and decisions. This is one feature of a positive behaviour support approach (e.g. Anderson and Freeman, 2000; see the section *Positive behaviour support* in Chapter 7) which aims to involve the target person and family members as well as a team of professionals. Such an approach allows the person and their families to describe their own goals (rather than these being assumed by others) and for a more comprehensive understanding of the person (for example, they may present quite differently in different contexts which might be missed by a sole professional).

We also make assumptions in Intensive Interaction. At a very fundamental level, I think that we practitioners and advocates of the approach assume that our clients who are not social are not this way out of choice. When we see people who are preoccupied with self-involved activities (such as object twiddling, rocking, head-banging) we assume that their experiences have led them to this point – in particular, that they have not been offered social interaction in a way that they want to engage with. We assume that if we can find the 'right' way of being with the person, we will draw their attention towards the social world. One danger of such assumptions is that we persist too tenaciously in the face of a negative client response. In such cases, supervision is vital to gain an alternative (and more objective) perspective on our assumptions and practice.

Attributions

'Attribution' is a term that is used in psychological literature and research and refers to the cause that we assign to an event. If I say that Peter hit me because he is a 'nasty old devil' I am attributing his behaviour (hitting me) to an aspect of his character (his nastiness). Much psychology research has looked at the types of interpretations that we make for our own behaviour and those that we make for others' behaviour (see, for example, Heider, 1958). One finding is that we are more likely to attribute our own behaviour to **external** causes – for example, I snapped at my partner (behaviour) because the kids had kept me awake all night (a cause that is external to me). In contrast, we tend to explain other people's behaviour in terms of **internal** factors – in the Peter example, his nastiness is an internal factor (something that is a part of him). If we are to practise Intensive Interaction successfully, we need to reflect on the attributions that we make for our clients' behaviour. We cannot, for example, have the necessary attitudes of open-minded enquiry and empathy if we see Peter as a nasty old devil.

There are lots of words that all mean pretty much the same thing as attributions, such as explanations (see the section *Explanations of behaviour* below) and interpretations (however, the reader should be aware that 'interpretation' can be used in a more technical sense to refer to the explanations that are offered by therapists working in the psychoanalytic tradition: this school of therapy is described in Chapter 7, in the section *Psychoanalytic therapies*).

Attunement and mis-attunement

If we are attuned to another person we are accurately sharing something of what they are experiencing. Different terms are used to refer to this interpersonal (between people) sharing. Stern (2000, p.144) notes that Trevarthen (eg. 1977) uses the term 'intersubjectivity'. This, however, has a different emphasis to attunement as it refers mainly to the sharing of intentions and motives (see Stern, 2000, p.131). Attunement, in contrast, is about the sharing of feelings – a precise term is **affect attunement** (Stern, 2000, p. 140). Stern (2000, pp.140–141) gives some great examples of infant–mother interaction that illustrate what the term means and one is reproduced here:

> A nine-month-old boy bangs his hand on a soft toy, at first in some anger but gradually with pleasure, exuberance and humour. He sets up a steady rhythm. Mother falls into his rhythm and says, 'kaaaaa-*bam*, kaaaaa-*bam*', the '*bam*' falling on the stroke and the 'kaaaaa' riding with the preparatory upswing and the suspenseful holding of his arm aloft before it falls. (p.140)

Stern (2000, pp.141–142) specifies three important characteristics of attunement:

1. Attunement involves a kind of imitation, but not a faithful copying of what the other person has done. Straight imitation would maintain attention on the external behaviours whereas attunement is about what is going on inside the person.

2. Matching tends to involve a different mode or channel to the original – in the example of the little boy above, aspects of the boy's arm movements were being matched by aspects of the mother's voice.

3. 'What is being matched is […] some aspect of the behaviour that matches the person's feeling state. The ultimate reference for the match appears to be the feeling state […], not the external behavioural event. Thus the match appears to occur between the *expressions of inner state*' (my italics) (p.142).

Attunement is seen to be vital for an infant's development: 'reflecting back an infant's feeling state is important to the infant's developing knowledge of his or her own affectivity and sense of self' (Stern, 2000, p.144).

When practising Intensive Interaction we will only be successful if we are open to reading our clients' internal states correctly. This means that we need to give them our full attention and put aside distractions. Often when we are at work we are rushing from one thing to the next and feeling hurried and harried. But we need to find a calm place for ourselves if we are to be open to our client and not caught up in our own thoughts and feelings. When mirroring, for example, we should not be just mechanically reproducing a client's behaviour but we should be picking up on their emotional tone (are they excited? pleased? puzzled? frustrated?) and reflecting this back in an attempt to achieve the attunement that is demonstrated between mother and infant. In so doing, we may ultimately be able to establish a connection and a dialogue with them.

It was noted above that attunement is vital for an infant to develop knowledge of his/her own emotional states and sense of self. This makes me think of how many of my clients with a learning disability have had a very poor sense of their own feelings and how many rely on other people to help them to manage negative feeling states (for example, to help them to feel calmer when they are becoming angry). This leads me to wonder whether the affect attunement aspect of Intensive Interaction has the potential to help such people gain a better understanding of their affective life and so be in a position to regulate their own emotions better.

Avoidance

We can avoid things in a concrete way (**behavioural avoidance** or **disengagement**) or in our thoughts (**cognitive avoidance**) or at an emotional level (**emotional avoidance**). Some staff may try to stay out of the way of people who are known to be particularly challenging – a form of behavioural avoidance. If we try not to think about something, this is cognitive avoidance and if we try to avoid our feelings, we are being emotionally avoidant.

Relating avoidance to Intensive Interaction, it is imperative that we recognize avoidance in ourselves and others if we are to work in a genuinely intensive way. Bender (1993) identifies a problem that he calls 'therapeutic disdain' for people with a learning disability. He identifies that therapists often avoid one-to-one work with clients who have a learning disability (behavioural avoidance) and attributes this to therapists finding them unattractive:

> psychotherapy involves intensely relating over quite a long period to another person – a certain kind of intimacy. The giving of this intimacy is more difficult, aversive and more energy consuming when the person is seen as unattractive. Instead of working on internalized aspects of prejudice, stereotyping and hostility, clinical psychologists, for the most part, along with other mental health professionals continue to deny that there is any moral obligation for them to provide such services. (p.11)

Cognitive and emotional avoidance are both covert, meaning that we cannot see them from the outside. I can apparently be working with a client, for example, but thinking about what I am going to have for tea (cognitive avoidance) or trying to suppress the hopelessness or anger or sadness that I am feeling in response to being with a client (emotional avoidance). If I am sticking address labels on a bunch of envelopes it is probably okay to daydream so long as all the envelopes need the same treatment. But when I am interacting with a person I need to be attuned to them and watching to see whether, for example, they are enjoying what I am giving them, whether I am doing it at the right pace or whether they need a break or to move on to something new. So I need to be aware of when I am avoiding the present moment and the person in front of me and return my focus wholly to them.

To improve our practice in Intensive Interaction we also need to be alert for any patterns to our avoidance and, if we spot them, try to understand them. It may be that our attention wanders in a random way since this is a natural occurrence. On the other hand, we may find that our attention wanders more with certain clients than others (we can then ask ourselves why we find this client particularly difficult to be with) or that we tend to ward off particular emotions when we feel them in clients (some clinicians may find that they ward off sadness, for example, whereas others may find anger hard to be with). We may find strong feelings threatening or overwhelming and should bear in mind that our clients with learning disabilities are particularly likely to 'hold' strong feelings. If we think about typical life experiences for somebody with a learning disability (such as repeated failure at school, inability to keep up with the achievements of peers or siblings, difficulty achieving independence and so on) then strong feelings of sadness and anger are to be expected. And as practitioners of Intensive Interaction, we need to be able to bear to be with these feelings (c.f. Sinason, 1992, pp.17–38 and the section *Empathy, congruence and positive regard* in Chapter 5 of this book).

Clinicians may also recognize avoidance in direct-care staff and their formulation (see definition later in this chapter) may identify this as an important area to work on. Such work is backed by research which has found that certain coping strategies used by staff working with people who are challenging increase the risk of staff burnout – these unhelpful strategies include forms of avoidance such as self-distraction, denial, substance abuse and behavioural disengagement (see, for example, Hastings and Brown, 2002). As these authors note, clinicians should be interested in this issue because burnout may lead to increased staff turnover which will indirectly affect quality of care through disrupting relationships between staff and clients, thus producing discontinuities in care. In addition, burnout is likely to directly diminish the quality of care that staff provide. Extrapolating to the emotional requirements for Intensive Interaction (such as affect attunemement), staff who have feelings of depersonalization (for example, treating people like impersonal objects) and emotional exhaustion are not in a place to meet them and so could not be expected to employ the approach successfully. Clinicians who are considering training staff in Intensive Interaction should be sensitized to the issue of burnout and whether this needs to be addressed before Intensive Interaction can be successfully rolled out.

Coping strategies

We all have strategies for getting ourselves through difficult times. These difficult times can be relatively minor – getting stuck in traffic, for example – or relatively major, such as the death of a loved one. Sometimes we cope by tackling the problem itself – if we routinely get stuck in traffic coming home from work, say, we might look at other routes or ask our boss if we can start and finish work at a different time. Sometimes we cope by managing our emotions – such as when we make time to grieve for somebody we have lost. Problems arise when we try to avoid our emotions through the use of unhelpful or damaging coping strategies. After a loss, for example, we may deny that we feel sad or angry and hide these feelings away. Hidden feelings, however, do not just go away but will build up and may be expressed unexpectedly and strongly.

A former client of mine, Dave, had a life history that was marked by repeated losses and abandonment and he was so incapacitated by this that he could not bear to be in a room with me. Based on his history and one brief contact (in which he was so anxious, he sweated profusely throughout), I believe that he was terrified of the possibility of talking about his experiences because the emotions felt so overwhelming that he did not feel he could bear them (and he may well have been right about this). Dave was very interested in history and a member of staff, John, offered to bring him in a DVD about the First World War. When John was next on shift, Dave immediately asked him for the DVD, but he had forgotten it. Dave spent the rest of that shift in his bedroom, refusing to talk to anyone. When the shift changed, Dave approached a member of staff and accused John of a serious assault. An investigation cleared John of fault completely and staff were at a loss to understand why Dave would have made such an allegation. Understanding his history, however, made it obvious that he had never grieved for his many childhood losses and so incidents in the present that left him feeling rejected or overlooked or uncared for re-awakened the powerful feelings from childhood which were then expressed in how he behaved. His allegation against John was an expression of his anger at having been let down by John and by all the people who had let him down before.

It is not only clients who have these issues – many of us might find that we react to things more strongly than we can make sense of immediately and, on reflection, we find that 'old' feelings that we had not dealt with were being re-awakened. Staff and carers who support people with a learning disability will have similar experiences, and unless we support them to be aware of their own emotional responses they will be at increased risk of burnout and unable to practise Intensive Interaction successfully. Existing coping skills are therefore an important area to consider for anyone planning training in Intensive Interaction for staff or carers.

It has been my experience that organizational level denial can exist about the emotional impact of supporting people who are challenging or very impaired and advocates for Intensive Interaction-type approaches in such organizations may well find organizational or personal barriers put in their way. In such situations, supportive and like-minded colleagues are essential, as is an acceptance of the difficulty of instigating any change in some systems.

Empathy

When we try to see and feel the world from another person's perspective, we are trying to be empathic. If we are successful, we will not just be able to understand the person's thoughts but also feel something of what they feel. It is often confused with sympathy which is a feeling of pity for somebody else's situation. Sympathy is about our own feelings (pity) rather than a connection to what the other person is feeling (empathy). There is an overlap in the meaning of empathy and attunement, but they are not synonymous. Stern (2000, p.145) makes the point that attunements 'occur largely out of awareness and almost automatically' (Stern is talking specifically about naturally occurring mother–infant attunement, and this is not to say that the Intensive Interaction practitioner cannot deliberately and consciously aim to achieve attunement with their interactive partner). In contrast, he describes empathy as involving thought and planning of a response (in addition to the affective component in which we feel something of what the other person is feeling – emotional resonance). Since Intensive Interaction involves deliberate and considered responses to our interactive partner, it can be seen to involve a blend of attunement and empathy – it is not as automatic and unconscious as mother–infant attunement and necessarily involves some thought (cf. Nind, 1996).

Empathy, and not sympathy, should underlie all our work with people with a learning disability. If I feel sorry for somebody else's difficulties, how does that help them? But if I am trying to share something of what the person is feeling I may be able to give them a sense that there is somebody who is genuinely alongside them and so create a sense of connection. To achieve this sense of connection is, of course, one of the aims of Intensive Interaction.

When we carry out Intensive Interaction, we should always strive to be empathic towards our partner, picking up on their emotional expressions and their reactions to our actions. We can demonstrate empathy by, for example, backing off physically when someone appears anxious and explaining what we are doing and why in a calm, soothing voice (even if the words themselves are not meaningful, the tone in which they are said may be soothing). Similarly, we can match our expression of emotion to that of our interactive partner. One of my former clients, Anne, used to hold up jointly created pictures very happily and say, with real enthusiasm, 'look at that'. In replying, we (a co-therapist and I) tried to match not just the emotion (smiling back to show that we shared her happiness) but also the intensity of the emotion (a big smile and enthusiastic praise for what she had made with us). We were sharing her feeling of delight and trying to show her this.

I have written in the preceding section on *Avoidance* about how we might resist closeness with people with a learning disability because we fear the strength of their negative emotions and we do not want to feel that level of pain or rage. This can be thought of as a fear of empathy.

Explanations of behaviour

In the earlier section *Assumptions* I wrote about a tendency to jump to conclusions about the causes of things. This tendency makes it difficult for us to observe situations objectively. Devoting time to looking at this issue, and helping staff to understand the difference between observations and explanations, is often time well spent (for a model that can be used to do this, see Coia and Handley, 2008, pp.108–109). This is a fundamental pre-requisite for staff to be able to practise Intensive Interaction since it enables them to generate testable hypotheses about their clients' behaviour, rather than make unhelpful judgements. If I think that George hits out because he has a 'nasty streak' all I can do is try to change George – and quite often this miracle is expected of a psychologist! Whereas if I stand back and observe I might notice that George is more likely to hit out when people get very close to him. I might ask if some people are more likely to get hit than others and observe that it is people who approach him from his left side who are most likely to get hit. I can then start to make predictions and test them out – if I work with George on his right side and keep at a comfortable distance, he should feel less threatened and be less likely to hit me. As well as being able to generate useful hypotheses, I am also likely to feel more empathy with George. If I see him as someone with a 'nasty streak', it is unlikely that I am seeing him accurately and unlikely that I will want to get to know him better. If I stand back and observe, I am more likely to see and feel his anxiety and discomfort and so begin to have some sense of connection with him and want to understand him even better. This echoes Zeedyk's (2008, p.15) statement that, 'in order for communicative exchanges to blossom, practitioners must accept their partner's existing behaviour, seeking to understand the meaning that the behaviour holds for them'.

To put aside explanations is a very big ask indeed. Partly this is because we (unconsciously) make explanations all the time in our everyday lives: it is second nature to say that an acquaintance has not been in touch for a while because 'she's never really been bothered' or our partner snaps at us because they are a 'miserable old sod'. And the gossip magazines play on our love of attributing causes to things on the basis of little or no evidence – 'Posh looks miserable, worried about Becks playing away' and so on.

I also think that people who work in learning disability services find it difficult to put aside explanations of their clients' behaviours because these explanations have a long history and over the years staff will have found lots of 'evidence' to support them. The problem is that evidence tends to get twisted to fit (support) explanations rather than being viewed objectively – this is known in the psychological literature as **confirmation bias** (Wason, 1968) which means that we notice, pay attention to and remember things that fit with our existing explanations and that we fail to notice, ignore and distort information that does not fit. Supporting direct-care staff to have an open mind is therefore likely to require sustained input over time to build on learning from training. In this respect, the practitioner will benefit from reading the Samuel *et al.* (2008) study which found difficulties in facilitating direct-care staff to become more reflective and proposes various measures to support this process (such as supervision from qualified professionals; see Chapter 10, the section *Effectiveness of training* for a more detailed summary of this study).

Formulation

Before a therapist offers therapy to a client, they should carry out an assessment and use this to generate a formulation. A formulation is the therapist's hypothesis about what has caused the client's difficulties and what is keeping them going, and these formulations vary in complexity. A **longitudinal** formulation will include three classes of factors – predisposing, precipitating and perpetuating (or maintaining). If parents only praise their child for doing exceptionally good work, this can be a **predisposing factor** for depression. Let's say this child fails her first year at university – this acts as a **precipitating factor** because she has learnt from her parents that she is only worthwhile if she is exceptionally successful. The failure at university leads her to feel unworthy and low in mood. She may feel so unworthy and low that she stops doing anything at all, not caring for herself or seeing friends or keeping her place tidy. Her unkempt appearance, deteriorating friendships and untidy surroundings serve as further evidence of her unworthiness and are therefore **perpetuating factors**.

To give an example from my Intensive Interaction work: Lorraine has lived in institutions for almost all her life. Her case notes revealed a tragic history in which her mother almost completely neglected her during the very early years of her life and then abandoned her (on Lorraine's admission to hospital, her mother had no further contact with her). As an adult, Lorraine has self-injured in extreme ways (such as severely burning her skin with boiling water) and when I met her she self-injured almost continuously at a relatively low level (for example, by pressing her hands and feet against hard surfaces). A previous psychologist explained her self-injury as a response to the deprivation in her childhood – specifically, it was hypothesized that the neglect that Lorraine had experienced (predisposing factor) meant that she had not learnt about the boundaries of her own body. Her self-injury functioned as a way in which she could experience herself physically (that is, she was able to feel herself when causing herself pain (perpetuating factor)).

I observed staff to take a very controlling attitude towards her, seeming to believe that they had to stop her self-injury at any cost. I offered her sessions of Intensive Interaction (in addition to other interventions), hypothesizing that this might prompt the care staff to become interested in a different way of interacting with her. Accepting the hypothesis that her self-injury was rooted in early neglect, I did not expect to impact on the frequency or severity of this. Rather, I wanted to see if it was possible to increase her quality of life regardless of the level of her self-injury. As the intervention progressed, it became apparent that Lorraine had many positive skills for instigating and sustaining interactions. The barrier to overcome lay in interesting staff in taking a less controlling approach – this required a re-assessment of the situation (for example, to understand the strength of the staffs' resistance), re-formulation and new intervention plan.

Functional assessment

An ABC assessment can also be called a **functional assessment**. This is because the practitioner is trying to establish the functional relationships between the three elements. The practitioner is asking questions such as:

- Does a particular demand function as a trigger for the challenging behaviour?

- Does the challenging behaviour function as a communication? (For example, is it the person's way of saying that they are distressed or tired?)

- What happens after a behaviour occurs that might reinforce or punish it? Are adaptive (useful) behaviours followed by responses that function as reinforcers?

Anderson and Freeman (2000) note that whereas traditional functional assessment has focused on ABCs, there is a move towards looking at broader lifestyle issues (for example, from practitioners adopting the positive behaviour support approach). Thus, functional assessments may include analysis of factors such as **setting events** as well as immediate antecedents. A setting event is a broader factor that increases or decreases the likelihood of an antecedent being followed by a particular behaviour. Let's say that the challenging behaviour is James throwing his breakfast bowl to the floor when asked to take it to the sink (antecedent). The behaviour is most likely to occur if James has slept poorly and least likely if he has slept well. We could then hypothesize that tiredness is a setting event and an intervention might involve investigating how to help James to get a good night's sleep.

An Intensive Interaction practitioner may use this framework to understand their clients' behaviours. If I think about clients who are very involved in what look like self-stimulatory behaviours (such as rocking, head-banging, twiddling objects very close to their faces and so on), my 'self-stimulation' thought is a functional hypothesis ('the behaviour functions to give the person some mental stimulation'). If I offer Intensive Interaction, I am asking if I can make myself interesting enough to draw the person's attention away from their internal world and onto me. If they allow me to join in with their existing activity (such as the object twiddling) then this becomes something shared rather than self-stimulatory. This could be understood in functional terms – that is, that the person is getting stimulation from a shared activity rather than having to rely solely on *self*-stimulation. This may then open the possibility for further shared activities which could come to replace some of the self stimulatory activities.

Self-efficacy expectations and self-esteem

A number of authors have commented on how the negative life experiences of people with a learning disability (such as repeated failure, social deprivation and rejection) are likely to lead to low self-efficacy expectations and learned helplessness (that is, having little belief in their ability to change things around them), low self-esteem, and an unwillingness to try (see, for example, Jones *et al.* 1997, pp.25–26). I can think of people whom I have met who I think have experienced the extreme limits of these factors. I am thinking of people who have lived most of their lives in institutions and who spend their lives doing very little – perhaps just rocking and meeting their physiological needs. My guess is that these people have learnt over years that they cannot influence what happens to them or around them and so they have given up trying to affect the world around them. I think that it feels safer to these people to retreat inside and ignore what is going on outside.

Such people are, I think, particularly likely to benefit from Intensive Interaction (indeed several of the studies that have found evidence to support the beneficial effects of Intensive Interaction have had institutionalized adults as participants – for example, Elgie and Maguire, 2001; Lovell, Jones and Ephraim, 1998; and Nind, 1996).

It is interesting to speculate about what underlies the positive effects of Intensive Interaction. For example, it may be the case that modelling somebody's behaviour leads to them developing the idea that they *can* have an effect on the world – their self-efficacy expectations are raised.

This may then lead to intentional behaviour (that is, the person acts to affect the world around them intentionally). In developmental studies involving ordinary infants, it is proposed that mothers responding to their infants *as if* they are intending to communicate is what leads to actual intentional communication (see the section *Stern, Daniel* in Chapter 7 of this book for a more detailed description). We can also speculate that Intensive Interaction will benefit people's self-esteem through a number of mechanisms such as their being treated with respect and as somebody of value, and through raised self-efficacy expectations. (Of course, this would be almost impossible to demonstrate in people who cannot articulate their self-view.) Similarly, we can expect low mood to improve with raised self-esteem and self-efficacy expectations – this may be evinced through such observables as increased smiling and motivation. These effects have indeed been demonstrated in the form of increased levels of contingent smiling (Leaning and Watson, 2006; Lovell *et al.*, 1998; Nind, 1996) and increased social initiation and/or engagement (Cameron and Bell, 2001; Kellett, 2000, 2003, 2005; Nind, 1996; Watson and Fisher, 1997). We might not be able to demonstrate improved self-esteem or mood conclusively, but I propose that we have evidence that supports these effects alongside a duty to think about these concepts in our therapeutic work with people with a learning disability.

Some Issues Associated with the Practicalities of Approach Use

Tell me, and I may forget; show me and I may remember; involve me, and I will understand.

Confucius (apparently!)

Graham writes...

In this chapter I look at some of the more practical issues that can come into play when engaging, or attempting to engage, in Intensive Interaction with someone with a social or communicative impairment. Reflection on these issues can make the process of Intensive Interaction more likely to be successful. Equally some of the issues addressed can become barriers to implementation of Intensive Interaction either in the short term, or over more extended periods. I did not think it possible, or even wise to cover all the possible issues that might pertain in all possible Intensive Interaction scenarios, but I have tried to include those that I think might be most useful for practitioners. The issues I have included look at matters such as practitioners' expectations of an Intensive Interaction intervention; the difficulties presented in having intangible Intensive Interaction goals; and issues related to the sustainability, or otherwise, of Intensive Interaction interventions. I have also addressed some more directly practice related issues such as timing, tempo, frequency and duration, and latterly I address issues related to structure, and suggest some strategies for disengagement, if that is problematic. Finally I look at more systematic ways of assessing a participant's level of engagement in Intensive Interaction activities, and also set out a planning tool that may be of some help in particular, more formalized circumstances.

'Expectations'...having realistic expectations

When going into an Intensive Interaction intervention, or preparing to support other people to use Intensive Interaction, I think that one important issue to reflect on is that of expectations. I think that we should be wary of raising people's initial expectations to too high a level. That is not to say that there won't be a rapid and significant change in the level of observable sociability for the person with a social impairment, and we undoubtedly need to project confidence that the process will achieve the desired results, as this will be vital in supporting and encouraging others who we are working with. However, I think that it can be counterproductive to project an expectation that results will always come easily and quickly.

That is not to discount the obvious possibility that sometimes some initial interactive work will generate immediate and demonstrably positive results. In most of the cases I have worked with, however, and especially so with people with profound and multiple learning disabilities, the changes that have accrued might best be described as 'evolutionary rather than revolutionary'.

This issue of remaining grounded, with realistic views of our own potential to make a difference, can at times be difficult if we compare our own efforts and subsequent results with training videos that show some of the more rapid and apparently 'revolutionary' changes in people engaged by expert practitioners (e.g. the changes seen in Gabriel when working with Phoebe Caldwell in *Learning the Language*, Caldwell, 2002). The use of such video footage is an invaluable tool in demonstrating both the potential benefits and the accessible, practical nature of the approach, and is something that I regularly use in training. However, when viewing such video footage, and especially when introducing novice interactors to the approach via such video footage, our expectations should be tempered by a realization that we should not always anticipate a replication of this kind of rapid initial accessing in our own work. We need to view, and we need to encourage others to view, such video resources with an analytic frame of mind, trying to find a balanced middle ground in which we accept the footage as instructive, without seeing it as setting an unrealistically high standard against which we might measure our own attempts.

This 'balanced' middle ground will lie somewhere between a fatalistic or pessimistic view that the person with a social impairment might only change slowly or not at all (and thus Intensive Interaction potentially being an effortful long-haul with little observable effect), and believing that we can effect a 'miracle cure'. If we, or the people we support, can keep within this balanced middle ground, where we remain genuinely optimistic of change and yet at the same time are still pragmatic and reflective (without being overly self-critical if change doesn't come as rapidly as we would wish), then I believe we are more likely to succeed more often in the longer term.

In summary, unrealistically high hopes dashed are much worse than cautious or conservative expectations exceeded.

'Unpredictable and intangible goals'...and dealing with them

Another potential difficulty that Intensive Interaction practitioners might encounter when starting to work with a new person, or when supporting others to use Intensive Interaction, is that much of what they seek to achieve can be difficult to predict accurately. Convincing others of the importance of Intensive Interaction can be tricky when the potential outcomes are not precisely known, not always easily quantifiable nor measurable, and the rate of any change is uncertain. Thus the intangible and unpredictable nature of Intensive Interaction can make any individual work, especially supporting novice others with individual work, a bit more complicated: we want to be continuously positive and enthusiastic, but are not always sure just how positive and enthusiastic it is wise to be.

Therefore, before starting any Intensive Interaction intervention, being transparent about the uncertainties involved in using the approach, and describing any potential outcomes in broad and approximate terms, is usually a prudent approach. Again there is a balance to be struck between projecting the necessary confidence to carry people with us and choosing the language we use to advocate for Intensive Interaction in terms that acknowledge the uncertainties and the intangible nature of any potential outcomes. Using terms like starting out on an 'interactive journey', or just saying 'let's see where this takes us' might appear somewhat woolly, but I believe that it is important to be realistic and honest. As stated above, it is my view that modest and realistic aims achieved (but possibly exceeded) are better than falling short of overstated or over-confident aims.

'Initiative decay': acknowledging the possibility of...

When initially using Intensive Interaction with a person with a social impairment, or embarking on an Intensive Interaction intervention, it might be useful to consider the real possibility of 'initiative decay' (Buchanan, Claydon and Doyle, 1999). 'Initiative decay' is the phenomenon of reduced engagement with, or declining application of a practice change initiative as time passes. This happens for individuals, or staff teams when 'change in working practices and procedures are abandoned as their novelty fades' (NHS Modernisation Agency, 2003, p.4). This 'initiative decay' has been especially identified when changes in practice are expected after training that only focuses on the necessary skills to complete a task, but does not cover aspects of policy or the necessary cultural changes required in the wider working context.

In my experience 'initiative decay' can happen after an initial period characterized by high levels of interest, practice and reflection associated with the introduction of Intensive Interaction. This tends to be followed by a gradual but sustained reduction in the interest, practice and reflection as time progresses. This is not a situation particular to Intensive Interaction: such 'initiative decay' is widespread across practice change initiatives (NHS Modernisation Agency, 2003). The lesson to be learnt from this is that, when setting up Intensive Interaction interventions, it is useful to acknowledge the possibility of 'initiative decay', and explicitly plan with sustainable practice change in mind. Such sustainable practice change will require longer-term support mechanisms for approach maintenance, specifically: access to continued further training or practice development opportunities (e.g. follow-up or refresher courses); the long-term availability of practical support and advice networks; access to literary or research evidence and articles; and, of vital importance, active and visible managerial support and supervision, including active modelling of the appropriate Intensive Interaction techniques.

In terms of individuals, there may also be particular times when 'initiative decay' may be more likely to happen. This may be especially so during the 'transitional phase' which potentially begins as any initial and easily discernible expansion of interactive behaviour associated with the early stages of using Intensive Interaction tails off (Firth, 2008). Such a transitional phase is described by Nind and Hewett, who use the term **'plateauing'** (2005, p.134), and is potentially a crucial period for practitioner support. This is because any previous, easily discernible interactive expansion, which is highly reinforcing for a practitioner's continued application of the approach, subsides into a phase of less easily discernible development.

Sessional or timetabled vs. integrated or opportunistic Intensive Interaction

The issues of when to engage someone with Intensive Interaction, and how this should be organized or scheduled, seem to be a recurrent theme around the use of Intensive Interaction. In my experience there tends to be two main variations on the scheduling theme. First, there is Intensive Interaction that is scheduled or timetabled to happen in discrete sessions at some relatively fixed point in the day, or sometimes even programmed weekly sessions. Second, there is the kind of Intensive Interaction that happens opportunistically at various unscheduled points during a day, and thus occurs as the most appropriate times present themselves. In some circumstances there can be some combination of the two types, and this may be advantageous, as it can combine the positives and counter the potential drawbacks of both at the same time.

Sessional Intensive Interaction has its advantages, as well as some possible negative aspects. If Intensive Interaction is regularly timetabled, with perhaps identified individuals given particular responsibility to do it, then it should be more likely to get done with the desired frequency. This can therefore help someone with a social impairment have reliable and regular access to Intensive Interaction. In some working scenarios, say schools, FE colleges or possibly some day services, having a sessional framework for Intensive Interaction is sometimes the only way it can be realistically managed. This doesn't mean that Intensive Interaction cannot be done at other times if someone is available to do it, but as the mainstay of their Intensive Interaction work, in some situations scheduled sessions fit the working context much better.

However, this has the obvious drawback that the person with a social impairment might not be ready, or willing to engage in Intensive Interaction at the scheduled time, for a variety of reasons. The reason could be a person's current mood, some illness or tiredness, epileptic activity, or it might just not be their best time of day (say after a meal when energy or arousal levels tend to drop away and drowsiness can sometimes creep up!). If Intensive Interaction is scheduled, and it is supposed to happen at a specified time, then there is a risk that the communication partner's agenda of 'it's Intensive Interaction time' might over-ride the wishes of the person being interacted with, whether they wish to be engaged or not. Some forward planning of the best times for sessional Intensive Interaction is worthwhile if the aim is to maximize its impact and reduce the chances of the person with a social impairment not being ready or in the right frame of mind for sociable interactivity.

Opportunistic Intensive Interaction has the clear advantage that it can be done at the most productive and favourable times, and it can be integrated into basic care routines. It can occur naturally and repeatedly throughout the day in a way that best suits everyone's current mood and arousal levels. However, if Intensive Interaction is left as an unscheduled activity, then there is the potential that no-one takes responsibility for it, and it can be the case that no-one actually does it. Opportunistic Intensive Interaction may be left for others to do 'sometime later', and this can lead to a situation where no-one actually gets around to doing it, especially if any potential interactors are busy or have a number of competing tasks to perform. Another potential drawback of an opportunistic strategy is that, if Intensive Interaction is integrated into other activity, or engaged in alongside another activity, there is a risk that it is not engaged in with the required levels of focus and intensity, potentially leading to 'less-than-Intensive' or superficial and time-limited interactions.

So, sessional and opportunistic Intensive Interaction both have their benefits as well as their drawbacks, and an optimum combination of the two strategies is probably the most productive way to proceed.

Tempo and response times

Even when we know the types of interactive techniques and strategies that work to engage an individual person with a social or communicative impairment, the successful execution of these techniques and strategies will depend on how they are applied. At times misjudged use of tempo, intensity and timing can have a negative impact on the effectiveness of the approach. One key ingredient in any successful application of Intensive Interaction is the tempo at which the techniques are employed; another is the amount of time allowed for some kind of response from the person with a social impairment.

Often, when novice practitioners attempt to engage someone using Intensive Interaction, the hardest thing for them to judge accurately is the pacing of their own activity, and their willingness or ability to allow sufficient time for some kind of response from the person they are interacting with. This is often, I think, due to a lack of confidence in their own practice combined with a genuine desire to see some tangible and positive responsiveness on the part of the person with a social impairment. Making moment by moment judgements on when to push ahead more quickly, or become more extrovert or demonstrative in one's own interactive behaviour (say when trying to initially gain someone's attention), or knowing when to temper or curtail the level of one's own interactive behaviour is not always easy.

Knowing just when to attempt to initiate interactivity, when to continue an interactive episode, when to press ahead with increasingly lively or vibrant interactivity, when to slow down and curb the tempo of interactivity, when to change the focus or even the form of interactivity, or knowing when just to sit back and do nothing and just make oneself 'available', and knowing which of these to do at any given point in time is, in my view, possibly the most complex type of judgement practitioners have to make. However, in areas such as tempo and response times, as with all other skills or crafts, we can improve our judgement making by gaining greater practical experience in surroundings that are both reflective and supportive.

This is an area in which the use of video recordings of good Intensive Interaction practice is indispensable, not just showing the techniques that might be used, but also demonstrating the tempo at which the techniques are employed. The wider the range of video footage seen, incorporating different interactive partnerships with different characteristics of tempo and response times, the more vicarious experiences people will have on which to base their own judgements and model their own practice. Asking Intensive Interaction trainees to watch video of Intensive Interaction and specifically asking them to look at and comment on the pace or tempo of the interactivity is something I now incorporate in our introductory training. Using certain passages of video to view and analyse episodes of Intensive Interaction that include periods of differently paced interactivity, such as the section showing Mohammed and Amanda on the Intensive Interaction DVD (Hewett, 2007), is useful. Such video can demonstrate how such periods of interactivity with different tempos can naturally emerge, and can be seamlessly integrated and flow together within an extended Intensive Interaction session.

It must also be acknowledged that there are some people who naturally seem to know which of these things to do, to what extent, and just when to do them, in a seemingly intuitive way. It is as if they have the requisite knowledge and skills to continually get the right balance of tempo and response times already latent within them, and this applies to people both with and without a diagnosis of learning disability.

Structured vs. unstructured activity

The identification of 'structure' within a period of Intensive Interaction is an interesting concept. Some types of structure might not be discernible to any outside observer, but that doesn't mean that there isn't a structure underlying the activity. Structure may be very subtle and may only be clear to the actual participants themselves.

Any such subtle structure within interactive exchanges between familiar people may involve particular sequences of actions, say a series of differently intoned vocalizations, facial expressions or body movements, and may incorporate timely pauses and specific repeated rhythmical movements or activity. Some structured activity may solely comprise of simple exchanges of fleeting eye contact or mirrored breathing rhythms, but so long as the activity has been rehearsed and repeated several times, then the 'structure' can develop from inside the interactivity and will thus be recognizable to the participants. Some regular interactions quickly develop a simple but clearly identifiable structure, say the participants taking deliberate turns to squeeze each other's hands gently (perhaps incorporating a pattern of repeating three short squeezes in each turn), or there may be different layers of structure within an activity, say a repeating non-verbal rhythmical vocal exchange concurrent with some rhythmical physical contact exchanges and some repeated periods of intermittent eye contact.

However, it is my experience that the lack of an easily apparent and familiar activity structure can make Intensive Interaction difficult for some carers or staff, and also for some people with a social or communicative impairment. Some carers or staff undoubtedly prefer an easily discernible and familiar structure to a period of potential interactivity, a structure that is recognizable from the outside, and that gives any inter-activity a task-like certainty and also a final and recognizable outcome. This desire for familiar and recognizable structure may be as much to do with a practitioner's confidence in what they are doing, rather than an issue associated with competence (although the two can be very closely interlinked). Such staff or carers prefer to construct interactivity in such a way that it gives them clear markers along the way so that they know if they are 'doing it right', and equally when they have finished. Sometimes such a recognizable structure can be intentionally imposed by staff or carers on a session of interactivity, and can sometimes even become a pre-requisite to any interactivity. However, an imposed structure requires some level of compliance, can lead to a form of task completion, and thus tends to reduce the equitable and also the creative nature of any interactivity. Any such requirement for an easily observable and predeter-mined structure will almost certainly curtail the level of negotiation and exploration within a period of interactivity that provides the vehicle for interactive development and progression.

In summary, structure may develop collaboratively within sessions of Intensive Interaction but practitioners should guard against imposing a structure.

Seamlessness!

Contrasting somewhat with the issue of observable structure is the issue of seamlessness. This term refers to the way that some interactivity can seamlessly move from one type of exchange to another. This type of seamless interactivity is, in my view, analogous with the way that a relaxed verbal conversation between friends can move easily and often quickly between widely differing topics.

The ability and willingness of both parties to switch seamlessly between different types of interactive behaviour is often something that comes with increasing familiarity and trust between an Intensive Interaction practitioner and a person with a social impairment. Interacting with someone who is flexible within an interactive session is a useful de-velopment, but it should not be forced on people who are not ready. In the early stages of Intensive Interaction (and the early stages of Intensive Interaction can last for a long time) frequent repetition of familiar ac-tivities can dominate. It has been my experience that such repetition can sometimes be a problem for an Intensive Interaction practitioner, especially a novice practitioner, although almost certainly not for the person with a social impairment.

Frequency and duration

The optimum frequency and duration of employing Intensive Interaction with a particular person can depend on a range of factors. These factors will include the person's cognitive and personal characteristics, their current mood and circumstances, the current working environment and the general culture of care. The optimum frequency and duration may also include such factors as the time of day or even the light conditions or temperature in the room.

The key task for practitioners is to be sensitive to the person's feedback. Getting it a bit wrong generally isn't such a disaster. For whatever reason, if someone isn't responsive at the time, then we can always try again later. We could also temper the pace and tempo of the interactivity if someone is less responsive, or try increasing the pace and tempo slowly as they begin to engage with us.

There are no concrete rules about frequency and duration, but we should guard against accepting too many reasons (or possibly excuses) not to engage a person with Intensive Interaction, whether it is a shortage of time, or staff, or something concerning the person's perceived mood or physical state. When considering 'frequency', we should be aiming for just that: frequent engagements, or at least frequent opportunities to engage being created. Ideally then, Intensive Interaction should be undertaken at least daily, and for most people it should become part and parcel of their normal daily routine. However, there is a danger that, as the frequency and integration of Intensive Interaction increases it may become diluted, no longer having the necessary focus to be truly 'intensive' interaction. If Intensive Interaction becomes integrated into normal daily routines, I would still advocate for periods during the day when it is used as a separate and singularly focused approach.

Duration is an issue that can also be influenced by a number of factors. We should be making continuous judgements as we go along about whether to continue or disengage from a period of interactivity based on the feedback we receive, and should ideally allow ourselves sufficient time to extend the session if it is going well. For some people it can take a while for them to engage or warm-up to a period of interactivity, and so if given insufficient time they would not engage as well as they might. A session is ideally carried out in a relaxed manner, with sufficient time to expand on or draw out previously successful activities, and without any pressure to curtail a session due to an overly brief time-frame.

I also think it wise to guard against any impulse, perhaps in the early stages of an Intensive Interaction intervention, to give unsustainable amounts of time and energy to it. This avoids Intensive Interaction being adopted in a 'flash-in-the-pan' type way. Realistic planning should aim for sustainability over the life-span of the person concerned.

Disengagement – finishing an activity that is going well

Some people experience problems when trying to disengage from or end a period of Intensive Interaction when it has been going well. It can be a problem for the person with a social impairment because they want the interaction to keep going if it is enjoyable, intensely stimulating or in some other way rewarding. Indeed, I have occasionally worked with people who have sometimes become challenging when the interactivity they have been enjoying has had to be curtailed, from their perspective for reasons they probably could not understand. Such an instance was a young woman whom I worked with who would get so intensely focused on a hand exploration activity that when the point came when I wished to disengage she would grip my hands more and more tightly, to the point of causing me pain and sometimes scratching my hands. It was when working with this client that I started to think about using a deliberate disengagement strategy, and with her it was to slowly wind the interactivity down and then redirect her into another, non-social activity that she could carry on alone.

Disengagement can also sometimes be a problem for Intensive Interaction practitioners who may also find a session of Intensive Interaction enjoyable, intensely stimulating or in some other way rewarding. Alternatively, they may feel guilty about terminating an interactive episode when their interactive partner clearly wants to carry on.

It can therefore be useful to develop a range of disengagement strategies that may be adopted if finishing a session of Intensive Interaction becomes difficult. Obviously, with the wide range of people engaged with Intensive Interaction, these strategies may vary, and could be as simple as saying 'okay' or 'one more time' to someone with sufficient symbolic understanding to take this on board. For other people, appropriate disengagement strategies might include slowly decreasing the pace of an activity, and slowly increasing the length of any pauses within it, so that a point is eventually reached when the activity just peters out.

The use of a 'final game' strategy could also be developed. This employs the deliberate introduction of a final activity, one that by design comes to precede the end of a session. With such a strategy it is probably advisable to use a more slowly paced activity to reduce the joint arousal levels of both participants, as this can ease disengagement. This activity then comes to act as a signal for the impending end point of a session, and so the disengagement doesn't come as an unsignalled surprise.

Another strategy that can sometimes be successfully employed is, when possible, to arrange for something both distracting and positive to happen just as the required time has elapsed for the Intensive Interaction session – this 'something' could include the arrival of tea and biscuits, or the appearance of another member of staff that the person likes or recognizes. Equally, an Intensive Interaction session could deliberately be timed to take place so that a natural break occurs around the time envisaged for the session to end. These natural breaks could be a preordained tea break, or lunch being served, or the arrival of an escort or the minibus home.

Assessing the level of interactivity during Intensive Interaction

It is useful to acknowledge that any assessment of the quality or level of intensity of Intensive Interaction is not an exact or objective process. It can be very arbitrary and subjective, especially so if any judgements are made by the person actually engaging in the process. However, one possible way to help with the process of assessment is to use a graded series of definitions specifically drawn up to correspond to particular levels of interaction. Such levels of interactivity, indicative of the quality of engagement that a person with a social impairment experiences within any given period of interactivity, can be judged more consistently with such definitions in mind. Such a systematic approach can help make any judgements more informative and reliable, and such a system could subsequently be used to highlight any interactive progression if used over a period of time.

The UK Qualifications and Curriculum Development Agency has devised such a system, the 'Framework for Recognising Attainment', which is based on the work of Aitken and Buultjens (1982), Brown (1996) and McInness and Treffry (1982) (see www.qca.org.uk/qca_1834.aspx) The defined levels within the system are:

- **Encounter:** an 'encounter' occurs when a person with a social or communicative impairment is present during an interactive episode, without any obvious awareness of its progression, e.g. when the person simply shows a willingness to tolerate a shared social atmosphere.

- **Awareness:** 'awareness' occurs when a person with a social or communicative impairment appears to notice, or fleetingly focus on an event or person involved in the interactive episode, e.g. when the person briefly interrupts a pattern of self-absorbed movement or vocalization to pay attention to the interactive partner.

- **Attention and response:** 'attention and response' occurs when a person with a social or communicative impairment begins to respond (although not consistently) to what is happening in an interactive episode e.g. when the person shows clear signs of surprise, enjoyment, frustration or dissatisfaction in response to the actions of their interactive partner.

- **Engagement:** an 'engagement' occurs when a person with a social or communicative impairment shows consistent attention to the interactive episode presented to them, e.g. when the person demonstrates sustained looking or listening, or repeatedly follows events with movements of their eyes, head or other body parts.

- **Participation:** 'participation' occurs when a person with a social or communicative impairment engages in sharing or taking turns in a sequence of events during an interactive episode, e.g. when the person sequences their actions with another person, or by passing signals repeatedly back and forth.

- **Involvement:** 'involvement' occurs when a person with a social or communicative impairment makes an active effort to reach out, consistently join in, or even comment in some consistent and meaningful way on the interaction, e.g. when the person sequences their actions with another person, and also speaks, signs, vocalizes or gestures in some consistent and meaningful way.

Disseminating individual Intensive Interaction techniques – using the SNAP system

The **Strengths and Needs Analysis and Planning** (SNAP) system was developed by Dr Jill Porter and Dr Penny Lacey (the School of Education, Birmingham University) to enable more effectively the cognitive and communicative progress of students with severe or profound and multiple learning difficulties. The system, demonstrated by Dr Lacey at the 2006 UK Intensive Interaction Conference, is simple, person-centred and practical, and it can be used to identify the current, or potential, communicative or cognitive strengths of a person with a social or communicative impairment. It subsequently articulates the kind of activities required to develop these communicative or cognitive strengths further. The system facilitates efficient sharing of such information with other people or services in an accessible and coherent format, and it also lends itself to successful collaborative working, as a whole staff team or group of carers can jointly construct it (Leeds Partnerships NHS Foundation Trust, 2007).

The SNAP system is split into two sections: first, statements of the person's communicative or cognitive 'strengths' followed by, second, associated statements of the person's communicative or cognitive 'needs'. The completion of the 'strengths' section requires a process of observations and discussion with colleagues, parents or carers. These 'strengths' are apparent in the person's engagement in activities and/or behaviours that are either social, or could potentially become social if engaged in alongside or with the participation of others.

Communicative 'strengths' that would be listed on a SNAP plan would be exemplars of the fundamentals of communication and sociability. These might include: the toleration or initiation of proximity/sharing personal space with others; the use of eye contact; visual focusing on the actions of others; the use of facial signalling to indicate an emotional state; engagement in exploratory or stimulatory physical activity; the use of non-symbolic vocalizations; engagement in rhythmical physical self-stimulation; initiation or engagement in social physical contact with other people; the sequencing of actions with another person; indications of consent or withdrawal of consent to the continuation of an activity.

In practice 'strengths' statements should be written in a succinct manner, but in a way that is also quite broad in nature. They might also contain brief descriptive examples of the skill, behaviour or activity. Examples of 'strengths' statements of clients I have worked with are:

> The use of eye contact: the person will engage in sustained eye contact with someone who is very close in and directly in front of them.

> The use of eye contact: at a distance the client will repeatedly engage in short periods of eye contact interspersed with looking away (and smiling or even laughing).

A list of a person's strengths statements (again, these are actual statements for clients I have worked with) might look like this:

1. Varied pre-verbal vocalization and laughter during some interactions.

2. Actively reaching out when [the client] senses someone in close physical proximity, especially on his right hand side, and subsequently initiating physical contact.

3. The use of his right hand (and also his left hand to a lesser degree) to explore and manipulate someone else's hands (including hand-holding) with sustained attention.

4. Responses to a variety of light physical sensations, e.g. tickling or blowing on to his arms, neck and face (under the chin).

5. Auditory sensitivity, listening to noises close by within his environment, especially the human voice.

6. The exploration of materials (often his own clothes) or objects, especially with his right hand, with sustained attention.

7. Using a clasp/grip reflex on various objects, e.g. holding various sensory balls, rubber quoits, etc.

8. Communication of displeasure/unwillingness to continue/join in with an interactive sequence by averting his attention.

Each SNAP document should only ever have the status of a working or draft document, and each document should be regularly re-evaluated and updated to include any more detailed or accurate 'strengths' statements. Such a re-evaluation should be conducted collaboratively with all those people who use Intensive Interaction with that person, and this process can create an ideal forum for open discussion and critical reflection on the interactive techniques employed.

Once the 'strengths' statements have been listed, the 'needs' section can be completed. The statements of a person's communicative, social or educational 'needs' should follow directly from each of the individual's identified 'strengths'. This is because through the use of Intensive Interaction we are endeavouring to engage and practise the person in using their 'strengths', and if our primary aim is developmental or educative we will also wish subsequently to develop their communicative or cognitive potential. Any communicative or cognitive development will be supported by the person's involvement in activities that are both within their competence and based on the activities or behaviours that the person already finds sufficiently motivating to engage in. Thus the kinds of activities to be listed as 'needs' statements are those designed to promote active engagement, participation and collaborative interactivity. The 'needs' statements should give a clear indication of the kind of interactivity that is both appropriate and developmentally valuable, but they should be written in a way that is not too prescriptive since we want the person with a social impairment to lead the interactions as much as possible. The 'needs' statements should be broadly stated and constructed in such a way that enables exploration, thus allowing for the possibility of increasingly sophisticated or even novel social experiences.

More detailed examples can be incorporated into the statements to give more practical guidance. An example: for a person for whom a strength was stated as:

> The exploration of materials (often his own clothes) or objects, especially with his right hand, with sustained attention.

the associated needs statement could be:

> To explore different objects or materials (with a range of surface textures and shapes) in jointly focused or sequenced activity with another person – supported physically, and if appropriate employing associated verbal or pre-verbal commentary. The items currently engaging the person most include: his shirt or jumper, various pieces of cloth, ribbons, curtain tassels, a blusher brush and Koosh-balls.

Another example: for a person for whom a strength was stated as:

Varied pre-verbal vocalization and laughter during some interactions.

the associated needs statement could be:

> Reflected vocalizations given in response to his own (even breathing sounds, but especially laughter), with appropriate timing and intonation (especially very close up near his face so that he can feel the breath on his skin around his neck/ears).

When using such a SNAP system with staff or carers who are unfamiliar with the system, or with Intensive Interaction itself, it can sometimes be difficult for them to perceive of certain behaviours or activities as positives i.e. as 'strengths'. Certain self-involved or repetitive and self-stimulatory behaviours may historically have been seen as pointless, distracting or even in some way 'off-putting' and thus negative behaviours. Such behaviours might include rhythmical or idiosyncratic body movements, repetitive exploration or manipulation of objects, or continually making non-symbolic vocalizations. Therefore some introductory work around re-conceptualizing certain behaviours as 'strengths' which may be potential access points and thus useful within Intensive Interaction may need to be undertaken.

10

Creating an Interactive Environment

Things gain meaning by being used in a shared experience or joint action.

John Dewey (1859–1952), American philosopher and educator

Ruth writes...

The term 'environment' tends to make us think about obvious, tangible, physical aspects and overlook such things as the organizational context within which people live and work, the quality of relationships between people, and sensory features (such as colour and patterning of furnishings). Unsurprisingly (I am an advocate for Intensive Interaction!), I value the interpersonal environment very highly and think that it has a massive impact on people's quality of life. The material that follows therefore contains a lot of reflection on various aspects of the interpersonal environment. These aspects include the 'person-centredness' of organizations and where interactivity lies in their hierarchy of priorities; whether the people receiving support have 'choices' imposed upon them or are allowed to make real decisions about their lives; whether the interpersonal context facilitates experiences of joy and fun; and whether this context allows people to be themselves and so start to experiment (for example, with being sociable). The aim is to provide the reader with food for thought (by sensitizing them to issues which they may usefully consider in their own work environments – for example, regarding difficulties in securing management support for an intervention plan) as well as some suggestions about strategies that may be helpful (for example, for managing anxiety in the face of unrealistically high expectations and carefully planning and evaluating any training that is offered).

The physical and sensory aspects of an environment are also important, of course, and in this chapter I share my thoughts on how some particular aspects of it can be affected to maximize opportunities for interaction. These include some very practical features (for example, how seating can best be organized) as well as those that are somewhat more nebulous (such as the general ambiance of a setting).

In order to maximize the impact of any Intensive Interaction intervention, the reader will want to consider all aspects of the environment that can potentially help or hinder. To assist in this, the scope of this chapter is therefore a broad one.

Being client-led or person-centred

Approaches to care can be crudely divided into those that are expert-led and those that are client- or person-led. The approach adopted by an organization will fall somewhere along this continuum and this will be an important determinant of how support is delivered. In Chapter 7, I described behaviourism as an expert-led approach: the behaviour analyst decides, for example, what behaviours need to change and how to intervene (see the section on *Cognitive and cognitive behavioural theories*). Positive behaviour support (for example, Anderson and Freeman, 2000) advocates a more person-centred/client-led approach in that the person themselves and their families are involved in the process of setting goals and deciding on the strategies that will help to achieve these.

Person-centred therapy, founded by Carl Rogers (see Chapter 7, section *Rogers' person-centred therapy*) is so-called because the person seeking help is seen as the expert in themselves and the helping professional is given the role of guiding them to find their own wisdom (rather than giving them direction about how to get better). Kirschenbaum and Henderson (1989) describe Rogers' central message as 'deceptively simple, yet profound in its implications':

> All individuals have within themselves the ability to guide their own lives in a manner that is both personally satisfying and socially constructive. In a particular type of helping relationship, we free the individuals to find their inner wisdom and confidence, and they will make increasingly healthier and more constructive choices'. (p.xiv)

Many services for people with a learning disability aim to implement a person-centred approach. In practice, this may involve meetings with the person and key others in their lives to agree goals and strategies, and reviews to see how well goals are being met, whether the goals are still relevant to the person and so on. My experience of such approaches is that they can work well for people who have good verbal abilities to say what they do and do not want. I have found that problems can arise, however, for people with fewer verbal abilities. My experience has been that those supporting such people assume that they want/need certain experiences on the basis of little or no evidence, often assuming that superficial inclusion in mainstream activities, such as shopping, is what the clients really want.

In contrast, Intensive Interaction has the potential to be genuinely client-led so long as the practitioner tries to find a way of being with the person rather than a way of changing them. To some extent this will involve resisting external pressures – for example, the thrust of national policy to get people into their communities. What the implementation of such policies often seems to ignore is the **meaningfulness** of community involvement/inclusion. If someone spends two hours walking around a shopping centre, and has no way of interacting with the people around them, how is this of benefit to them? I argue that it may be more benefi-cial to spend the same time in an Intensive Interaction session whereby someone aims to get to know the person, and how they communicate.

In order to remain person-centred, the Intensive Interaction practi-tioner needs to practise reflectively. They should continually question how they are being with clients, asking, for example: Am I being person-centred? Am I projecting my own desires or wishes onto the client? Am I responding to external pressures rather than what the client wants? Am I accepting the whole of the person, including their disability and negative emotions? For many practitioners it will be especially hard to put aside the wish to change the person – many of us have been trained to believe that we can and should actively try to change people for the better. It is quite a challenge just to let somebody be and accept them as they are – person-centred approaches, however, tell us that it is precisely when we create a context in which somebody can genuinely be themselves that they are most likely to change. This change is not imposed on the person by the therapist, but occurs spontaneously within the person.

I have not worked in or with a service that could honestly call itself wholly person-centred (although I have worked with some that are trying very hard to be). Rather, I have found that they have been led by a variety of other things. One service was very much staff-led. Staff decided what the priorities were and made a lot of decisions on behalf of the people being supported. The priorities were largely about cleanliness (there were lots of rules about how often the floor should be mopped and the bed linen changed) and the people had very restricted choices about what they could eat, where they could go, and what they could wear. It was common for staff to decide if the clients were too heavy and should go on a diet. One of the young women, Janet, living in this service was very compliant and unassertive and spent much of her time looking after her peers and doing jobs 'for' staff. Towards the end of my time there, we went on holiday – Janet, one of her peers, me and one other staff member. This member of staff and I were of the same mind that Janet and her friend should spend their holiday as they wanted and for the five days that we were away, this is exactly what happened. And they had a ball – playing on the amusement arcades, travelling in horse-drawn carriages, and singing karaoke. Janet really blossomed and I love to look back at photographs of this holiday and see her beaming smile. I was told later that she had really changed once back at home – giving up her college course and saying that she wanted to have a job instead and no longer being the 'skivvy' for her peers and staff. This is just an anecdote, but this experience gave me a strong belief in the power of giving choice and self-determination to people with a learning disability and in the power of creating the conditions for change rather than attempting to impose change on people.

What would have been needed to make this service person-centred? Most importantly, I think, the manager needed to be present more (she had a huge amount of work to do and so was only rarely about) and have a real feel for what was driving care on the ground (that is, the in-formal staff culture). Only with this awareness could she have led staff to operate from a different philosophy. She would have needed a strong personal commitment to a person-centred approach and been prepared to challenge all practice that did not meet this standard. This would need top-down support from senior managers and training to equip staff with the skills to deliver a person-centred approach. It is easy to have a policy that says 'we strive to deliver person-centred care', but very difficult to ensure that everyone in the service really understands what this means and has the knowledge, skills and attitudes to deliver it. It also seems to hold in many services that staff are punished for getting things wrong, but rarely praised when they do things well. This has to change if we are to affect staffs' practice positively.

Joy and fun

Joy is a profound emotion that gives meaning to life, and it is hard to imagine experiencing joy in a context that does not involve another person. When I think about my own life, feelings of joy are connected to my intimate relationships – I feel joy, for example, when my little girl gives me a kiss or a cuddle or shrieks with delight when I tickle her or when I hear from a friend that she has had a baby boy and that they are both healthy and heading home. I can certainly have very pleasurable experiences when I am alone (for example, floating in a warm bath and feeling deeply relaxed and contented), but I cannot think of any that I would call joyful. Daniel Stern (2000), a psychoanalytically trained psychiatrist (see Chapter 7), very evocatively describes the interpersonal experience of joy for infants:

> during a 'peek-a-boo' or 'I'm going to getcha' game, the mutual interaction generates in the infant a self-experience of very high excitation, full of joy and suspense and perhaps tinged with a touch of fear. This feeling state, which cycles and crescendos several times over, could never be achieved by the infant alone at this age, neither in its cyclicity, in its intensity, nor in its unique qualities. Objectively, it is a mutual creation, a 'we' or self/other phenomenon. (2000, pp.101–102)

I suggest that experiences of joy are similarly 'we' creations for adults. And without these experiences of joy, life would be so much flatter – moments of joy are the sparks that light life up, that give it sparkle and meaning. Intensive Interaction does not guarantee that somebody will have such joyful experiences, of course. It does, however, promote the sorts of relationships within which there is the possibility of people feeling joy.

Having **fun** is another experience that gives a lightness to life and so makes it more worthwhile. It is not such a profound feeling as joy, but I think that it is one that most of us can experience more regularly. And we *can* have fun on our own (we might choose to go out and jump in puddles, for example), but I think that we are more likely to have fun with other people and that the sharing of the experience increases the feeling of fun. One of the defining features of Intensive Interaction is that it should be mutually enjoyable for both parties – and if we're enjoying something, then there's a good chance that it will be fun. Fun seems to be a step up from enjoyment: whereas enjoyment can be quite subdued, there's something more upbeat about fun. Fun is about letting go (of our agenda, of having to be 'adult'), being in the moment, sharing, finding the child in us that likes to play; doing something because it feels good and gaining a real sense of freedom (from the pressures of being adult and having to achieve).

How often do the people with a learning disability that you know have fun? Do they have the opportunities to experiment and find out what feels like fun for them? Do they get to share experiences rather than having experiences imposed on them?

Intensive Interaction creates the possibility for people to have fun. The practitioner needs to be able to allow this to happen (creating opportunities and watching for feedback) rather than trying to *make* it happen. And if the person who struggles to be social starts to find interacting fun, then they should start to want to interact, thus creating a virtuous circle between the person and their environment.

Service or management factors

If we want to create an environment that supports Intensive Interaction, a crucial element in services is management support. I have most experience of residential settings for adults. In my work as a clinical psychologist, I would typically receive a referral for an individual client, but most often I found service-wide problems that affected all of the people living there. Such problems have included a lack of compassion towards the service users (staff seemingly blaming them for the problems that they have); an insistence that people have a 'normal' life regardless of whether this is in their best interests; and an over-reliance on control and containment. In these various settings, I have considered the use of Intensive Interaction as one part of an intervention strategy. This strategy, however, has also had to involve assessing management support for the plan and intervening at this level too. Issues that I have encountered with management support have included:

- managers being unaware of what is driving care on the ground (the informal staff culture) and so unable to influence this

- managers being unwilling to tackle poor care practices

- managers being fearful of change and resistant to any alteration to current care practice

- managers lacking support from within their own management structure, resulting in little confidence to deal with issues decisively (such as poor care practices and introducing new ideas)

- staff having little confidence in their manager (for example, managers with very little experience or expertize) and resisting the manager's attempts to influence their practice

- managers lacking knowledge about interventions that could benefit the people that they support

- managers lacking a clear idea of direction for their service and consequently failing to give clear guidance to staff.

If there are difficulties in securing management support for any intervention plan, these obviously need to be assessed and addressed first. It is not helpful, for example, for the practitioner to introduce a staff team to Intensive Interaction when there is little or no management backing for it. This is likely to lead to staff ultimately feeling powerless and demoralized – for example, when their manager refuses to protect any time for them to practise Intensive Interaction or to hear about the changes that it has made in the way that somebody is supported.

Professionals working into services will also need to consider the broader agenda of the organization and how this will impact on the likelihood of Intensive Interaction being successfully adopted – for example, I can think of one organization that was so wedded to a very literal understanding of Normalization (service users had to be accessing the community or developing daily living skills in practically every waking moment) that home managers could not even contemplate some of the ideas of Intensive Interaction (spending time at home getting to know someone when they could be out, 'accessing the community'). In this case, it would have been fruitless to continue to address things with home managers – more senior managers needed to be involved.

Physical and sensory environment

An Intensive Interaction practitioner should give some thought to shaping the physical and sensory environment to create maximum opportunities for interaction. Some specific issues that I have encountered and that may be helpful for practitioners to reflect on are:

- **Seating arrangements**: In one service, staff tended to sit around a table whereas the service users sat on sofas. I recommended removing the table so that the staff had to sit with the service users. Practitioners may also consider the types of seating that are available – for example, would mats or large beanbags make interaction easier than chairs?

- **Availability of interactive resources**: Many services have lacked the resources that might facilitate interactions. Such resources do not have to be expensive. Rather, they should take into consideration the preferences of the service users. For example, if somebody enjoys tactile experiences, staff might buy various materials cheaply from a charity shop and use these in joint exploration of feel/texture. Mirrors can be useful in establishing contact with some people (since eye contact, for example, can be explored in an 'indirect' way) and having photographs of familiar people around can be a useful prompt for interaction. Interactive materials should be freely available to the service users – this will obviously need consideration in individual cases since materials may also need to be protected from damage. Care must be taken, however, to ensure that equipment does not become an end in itself since its power to facilitate interaction can be lost if it is allowed to become a solitary occupation (Caldwell, 1996, p.16).

- **General ambiance of the physical environment**: I have been into many services that quickly led me to feel flat and oppressed – this may be due to lack of light, the colour of the paint on the walls and/or signs that the furnishings and furniture are uncared for. If I feel like this on a visit, the effect will be much greater on those people who live there. Feeling flat, oppressed and devalued will lower motivation to interact (or do anything at all). Similarly, practitioners will need to be mindful of people's sensory sensitivities (especially for people who have problems on the autistic spectrum) and whether they are being over-aroused by sensory stimuli such as the colour and/or patterning of walls and/or furnishings.

- **Noise levels**: I have been in a number of services where I have felt frazzled (over-stimulated) in minutes because of the noise levels, sometimes caused by the physical characteristics of a building (such as hard floors that did not dampen sound), or by blaring televisions or radios, or staff chatter. This can be so distracting that focusing on any interactive work becomes near impossible. Practitioners who find themselves in comparable situations will need to find ways of addressing the problems before undertaking any Intensive Interaction work.

- **Space**: Some people need more space than others to feel comfortable. This can be in terms of their physical distance from others and/or in terms of having a quiet space of their own to retreat to. Practitioners should also remember than when somebody is already feeling anxious or angry, they need an even greater degree of personal space than usual and that encroaching on this space will escalate their negative feeling(s) and increase the likelihood of some kind of challenging behaviour. Practitioners consider how best people's needs for personal space can be met.

- **Television**: I have been into many homes where the TV dominates the living area and seems to be constantly switched on. It is such a killer of interaction! If you have power over the remote control – *turn the tv off!!* If you do not, use whatever tactics you can to get the TV turned off more often. For people who really do like to watch TV, try to make it more interactive – for example, use it as a joint-focus type activity and talk about what's being watched.

- **Availability of a video recorder**: I believe that this is essential in the effective development of practitioners' competence in the practice of Intensive Interaction. Samuel and Maggs (1998), however, found that this did not fit easily with using Intensive Interaction informally (p.135) and that it impacted negatively on the quality of interaction (p.133). They preferred a more subjective form of recording recommended by Melanie Nind (Nind and Hewett, 1994; Nind, 1996, 1997; cited in Samuel and Maggs, 1998, p.133). My own view is that it is only with a visual recording that practitioners can really see what they are doing (rather than what they think they are doing) and receive constructive feedback that is based on what they are actually doing. I am aware, however, of the huge anxiety that this process can generate as well as the tremendous benefits that can come from it. I think that all professionals should make regular videotapes of their Intensive Interaction sessions since they have an obligation to improve their practice continually. Practitioners who aim to support others to use video should take account of the likely resistance that they will encounter. For example, in a study by Samuel *et al.* (2008) which looked at using video as part of an Intensive Interaction intervention, all the staff involved were reluctant to watch their own videos.

The social environment

The social environment is key to promoting positive interactions and staff need to be equipped with the right knowledge, skills and attitudes to be successful. One essential skill is being able to share control with the person with a learning disability (see, for example, Ware, 1996). This sounds easy, but is actually very difficult – not just for direct-care staff, but also for therapists who are attempting to offer therapy from a non-directive stance (see, for example, the discussion of this issue in Chapter 7 of this book, in the section *Cognitive and cognitive behavioural theories*).

> [m]any studies have shown that even those who believe that they are mostly being facilitative in their behaviour are often more directive than they realize. For example, therapists and teachers who assert that their clients and students speak for the majority of time in the counseling session or class often discover, when observed, that they themselves are doing most of the talking. (Kirschenbaum and Henderson, 1989, p.xv)

Ware (1996), writing about how practitioners can create a responsive environment for people with profound and multiple learning difficulties, likewise recognizes this difficulty and provides practical advice to help the more expert partner to be less dominant in interactions (see Ware, 1996, pp.68–70). Ware suggests that the practitioner could, for example, deliberately use pauses, wait for the other person to start, use imitation, and should also be sensitive to the person's wish to stop the interaction. This work, *Creating a Responsive Environment for People with Profound and*

Multiple Learning Disabilities, is a really useful and comprehensive book for anyone who wants to enhance the social environment for service users.

My own clinical experience echoes that of other authors who have found that some staff appear to be doing Intensive Interaction intuitively. For example, Hewett and Nind (1998) write:

> [w]e have so often had the experience of staff at Intensive Interaction workshops declaring that we had simply put a name, a structure and some legitimacy to what they were already doing naturally with some of their service users. [...] Many staff arrive at a responsive, process-oriented way of working with people who are pre-verbal because their intuitions about communicating get them there. (p.84)

Hewett and Nind describe this in terms of there being a good fit between the personalities of these staff and an interactive approach. There are also those who find the approach more difficult to take on board, but who can develop skills over time. Hewett and Nind (1998, p.84) have found that this learning process can be facilitated by these people observing a skilled practitioner and their being part of a supportive and communicative staff group.

If we are to be responsive to our clients, we first have to be able to really see what it is that they are doing (without jumping to conclusions about this, or dominating the interaction with our own behaviours). Ware (2003) recommends that the practitioner familiarizes themselves with the sorts of things that a person might do so that they (the practitioner) are then more likely to spot that behaviour when it occurs. She also talks about amplifying a behaviour so that it is more likely that it will be noticed and responded to. She gives a case example of Carol who was observed to raise her arm when a familiar adult was nearby, perhaps as an attempt to attract attention. Ware continues:

> [i]n Carol's case we found that staff becoming aware that this was what she did was sufficient to make sure she usually got an appropriate response [...] when she raised her arm. Amplifying behaviour makes it easier to respond to things you might otherwise miss.

Once staff have begun to acquire the skills to observe objectively, they are then in a position to respond to what they see. Hewett and Nind (1998, pp.86–87) enjoin staff to:

> [r]espond particularly to any attractive-seeming behaviours produced by one of the people you are teaching or caring for. Respond frequently, 'celebrating' (Nind and Hewett, 1994) in your behaviour what the person just

did. [...] After your response to something the other person just did, look carefully for the effect of your response. If a response to your response is evident, respond to that. You have started turn-taking sequences.

Being responsive, however, does not mean that the practitioner is completely passive, responding only when the client does something. Rather:

[s]taff prompting, doing something judged and crafted in order to 'light the other person up' need not be at odds with the overall issue of responsiveness. It can be seen as part of it. Put simply, it is all right to do something, offer something that you judge the other person will respond to. If she/he responds to what you did, then a behaviour has been produced to which you can then respond. (Hewett and Nind, 1998, p.92)

This echoes Ware's view (2003) that a responsive environment is one in which people get responses to what they do and get the opportunity to give responses to other people.

Hewett and Nind (1998, pp.90–91) briefly outline the ideal elements of the social environment that will facilitate connecting with people who are socially remote:

[b]e relaxed and informal; enjoy yourself and make sure that the activity is clearly intended to be enjoyable for you and the other person; don't do too much, put on too much of your own behaviour; use pauses and allow inactivity, thus allowing time and space for the other person to do things to which you can respond; don't try hard in one session for a long period of time; rather, have frequent attempts; be imaginative; be patient about lack of success.

It will repay the reader to spend some time reflecting on how well the social environments that they work in, or find themselves, meet these criteria. Some of my own reflections are that:

Be relaxed and informal: As a professional who most often tries to help with people's challenging behaviour, I am frequently aware of carers' or staffs' unrealistically high expectations of me, and this makes it hard to be *relaxed and informal.* If I am doing a session of Intensive Interaction with staff present, the more anxious or embarrassed I feel, the less able I am to be fully present with the client and to go with the flow, and the more likely I am to become directive and controlling. I try to manage any negative feelings that I have by being aware of them (like waves, if I allow the feelings to be, they will peak and then dissipate, but if I hold them back their power will remain undiminished) and by re-evaluating the thoughts that give rise to them. Rather than thinking, 'I've got to make this work' I might try to think, 'I cannot *make* this work. I can be observant and sensitive to what my client is doing and feeling, and responsive to them, but I cannot make the client engage with me.'

Make the activity enjoyable for yourself and the other person: a good question to ask is: 'what can I do to support my interactive partner to do something that is fun?' It might be that some staff teams or carers need additional support to ask and constructively answer this type of question. Carers and staff may need to realize that many people with a learning disability need to be supported to have fun, as much as they need support to develop in other areas.

Don't do too much: I have seen many staff who try to do too much – particularly they chat or talk to (rather than chat with) their clients, often in sentences that are way too long and complex. I have also seen staff who do too little – spending much of their time interacting with colleagues rather than the people that they should be supporting. Supporting other people to make any lasting change to their behaviour (whether that is to do less or more) is an extremely difficult process that cannot be easily accomplished by a single professional or intervention.

Use pauses and allow inactivity: people typically feel very uncomfortable in conversational pauses and rush to fill the gaps. It is a real skill to be able to sit back and allow pauses to happen. This ability, to allow for and feel comfortable within conversational or interactive lulls, is often related to experience and confidence, and tends to develop over time. Doing nothing can be one of the hardest skills to learn and use effectively.

Have frequent sessions rather than trying too hard in one session: Jaqui Maggs (an occupational therapist) made an interesting observation concerning her Intensive Interaction work with a client, Alice:

> [w]e sometimes strung out the formal sessions too long in the initial stages rather than responding sufficiently to Alice's signals to

end. This was possibly because visiting the house on limited occasions led to an expectation to achieve a lot in one visit. (Samuel and Maggs, 1998, p.136)

More frequent, shorter sessions are the ideal for many clients. We should therefore keep this in mind when planning how we collectively (that is, staff, carers and visiting professionals) plan and enact an Intensive Interaction intervention.

Be imaginative: This seems to be a paradoxical situation where the harder you try, the less successful you are. As soon as I ask myself, 'how can I be imaginative?' my mind goes blank! I think that we need to be alert to ideas that come to us in our 'down time' (when having a bath, dozing off, etc.) and not to dismiss ideas straight away because they seem too wacky or because other people are not immediately supportive. Sometimes the best ideas can come 'in the moment' when carrying out Intensive Interaction because we are embedded in the situation, and so thoughts that come then are contextually prompted and framed. They would be literally inconceivable at other times.

Be patient about lack of success: This is difficult to achieve, being so contrary to our wider culture (where it seems that people are only judged to be worthwhile if they are succeeding) and current competitive workplace cultures (for example, Payment by Results in the NHS). This may be a particularly difficult issue for practitioners who are employed by the NHS and work into services (psychologists, speech and language therapists, occupational therapists and so on) – at a very practical level, they have to assess continually whether to continue input when there is little or no evidence of benefit. Demand for these services typically outstrips available resources, and being patient about lack of success has to be balanced against the rights of those people on the waiting list to receive a service.

'Good enough' services

In an evaluation of the quality and costs of services for people with severe learning disabilities and sensory impairments, Hatton *et al.* (1995) describe what such services need to be 'good enough'. This includes:

appropriately skilled, trained and motivated staff; a clearly defined management structure; supervision, support and feedback for staff; a mission to provide individualized care; and mechanisms to review the quality of care being provided. I would add 'an environment in which Intensive Interaction underpins every encounter between staff and clients' to create a wish list for a 'good enough' interactive environment.

The unfortunate reality is that many services fall short of such an ideal. A vital aspect of providing truly individualized care, for example, is to communicate with people in a way that they understand and are comfortable with. As Samuel and Maggs (1998) powerfully illustrate, however, good (or even adequate) interaction can be a long way down the list of many organizations' priorities:

> [i]ncreasing legislation and residential home registration requirements, and the consequent wrath of management via disciplinary procedures, exist for badly kept drug records, the mal-administration of money or poor food hygiene etc. rather than for when a client has not been interacted with in a way they have understood between breakfast and lunch. (Samuel and Maggs, 1998, p.123)

Many of the services that I have worked into also depend on bank or agency staff who have often appeared motivated just to get through their shift with as little difficulty as possible. They cannot get to know the people that they are supporting in the same depth that is possible for regular staff and they are not full members of the team. This weakening of consistency and a team approach can only serve to undermine the overall 'interactivity' of an environment.

Effectiveness of training

Hatton *et al.*'s (1995) recommendation that 'good enough' services need appropriately trained staff raises the question of evidence for the effectiveness of training. Samuel *et al.* (2008) report on a study which involved 12 novice practitioners (home-care staff who had had no previous involvement with Intensive Interaction, and who were supporting adults with profound intellectual disabilities). The study involved a variety of interventions to help the home-care staff develop their practice: a half-day workshop facilitated by an expert practitioner; the provision of *A Practical Guide to Intensive Interaction* (Nind and Hewett, 2001); service guidelines; reflection record forms; a support group; and brief reflective conversations with an assistant psychologist. Following Intensive Interaction sessions between the novices and their clients a variety of measures (video observations, assessment schedules and staff questionnaires) were taken to examine two hypotheses: first that the novices could learn to use the principles of Intensive Interaction and second that there would be a positive impact on the quality of the relationship between the staff and the people they were supporting. The first hypothesis received the most robust support – video data indicated that the staff had learnt to use mirroring of movements and vocalization and were using contingent responding more. On the negative side, however, completion of reflection records declined over time (in detail and frequency); only half the novices attended a support group; all were reluctant to view their own videos; and there was no evidence of progression in the use of principles of Intensive Interaction. In relation to the second hypothesis, there was little evidence to indicate an improvement in the quality of the relationship between staff and client.

The authors note some methodological problems with the study that weakened any claims in support of the first hypothesis (such as the lack of any stable baseline in staff interactive behaviours) and the difficulties in engaging staff in reflecting on their practice. They suggest that more skilled supervision of the novices (rather than from an assistant psychologist) may have facilitated this aspect of their practice. They also note the challenges that are involved in real life research of this type involving a complex, multi-component intervention where there is a huge amount of variability that cannot be controlled (for example, the novices' willingness to complete reflection records and attend a support group). The authors suggest that replication might be attempted with more attention to practitioner skill, a longer duration and across settings.

For any expert practitioners or professionals who offer training in Intensive Interaction, this study illustrates that such training needs to be carefully planned and evaluated. Questions that will need to be asked concern resources – for example, is there sufficient time and/or resources to offer adequate training, supervise trainees and evaluate the intervention? Trainers should also be very clear from the outset about the aims of their training, identifying what they are trying to achieve, targeting the training intervention accordingly and carefully assessing to what extent different aims are realized.

Staff selection

One way of improving the social environment for our clients would be via a clearly defined and effectively implemented process of staff selection. In an ideal world, staff would be selected on the basis of the quality of their interactions with the people that they are intending to support. I am aware of some selection processes that include an element of this ideal – for example, I have sat on interview panels that have included a service user representative and so it has been possible to see how interviewees interact with them. The limitations of this are that the representative has always been verbally able (since they are sitting on a traditional interview panel and so need to ask questions) and that the assessment period is very brief. An ideal scenario, I think, would be to have prospective employees spend a longer period of time (perhaps a full day) with some of the people that they would support if appointed. This would open up the possibility for their non-verbal interaction skills to be observed and assessed and for assessors to look at how the people-to-be-supported respond to the person (so that people do not have to be verbal to have a 'say'). Such a process, although potentially difficult to organize and implement, would at least give employers some useful insight into a prospective support worker's inherent interactivity, and so be a useful basis for an offer of employment. Such a strategy would only make sense, of course, if there is a pool of prospective employees to choose from. The size of this pool, and the quality of the people in it, can only be enhanced if organizations increase the pay that is offered to direct-care workers.

11

Issues Associated with the Socio-political Environment

Example is not the main thing in influencing others, it's the only thing.

Albert Schweitzer (Philosopher)

Cath writes...

When Intensive Interaction was first introduced into learning disabilities services, those services were largely dominated by two major issues. One of these issues was the behaviourist practices which sought to reduce problem behaviour by a variety of methods. The other major issue was the philosophy of Normalization which sought to promote more culturally normal lives for people with learning disabilities and/or autism. The conjoining of these two issues can be demonstrated in many scenarios which affected the lives of people with disabilities. For example, 'socially acceptable behaviours' were seen as something to promote in order for people to access the community. Therefore behavioural methods were used to modify the behaviour of people with learning disabilities so that they might be more readily acceptable in the eyes of the general public. This led, for example, to people who desperately needed physical touch as a communication and reassurance being denied this simple human need, just in case a member of the public was accidentally hugged as a result of a culture of touch within their homes.

Added to the pressures on people with disabilities to conform was the introduction of the National Curriculum in schools, including special schools. While Intensive Interaction had been slowly and cautiously accepted into some services as a realistic place to start for many students who did not yet understand the fundamentals of communication, the National Curriculum was less realistic in how to approach this teaching. However, today the socio-political environment is a very different place. There are still some challenges to the sustainable implementation of Intensive Interaction but it is a much less hostile place than it was 20 years ago. This chapter examines some of the issues and philosophies that support and/or challenge us when seeking to introduce and support the use of the approach with people for whom it is appropriate.

The subject matter of this chapter would justify a complete book so the content includes only some brief discussion of the effect of recent past issues like age appropriateness and Normalization. I use the 'recent past' with a little caution since many, but not all services have re-examined these issues in the light of another area of included discussion – person-centred approaches. The apparently increasing trend in modern organizations, particularly the health service and education, to demand target driven accountability is also discussed.

The chapter also includes a brief examination of areas of human development that have emerged and are increasingly relevant in psychological fields. Those chosen for discussion are emotional intelligence and mindfulness, and Intensive Interaction practitioners may find these subjects useful in expanding their understanding and use of the approach.

Accountability

Most people who work in learning disability and/or autism services are funded from tax payers' money and accountability is increasingly and justifiably important. It may be useful to discuss what we mean by accountability since every profession will have expectations to provide evidence that what they are offering is effective and of best value.

A problem that regularly arises in many services is that any measurements made do not reflect the work that is done. As an example, specialist speech and language therapy within learning disabilities has for a long time been promoted by the Royal College of Speech and Language

Therapists as an assessment, consultative and training role, but the NHS still requires statistics that measure face-to-face sessions. Speech and language therapy departments are under pressure to demonstrate that they have fulfilled the expectations of the NHS, but a cascade model of skills development has been shown to be more effective than hands-on work (Granlund, Ternby and Olsson, 1992). Staffing levels in most speech and language therapy departments barely provide adequate time for the role to be undertaken as promoted by the Royal College and few departments have the staff to do anything other than assessment, consultation and training. It is hardly surprising that there is resistance to the idea of accountability since a great deal of energy and creativity is used in adjusting the statistics to reflect and justify effective ways of working. I'm sure this sad waste of time and energy is also relevant in many other services. And yet, providing evidence of the efficacy of Intensive Interaction is imperative to the sustainable use of the approach.

Perhaps one of the difficulties of being accountable in practice is that Intensive Interaction doesn't necessarily 'tick the boxes' of many pre-formatted statistical measurements and does not fit in with the idea of programme planning and goal setting. Targets cannot be predicted but measurements of progress can still be undertaken retrospectively.

Thus we need to be creative in the way we demonstrate accountability. Accountability involves open and honest reflection, good quality and realistic evaluation and action research to inform our practice. I work in parts of the world where this is not an expectation for professionals, so it is not uncommon to work alongside speech therapists who are still attempting to teach children speech sounds even though the children have an apparent aversion to being with other people and little desire or motivation to communicate. Because of these experiences I am keener than ever that my practice is informed and effective.

My work in the UK involves implementing Intensive Interaction projects that are sustainable over time and well accepted within the whole organization at every level. This involves accountability over time and at every level of the organization. In Chapter 2, I emphasized the importance of record keeping, not only to inform our own practice but to reassure managers that what we are doing is worthwhile. One powerful source of record keeping is video footage that has been analysed for specific strands of progress. This is meaningful accountability for both of the individuals involved in Intensive Interaction and is a significant way to promote and celebrate the ongoing use of the approach. Annual reviews for people with very little understanding of language are usually full of language. How much more appropriate it would be to have an edited DVD with clips of Intensive Interaction demonstrating progress – with some guidance for people attending the meeting who may struggle to appreciate the small steps of progress in the person's acquisition of the fundamentals of communication and sociability.

In busy services there could be a temptation to put staff onto training courses then tick the list that indicates they have attended. Training alone is unlikely to change people's behaviours in the workplace and so is not always effective in introducing Intensive Interaction into the care environment. As Georgiades and Phillimore wrote in 1969:

> The assumptions behind training as a strategy for inducing organizational changes are based upon the psychological fallacy that since work organizations are made up of individuals, we can change the organization by changing its individual members.

Therefore, for people offering the training there is an accountability issue in whether or not their training is effective. Accountability means finding ways to make training and support more effective. For Intensive Interaction this means finding ways to encourage the use of the approach in day-to-day life for the people who need it. In Crabbe's *The Intensive Interaction Research Project...and Beyond* (2007) the author reflected on the training and support practices used within an Intensive Interaction intervention and found that, despite training and on-site supported implementation of Intensive Interaction for six months, the use of the approach declined. This decline was reported as a result of other pressures on the services like cleaning or shopping, personal barriers to using the approach or confusion about how Intensive Interaction should be offered. Crabbe and Firth responded by doing things like reviewing their training, liaising with children's services, extending the information/training offered to a wider group of people and setting up support groups. This is a great example of accountability, reflection and action.

In 2005 I was undertaking a project in one authority which involved either teaching or supporting Intensive Interaction coordinators in teaching a one day Intensive Interaction course. Since this phase of the coordinators' training involved disseminating the approach to 348 other people it was a great opportunity to find out what people needed in order to use what they had learned. Evaluation forms all indicated that the course had been enjoyed, was informative, everyone had learned something and were supportive about the introduction of the approach into their services. Now, I'm cautious about taking course evaluation forms too seriously. Most people at the end of the day want to get home and most people are loath to put anything negative about the course or the trainers, so some of the questions were intentionally open-ended. The most helpful, and most often expanded upon section of the evaluation form was 'Do you have any comments on using Intensive Interaction in the workplace?' The responses were revealing:

- 73 per cent reported that they would require management understanding and support

- 46 per cent said they would like written supporting policies on consent to video, physical contact or age appropriateness

- 28 per cent said they would struggle to find the time to use the approach

- 26 per cent said they would need on-going support

- 21 per cent said they would feel vulnerable in the face of criticism from other staff and a lack of confidence in their own abilities and knowledge.

The results of this exercise informed our ongoing practice. In order for us to implement Intensive Interaction in a sustainable manner that provided accountability and efficacy we had to increase our levels of participation with the managers of the service. This involved educating and gaining their active support and involvement. Managers became involved in negotiating and writing practice guidelines which would give the staff freedom to use Intensive Interaction without being hauled up for being too physical or playful. Managers also became involved in restructuring services to give greater time for the approach to be used. Intensive Interaction coordinators agreed some support strategies to help staff overcome the initial hurdles of trying Intensive Interaction for the first time and reflecting on video. A 'pass it on' course was designed which guided people through the first steps of using the approach and had an expectation that the person would evidence their practice.

Intensive Interaction is largely a spontaneous and fun approach but we must never lose sight of the fact that governments, tax payers and services are entitled to know how their money is being spent and how effective this spending is.

Age appropriateness

In the early 1980s people with disabilities were often referred to as children, and treated in a manner that reflected this label. The TV film 'Silent Minority' made by Anglia Television revealed that staff routinely called the people with profound learning disabilities 'the babies' and as such placed them in a separate space to occupy their own time with no expectations that anything could be done to improve their lot. I have memories as a child of seeing fully grown adult ladies with Down's syndrome wearing child-like clothes which included short white frilly socks and strap-across shoes.

Something had to change in order to give people with disabilities some respect and dignity and the change that happened was the philosophy of Normalization. This thinking was a driving force in changes for people with disabilities and was largely responsible for getting people out of institutions and into community placements. Normalization was greatly misinterpreted and misunderstood at times and one of the confusions that occurred was the assumption that people with disabilities should be expected to participate in a 'normal' life whether this was meaningful to them or not. For people with profound learning disabilities this must have been somewhat perplexing.

When the idea of developmental approaches to working with people with profound learning disabilities was first aired in the late 1980s, there was a philosophical mismatch between this and the advocates of Normalization. Offering adults with learning disabilities and/or autism opportunities to participate in episodes of Intensive Interaction often used to be perceived as offering them something that was inappropriate for their chronological age. The suitability of Intensive Interaction during this period of time could be deemed appropriate or inappropriate depending on how it was represented and perceived. For example, if the approach was seen as play, this may have been unacceptable. If the approach was perceived as a conversation perhaps this was okay. Sometimes the objections may have been around using simplified, or even no language in organizations that communicated mostly with verbal outpourings.

Fortunately we are now in an era where developmental approaches are more acceptable and age-appropriate practices and expectations have been re-examined in the light of person-centred practices. This does not mean we can now return to treating people like children. It means we treat people with the respect and dignity of a fellow human being – and part of this respect is to communicate and interact with them on a level that they can understand and participate in. Intensive Interaction is not patronizing but empowering.

Community integration/inclusion

Community integration has largely been achieved in most services in the UK with most people with disabilities and/or autism living either at home or in small community homes. Community inclusion is another issue. The government White Paper of 2001, *Valuing People* (DoH, 2001) had inclusion as one of their main principles along with rights, independence and choice. Their view at the time was that:

> In the 30 years since the last White Paper – *Better Services for the Mentally Handicapped*, progress has been made in closing large institutions and developing services in the community, but more needs to be done. (p.2)

> People with learning disabilities are amongst the most socially excluded and vulnerable groups in Britain today. (p.14)

In consultations with various groups they were told that:

> People with learning disabilities often feel excluded and unheard... People with severe learning disabilities and complex needs are more likely to receive poor quality services. (p.11)

Valuing People aimed to target lack of community inclusion by helping to develop leisure opportunities, friendships and relationships. There is new legislation around accessibility for people with physical disabilities on public transport and new standards for toilet/changing facilities thanks to a campaign called 'Changing Places' (www.changing-places.org). The process of modernizing day services – also a *Valuing People* recommendation – has seen many day facilities being closed or attendance greatly reduced. Many more people are accessing direct payments where they have a personal assistant appointed by themselves or advocates. The PMLD Network Forum responded to *Valuing People Now* (DoH, 2009) with the following statement:

> We are concerned that the lack of availability of a suitably skilled workforce and the fact that local authorities often refuse to pay for skilled staff support are major barriers to the inclusion for many people with PMLD. (PMLD Network 2008, pp.6–7)

The PHLD Network forum (www.pmldnetwork.org/about_us/join.htm) requested services to:

> Invest in a workforce that is both sufficient and skilled to meet complex health needs and non-formal communication techniques.

In some places this request has not been met and many of the people who are being appointed as personal assistants have little or no training and direct payments to the individual do not always cover the cost of assistants receiving the necessary training and support. Furthermore, as they are working on a 1:1 basis with their client the opportunities for learning through role modelling are also reduced.

The same PMLD Network Forum requested:

> day time activities that are stimulating and meaningful to the individual, support people's physical and health needs in a dignified manner, access the community by taking part in activities that the person finds genuinely enjoyable and recognize that many people with PMLD experience the world largely on a sensory level and develop activities that take this into account.

One parent on the forum commented:

> Full on inclusion tends to lead to people being more marginalized and isolated (with exceptions) because they have not been enabled to have the necessary life skills to cope in an open environment. If you complain about closure of services with no replacements or alternatives you are 'labelled' as being against 'independence'.

A further appeal from the PMLD Network Forum requested: '[s]upport which helps people make friends and relationships.' This would appear to be where the use of Intensive Interaction could help in increasing inclusion for the people for whom the approach is appropriate.

In the past I've had regular discussions with various staff groups about whether or not they would engage in episodes of Intensive Interaction in the middle of a shopping centre. The responses vary from indignation that this may be expected to total acceptance that the types of conversations that are held in private would naturally be extended to a public place. There is room for a useful piece of research in gauging the public's attitudes to two different scenarios: first, seeing someone with PMLD and/or autism sitting vacantly in the middle of a shopping centre accompanied by a member of staff who is alternately 'doing things to', 'talking at' or ignoring the person, or second, two people having a mutually pleasurable time.

Emotional Intelligence

The concept of Emotional Intelligence was popularized through the publication of the Daniel Goleman (1995) book, *Emotional Intelligence: Why it can Matter More than IQ.* However, the possibility of an intelligence that is not purely cognitive and easily measured has been around for many years. Indeed it was one of the major proponents of IQ (intelligence quotients) who first raised the possibility that cognitive intelligence tests could not wholly predict a person's success in life. E.L. Thorndike (1920), a psychologist who is commonly accredited with building the foundations of IQ testing, suggested that IQ tests did not account for what he called a 'social intelligence' which is 'to act wisely in human relations'.

Wechsler, of the Wechsler Intelligence Scale for Children (Wechsler, 1949) and the Wechsler Adult Intelligence Scale (Wechsler, 1955), argued that the influence of 'non-intellective factors', such as personality, contributes to the development of each person's intelligence and models of intelligence would not be complete until these can be adequately described (Wechsler, 1940).

The psychologist Howard Gardner (1993) introduced the idea of 'Multiple Intelligences' which included interpersonal and intrapersonal intelligences. Interpersonal intelligence is concerned with the capacity to understand the intentions, motivations and desires of other people. Intrapersonal intelligence is the capacity to understand oneself, to appreciate one's feelings, fears and motivations.

Salovey and Mayer (1990) define Emotional Intelligence as '...a type of social intelligence that involves the ability to monitor one's own and others' emotions, to discriminate among them, and to use the information to guide one's thinking and actions'. Salovey and Mayer categorize abilities into four domains:

- **Perceiving emotions:** The ability to perceive emotions in oneself and others as well as in objects, art, stories, music, and other stimuli.

- **Facilitating thought:** The ability to feel and use emotion as and when necessary to communicate feelings or employ them in other cognitive processes.

- **Understanding emotions:** The ability to understand emotional information and communication, to recognize how emotions combine, vary and evolve over time and relationship transitions.

- **Managing emotions:** The ability to be open to feelings, including negative feelings, and to regulate them in oneself and others to promote personal understanding and growth.

In the most accessible publication by Goleman (1995) he outlines five main Emotional Intelligence constructs:

- **Knowing one's emotions:** the ability to recognize one's own emotions and their impact.

- **Managing one's emotions:** the ability to manage one's emotions so they are appropriate.

- **Motivating oneself:** marshalling emotions in the service of a goal.

- **Recognizing emotions in others:** having empathy and social awareness.

- **Handling relationships:** the ability to manage emotion in others.

The subject of Emotional Intelligence, the definitions, differing models and measurements is a diverse, unfolding and controversial field but regular Intensive Interaction practitioners will be able to relate to most of these definitions and see the relevance of Emotional Intelligence in their day-to-day practice. Goleman argues that Emotional Intelligence can be enhanced by practice and opportunities for insight into our own emotions. Reflective Intensive Interaction practitioners will, no doubt, be in agreement as they learn increasingly to 'read' the person they spend time with, and learn more about their own feelings by reflecting and reviewing the time they spend with another person in interactions.

Precise measurement of Emotional Intelligence would be a useful tool for managers in recruitment for services where Intensive Interaction is promoted. Unfortunately, much of the contention in the field of Emotional Intelligence is about tools and tests to measure this aspect of a person. Many of the tests are 'self-report' tests where participants with a small degree of knowledge of the subject could identify most of the 'correct' responses and are, thus, a test of the person's perceived views rather than their abilities.

Mindfulness

> Until we deliberately listen for it, we usually pay little attention to the fact that there's the constant chatter of a monologue – often idiotic – running in our minds. When we really lose ourselves, we can even work it up to a dialogue. Our minds jabber to themselves much of the time... (*Buddhism Plain and Simple* by Steve Hagen, 1997, p.102)

Mindfulness originates from Buddhist meditation techniques but is increasingly used in modern clinical psychology and psychiatry. In fact, mindfulness counselling is prescribed by doctors and is now recommended in the guidelines of the National Institute of Clinical Excellence (NICE) as a treatment of choice for recurrent depression. Mindfulness-based Cognitive Therapy (MBCT) is based on Jon Kabat-Zinn's Mindfulness-based stress reduction programme (Kabat-Zinn *et al.* 1992). The MBCT programme was designed specifically to help people who suffer repeated bouts of depression.

Mindfulness at work is also an expanding strategy for reducing stress, improving well-being, and the ability to flow with a given situation, enabling staff to react with the appropriate emotional response. Mindfulness is being fully involved in the present moment, giving total focus to the 'now', being present, aware, non-judgemental and accepting. Mindfulness is applied to both bodily actions and the mind's own thoughts and feelings. Being aware of rotating and persistent thoughts means having a choice as to how to respond to things rather than reacting automatically or from habitual patterns.

The relevance of mindfulness to Intensive Interaction practitioners is clear: being in the moment, attending fully to what is happening between the two partners, being unaffected by irrelevant thoughts in the focus of the interaction. The growing interest in mindfulness may also help Intensive Interaction practitioners to justify the tasklessness that is a feature of the approach.

Readers who are interested in mindfulness may also be interested in the psychology of flow. Positive psychologist Mihály Csíkszentmihályi (1990) wrote about this in his book, *Flow: The Psychology of Optimal Experience*.

Normalization

Normalization has been referred to a number of times throughout this book and this possibly reflects the enormous impact the philosophy has had on learning disability and/or autism services. The concept originated in Denmark as a result of government legislation in 1959 that aimed to 'create an existence for the mentally retarded as close to normal living conditions as possible'. This idea was then picked up, extended and theorized about ever since with the four main protagonists being Nirje (1969), Wolfensberger (1972), Bank-Mikkleson (1980) and O'Brien (1980).

Normalization gave some structure and understanding to the process of deinstitutionalization and moving services away from a mainly medical model to a more social model of delivery. There is much to be grateful for in the way in which the philosophy aided people with disabilities to have a more substantial presence and acceptance in communities. However, the Normalization agenda became so confused and widely interpreted that there were misunderstandings about what the 'normal' referred to – were settings for people with disabilities supposed to be more normal and community based, as opposed to isolated and specialist, or were we supposed to be advocating that people with learning disabilities should be more normal? The latter interpretation caused immense pressure on people with disabilities to conform and participate in society. In 1985 Perrin and Nirje wrote 'normalization as originally defined is based upon a humanistic, egalitarian value base, emphasizing freedom of choice and the right to self determination'. [AQ]

So, initially the Normalization debate was about the rights of people with disabilities to be treated as equal citizens and the responsibilities of society and services to provide these rights. However, the interpretation began to be focused on expecting people with disabilities to live like everyone else – with jobs and responsibilities to contribute to society. The responsibility somehow transferred itself from society's obligations to the person with a disability, to the person with a disability's obligations to conform to society. Many families and people working within services were disturbed by this thinking but it was, at times, difficult to express these concerns. There was a temptation for committed advocates of Normalization to view any disquiet or reservations as resistance to the much-needed changes that were occurring within services. The misinterpretations of Normalization prompted Wolfensberger to rework and rename his thinking as 'Social Role Valorization' in an attempt to change the emphasis from making people more 'normal' towards making environments and life circumstances more normal. However, this term never really got into the day-to-day language of most services in the UK, perhaps because, as with the whole Normalization agenda, this language appeared inaccessible, jargonistic and elitist.

Whilst there is much to be grateful for in terms of people with disabilities having a more community-based life and extended opportunities, Normalization is now largely seen as having done its job and person-centred approaches have become the main focus of most services. This is an especially welcome move for those people with more severe or profound disabilities for whom the Normalization agenda was frequently irrelevant.

O'Brien's five service accomplishments

In the UK, the philosophy of service that was more widely accepted and influential was that of O'Brien's 'five service accomplishments'. There were not vast differences between Normalization, Social Role Valorization and O'Brien's accomplishments in terms of definition or underlying theory, except O'Brien's emphasis was mostly aimed at service provision rather than creating pressures on individuals to conform. O'Brien's (1987) accomplishments placed individual choice at the centre of his ideologies rather than the needs for the entire devalued group to be accepted, acceptable and valued.

The five service accomplishments are:

- community presence

- support for making choices

- helping the person to develop competent skills that are functional and meaningful in community settings and relationships

- engendering respect by maintaining a positive image for people with disabilities, and

- ensuring participation in community and family life.

Again there are elements in the five accomplishments which could be misinterpreted to put the person with disabilities under pressure to conform. There are still times when people with acute sensory sensitivities are expected to go to the big, bright, overwhelming and potentially painful supermarket because they must participate in life and be a presence in the community.

To apply the five accomplishments alongside Intensive Interaction is entirely possible and realistic depending on staff confidence in using the approach in public and the public's acceptance of this type of interaction as functional and meaningful. Intensive Interaction certainly has a long-term aim of understanding and extending a person's communication which may include making choices and greatly aids the possibility of a person with profound learning disabilities participating in family life.

Person-centred approaches

If there is one thing that has changed the political landscape in the favour of Intensive Interaction it is person-centred approaches. Person-centred philosophies have helped us to re-examine policy issues that have previously blocked Intensive Interaction – policies like no touching or no playing. Person-centred planning isn't a clearly defined process but a general belief that an individual with disabilities has a right to be listened to, however the communication is transmitted, and that the messages received by the people around them should be acted on. The label 'person-centred approaches' grew out of a belief that previous planning for people with disabilities was done with the needs of the service as the priority and therefore the individual was expected to conform to the service rather than have what was best for them as an individual taken into consideration. John O'Brien (1987), who also featured in the discussions around Normalization and the five service accomplishments, was among one of the first people to name and describe person-centred planning.

Person-centred planning and thinking has been at the heart of recent government documents for people with learning disabilities and has begun a slow change within many services. The 2000 Scottish Executive paper, *The Same as You?* advocated Personal Life Plans. In England, the White Paper *Valuing People* (DoH, 2001) stated that it was a government objective:

> To enable people with learning disabilities to have as much choice and control as possible over their lives through advocacy and a person-centred approach to planning the services and support they need. (DoH, 2001, p.26)

Valuing People also stated that:

> A person-centred approach to planning means that planning should start with the individual (not with services), and take account of their wishes and aspirations. Person-centred planning is a mechanism for reflecting the needs and preferences of a person with a learning disability and covers such issues as housing, education, employment and leisure. (DoH, 2001, p.49)

More recently, in *Valuing People Now* (DoH, 2009) the government stated that:

> Good services for people with complex needs start with person centred planning, and with the assumption that everyone can benefit from direct payments and personal budgets. (DoH, 2009, p.9)

Person-centred planning uses a variety of strategies and techniques for helping people get their message across so that they can be actively listened to. The British Institute of Learning Disabilities factsheet on person-centred planning (Sweeney and Sanderson, 2002) reports, 'There are three tried and tested approaches that are commonly used and are well backed up in terms of resources, training and literature (www.bild. org.uk). These tools are Essential Lifestyle Planning, PATH (Planning Alternative Tomorrows with Hope), and Personal Futures Planning.'

Person-centred planning can be done without any of these accepted tools in a format that is meaningful to the individual. All strategies have in common that they attempt to place the person with the disability at the centre of any decisions that are made about their lives. Person-centred planning and person-centred approaches have a major likeness to Intensive Interaction in that they are both about process (what happens during the intervention being the main focus) rather than product (where an identifiable end result is the main focus). As such both person-centred approaches and Intensive Interaction are affected by the structure and culture of services, resources, time, staff skills, staff turn-over and attitudes to risk.

There may be a temptation within services to delay the use of person-centred planning for the kind of people for whom Intensive Interaction is appropriate. For this reason the PMLD Network (2008) response to *Valuing People Now* requested that:

> People with profound and multiple learning disabilities (PMLD) should be given priority for person centred planning. Staff should be properly trained in engaging with people so that people with PMLD are involved meaningfully in their development. (p.9)

It can be difficult to interpret the wishes and preferences of many people with profound learning disabilities and/or autism and making choices is an experience that can appear to be alien to this client group. The process with any individual could take a long time and may require many observations, discussions and opportunities for the individual to experience a variety of options to inform their choice in a meaningful way. Irvine (2001) found that once simple choices were consistently, simply and repetitively offered people with profound and multiple learning disabilities were able to learn to make choices.

The use of Intensive Interaction is useful and complementary to person-centred thinking. As one member of staff said after attending a week's hands-on Intensive Interaction course 'I've worked with Sarah for 18 years. I thought I knew her, but now I realize I only knew about her. Only now am I beginning to get to know her.' This has got to be a good start to using true person-centred thinking.

Person-centred approaches and Intensive Interaction are also similar in that their advocates can be passionate about their subject matter to the extent that objectors may be too afraid to voice concerns in the face of government support and an emphasis on positive change. However, just as in the days of Normalization, people with reservations need to be listened to or changes will be driven by the person-centred philosophy rather than being driven by the person at the centre of change.

Lack of time

In the informal study I undertook with course participants in 2005 (see the section *Accountability* in this chapter), 28 per cent of people felt they would not have time to implement Intensive Interaction. This is a recurrent theme of feedback from training and staff discussions in projects I am involved in. Some of the complaints about lack of time are valid, but many environments can accommodate Intensive Interaction by a re-examination of priorities in terms of housework, activities that people with learning disabilities are engaged in – that may or may not be meaningful to the individual – and good teamwork. There is no doubt that time can be an issue for some people wishing to introduce the approach and this needs to be addressed with managers. Educating inspection bodies about the need for Intensive Interaction and the effects it can have on individuals' lives can often help to refocus the importance of super-clean environments versus bored tenants/students.

In some services where there is a service expectation that a diary full of activities will take place it may be necessary to put definite sessions of Intensive Interaction into the timetable (with the understanding that interactivity can and should happen at all other times). One service I worked with completed the timetables with 'multisensory room/personal care/music group...and Intensive Interaction' for every activity. This created a built-in expectation that staff would be thoughtful of the approach at every point of the day.

There is no doubt that people working in public services are under increasing time pressure with more demands to spend time doing paperwork. Recently I heard of a service where a lady with severe learning disabilities had been so clearly under-funded for the support she required that she spent a great deal of time alone in her own flat with assistive technology that told her to go back to bed if she got up too early and go back into the house if she opened the front door. When people who have enormous needs to learn about being communicative and social – beside the human needs to be acknowledged and nurtured – this type of care is completely unethical and should be challenged at every level. Time is the most precious thing we can offer to people and time to interact needs to be regularly flagged up as a human right.

12

Issues Associated with Approach Development and Dissemination

Nobody can go back and start a new beginning, but anyone can start today and make a new ending.

Maria Robinson, author

Graham, Ruth and Cath write...
In this chapter we look at the current position of Intensive Interaction with an acknowledgement of the emerging research base, and the position and profile of the approach amongst individuals, services, and also the UK government. We also try to look at the future of Intensive Interaction, and try to focus on some of the potentially contentious issues that might impact on individual practitioners and services who wish to work in the Intensive Interaction way. It is our view that, as Intensive Interaction continues to become more recognized and more widely practised, such issues might well include capacity and quality of the available training, differentiation or moderation of training for different groups of practitioners, standardization and accreditation for training, and potentially a more formalized and overtly structured support network.

Intensive Interaction: the current position

The strength of Intensive Interaction's current position is that it has been very well received by the most important people involved with it use — that is, those people with social or communicative impairments and their direct carers. However, since many different people and professions are increasingly involved in the use and progress of Intensive Interaction, the future development and dissemination of the approach could well take us all on a number of different paths.

There is now increasing recognition of Intensive Interaction amongst a wide range of concerned professionals, including teachers, psychologists, speech and language therapists, occupational therapists, music therapist and others. The future course of Intensive Interaction will certainly be influenced by a number of issues (organizational, cultural, political, economic, etc.) but our view is that the most over-riding matter will be the resourcefulness and drive of the individual practitioners who become members of the informal 'community of Intensive Interactors'.

Advancements in any area or discipline tend to be built on the cumulative work of those that have gone before, and there are some major figures who have had huge influence on the early development of Intensive Interaction. Most notable are Dave Hewett and Melanie Nind who did the early research and wrote the original treatise. Acknowledgement should also be given to the seminal work of Geraint Ephraim on 'Augmented Mothering' (1986) and latterly Phoebe Caldwell who has published widely on Intensive Interaction and also produced the first training video (*Learning the Language*, 2002). Since the original work of Nind and Hewett, the increasing positive regard given to Intensive Interaction has been strongly influenced by the fact that its development and dissemination have remained very much practitioner focused, i.e. a 'bottom-up' process. Thus the approach is often owned and directed by those very people who practice it, and it has not generally been imposed on people from a remote managerial or academic position.

For people who support those with communication and social impairments Intensive Interaction has provided answers to questions that had not previously been asked or addressed. These questions, which are still the most important questions to address, are concerned with effective two-way human communication, with the processes of forming human relationships, and with what can successfully promote a person's feelings of connectedness and happiness. As Nind and Hewett state:

...we believe it is the most important area to work on to make a difference to someone's quality of life. (2001, p.3)

The research evidence for Intensive Interaction (its validated 'effectiveness' or 'efficacy')

Before looking at the body of research into Intensive Interaction, it might be useful to explore briefly the difference between claims for an interventions 'effectiveness', as opposed to its 'efficacy'. The two things are similar, and the terms can sometimes be mistakenly used interchangeably. The major difference is that efficacy is a measurement of the outcomes of an intervention carried out under traditional research conditions (i.e. in randomized or comparative trials). This means that measurements of efficacy are usually undertaken in tightly controlled environments so that as few potentially confounding variables as possible come into play. Effectiveness, however, is a judgement made on the outcomes of practice carried out in 'routine settings' (Barkham *et al.*, 2005), in the type of environment where the intervention would normally be used. Confounding variables therefore inevitably come into play. It is generally practice-based effectiveness that we, as Intensive Interaction practitioners, are concerned with: we want to know what works in real life scenarios.

Research evidence for the effectiveness of Intensive Interaction

Published research evidence has been vital in supporting practitioners' anecdotal claims of the effectiveness of Intensive Interaction and in promoting its increasing acceptance amongst professionals and academics. There is an increasing body of research evidence, albeit mainly from practitioners investigating interventions that they themselves have organized, that has helped describe and so define the possibilities of Intensive Interaction.

The body of peer reviewed and published research falls into a number of categories: some research studies have involved children (most often in special schools) and other studies have involved adults, most often in long-term residential care or attending some kind of day services (see Research papers, after References). The research also tends to fall into two categories with respect to the length of time over which the Intensive

Interaction intervention was studied, with child-focused studies tending to be longer than adult residential studies.

These studies have employed different methodologies, quantitative or qualitative, and the research has been carried out in a variety of settings (e.g. special schools, a hospital school, day service settings or various residential settings). However, across all these research studies emerge findings of improved or novel interactive responses by the child or adult participants. This increased or novel interactivity has been evinced in the following ways:

- increased social initiation and/or engagement (in Cameron and Bell, 2001; Kellett, 2000, 2003, 2004; Nind, 1996; Watson and Fisher, 1997)

- increased levels of contingent smiling (in Leaning and Watson, 2006; Lovell et al., 1998; Nind, 1996)

- increased levels of eye contact or looking at another person's face (in Cameron and Bell, 2001; Kellett, 2000, 2003, 2004; Leaning and Watson, 2006; Lovell et al., 1998; Nind, 1996; Watson and Knight, 1991)

- increased levels of socially significant physical contact (in Elgie and Maguire, 2001; Firth et al., 2008; Kellett, 2000, 2003, 2004; Lovell et al., 1998)

- increased toleration of, or responsiveness to, physical proximity (in Firth et al., 2008; Nind, 1996)

- improved levels of joint attention (in Kellett, 2000, 2003, 2004, 2005; Leaning and Watson, 2006; Lovell et al., 1998; Nind, 1996)

- increased use of vocalization (in Cameron and Bell, 2001; Elgie and Maguire, 2001; Kellett, 2000; Lovell et al., 1998; Watson and Knight, 1991).

Despite this quite compelling evidence for the effectiveness of Intensive Interaction, there is always a continuing need for further research and publications. Continuing further research will push forward our understanding of the effectiveness and breadth of the approach's potential application(s). It will also help to create an increasingly well-informed and thus insightful debate on such possibilities, as well as the potential difficulties and limits to the use of Intensive Interaction.

Further research into the use of Intensive Interaction with different groups of people with social or communicative impairments can only increase our understanding of just where and when Intensive Interaction can effectively be used. In our view, such future research might usefully focus on the following areas:

- The use of Intensive Interaction with people with late stage dementia to determine its ability to promote social interaction and reduce distress as people lose the ability to use symbolic language to communicate (there is one published exploratory case study looking at the use of Intensive Interaction with somebody with very advanced dementia (Ellis and Astell, 2008)

- The use of Intensive Interaction with pre-school infants with learning disabilities and/or autism to look at whether earlier intervention carries enhanced benefits.

- Its use with children who have experienced early deprivation/ institutionalization to assess the potential efficacy of Intensive Interaction, especially in terms of meeting their emotional needs (there is already some published evidence regarding the use of Intensive Interaction-type interventions with institutionalized children – Davies, Zeedyk, Walls, Betts and Parry (2008, pp.84–101), for example, report on the effectiveness of their intervention (imitative interaction) with children who are receiving state care in Romania).

- The role of parents in supporting the use of Intensive Interaction for their children – whether this enhances the benefits from Intensive Interaction provided in schools.

- The use of Intensive Interaction in services for people with severe challenging behaviour to see whether the benefits from Intensive Interaction generalize to other times/settings.

- The effectiveness of differing training models and methods to support Intensive Interaction practice (see the specific recommendations made in the Samuel et al. (2008) study).

- The effectiveness of structured supervision in supporting the quality of Intensive Interaction interventions.

The most credible evidence for the psychotherapeutic potential of Intensive Interaction has come from studies carried out in educational settings (Nind, 1996 and Kellett, 2000, 2003, 2005). These have employed the most robust research methodology of the published evidence. Typical of the cases presented is Jacob (Kellett, 2003) who is reported to have shown significantly decreased levels of self-injury and stereotypical behaviours pre- to post-intervention. The staff who knew him well also saw him as a much happier child and reported what can be seen as a change in his personality: 'they had discovered a delightfully humorous, mischievous side to his character that they had not known before.'

Using psychotherapeutic terminology, we can suggest that the Intensive Interaction intervention enabled the worker to develop a meaningful relationship with Jacob and that this promoted his psychological well-being (made him happier) and enabled him to show something of his potential (humour and mischief – see Chapter 7, the section *Humanistic theories*). It is also interesting to speculate whether the staff who knew Jacob well would have described his pre-intervention state as 'depressed' had he not had a learning disability – before Intensive Interaction was offered he was described as a withdrawn boy who spent much of his time engaged in self-injury.

Research that has been carried out by clinical psychologists has involved the study of single cases, but has provided consistent support for the psychotherapeutic potential of Intensive Interaction. Elgie and Maguire (2001), for example, found that their client Anna reached out to them as therapists during Intensive Interaction sessions (something which she had not done at all during the pre-intervention baseline phase) and Lovell *et al.* (1998) found that their client W. became happier and started to find enjoyment in interacting.

What is needed now are studies which set out to directly test hypotheses about the psychotherapeutic potential of Intensive Interaction and which employ robust methodologies. For example, studies might use standardized measures of psychological distress (pre- and post-intervention) to test for change on these variables (this would provide more credible support for the anecdotal evidence that Intensive Interaction can alleviate features of depression and make people happier). Similarly, it would be useful to develop a measure of the quality of the relationship that is developed in Intensive Interaction (one which an observer could use to rate factors such as warmth, practitioner's attunement to the client's emotional state, practitioner's reflection of the client's emotional state, practitioner following the client's lead, client's interest in the practitioner, client's level of enjoyment) and use this to track the development of such relationships and how this relates to psychotherapeutic changes. This would enable testing of the hypothesis that the development of a warm, meaningful relationship is associated with the psychotherapeutic benefits of Intensive Interaction.

High quality research, however, is time and labour intensive and the majority of professionals who deliver psychotherapy to people with a learning disability do not publish anything about their work. Changing this situation requires bottom-up and top-down changes. From the bottom, individual therapists need to be encouraged to get interested in Intensive Interaction and then advocate for protected time to carry out research. The recently established Regional Intensive Interaction groups may become fora where interested people can meet and devise collaborative research projects, thus sharing some of the burden. Some training courses (such as the professional training for clinical psychologists and speech and language therapists) include a research requirement and need to employ staff who have the expertise and enthusiasm to supervise research into Intensive Interaction. Top-down, senior management within organizations needs to genuinely support progress towards more person-centred working and devote resources (people, time, money) to relevant research (research into Intensive Interaction being one example). In an ideal world, the government would not just advocate Intensive Interaction in documents but would back this up with dedicated research funding.

Evidence for the effectiveness of training in Intensive Interaction

Samuel *et al.* (2008) published the first (and, as yet, only) study which looks at the effectiveness of training direct-care staff in Intensive Interaction (for a more detailed summary, see Chapter 10, the section *Effectiveness of training*). The results showed that the novice practitioners learned to use some specific techniques of Intensive Interaction (such as mirroring) and that there were gains in the communication and social abilities of the people (with a learning disability) that they were supporting. Less positively, only half of the practitioners attended a support group and they were all reluctant to watch videos of themselves doing Intensive Interaction. The authors note that this reduced the potential for them to learn through reflective practice and that this might have been better facilitated by more skilled supervision (c.f. Irvine, 2001) – the assistant psychologist who led the support groups was herself a novice practitioner. In terms of future research, an independent replication of this study (incorporating the authors' suggestions for improving on their own study) would be a very useful step forward. In addition, issues of how to promote the sustainability of gains from training and 'what might be considered the minimum requirements for good enough practice' (Samuel *et al.*, 2008) would be areas for future research with high relevance for practice.

Evidence from other 'non-research' sources

A lot of evidence for the effectiveness of Intensive Interaction comes from non-research sources, such as unpublished degree theses and case reports, action research studies and practitioner anecdotes (including the anecdotal reports of trainees and experienced practitioners). Although such evidence does not carry the same epistemological validity or evidential weight as that derived from peer-reviewed research, we would argue that it is still evidence of real life experiences and should not be readily dismissed. If you work with people who use Intensive Interaction, then you are likely to hear repeated and clear testimony of its effectiveness in terms of accounts of successful 'real life' practice and associated positive outcomes.

The sheer weight of this kind of evidence from those who practise Intensive Interaction supports the proposition that it is not necessary to be highly qualified to succeed effectively in using the approach. Instead, taken together, this body of narrative or anecdotal evidence suggests that effective Intensive Interaction is readily achievable by very many people, in a wide range of different contexts and environments, the common requirement being the will to work with the necessary creativity, sensitivity and perseverance, and for practitioners to have access to some basic training and continued support.

'Position papers' on Intensive Interaction

As well as empirical research papers, there have been a number of signifi-cant expositional papers about particular aspects of Intensive Interaction. Such papers tend to present an argument in favour of Intensive Interaction, and some tend to focus on particular theoretical analyses or certain prac-tical aspects of the approach (see Research papers, in the Further Reading section). These papers are useful to read to inform practitioners' prac-tice and their understanding of the positioning of Intensive Interaction within particular professional disciplines (educational, psychological, therapeutic and care/residential). This body of work illustrates the wide acceptance of Intensive Interaction across different disciplines which concern themselves with the support and development of people with a social or communicative impairment.

A theme that comes through these different papers is that there is much more that we have in common than there is that divides us in terms of seeing Intensive Interaction as an effective and valuable ap-proach. Although there may be differences between professions in some of the details (for example, the aims for Intensive Interaction are likely to differ between educationalists and therapists), they are united in seeing Intensive Interaction as an approach that benefits people with communi-cation and social impairments. Advocates for the approach are therefore working towards the same goals regardless of their profession – namely, to provide Intensive Interaction to as many people as might benefit from it and to develop its potential as far as possible.

'Champions' of Intensive Interaction (and the 'hero-innovator' problem)

In situations where change is desired, a person who is seen as a 'cham-pion' for the cause is often given or takes on the responsibility to lead and subsequently sustain the process. Sometimes a single person is asked to cascade the information or skills that they have garnered from some training package, so that all the staff of an organization come to un-derstand the need for, and gain the necessary skills to, implement the desired change. This has indeed been the case for some people who have come to use Intensive Interaction, and who have individually tried to persuade or encourage others across their organization to do the same. However this type of dissemination strategy, focused on one individual taking on the role of a 'champion' (or 'hero-innovator' as characterized by Georgiades and Phillimore, 1969), is one that can be laden with difficulty. Unsurprisingly, this kind of individualized strategy is much more likely to fail in the longer term than a strategy focused on collective or collaborative change.

Such an individualized strategy for driving forward change can also be a fraught and disaffecting experience for the person cast in the role of 'champion'. It leaves them vulnerable to the possibility of being undermined if they are perceived to fail in any way. This could occur for a variety of reasons, such as the resistance that is typical of organizations and individuals in the face of unsolicited change coming from an 'outside' source. Such a situation is not perculiar to Intensive Interaction: it is just how we as individuals, and the organizations we work within, tend to operate. Changing working habits and well-established practice is notoriously problematic, and it is generally very difficult for an individual to single-handedly achieve long-term change across a service or organization.

Practitioners who are aiming to bring about change in others are advised to seek out and then work alongside other people who share the same goals. This is certainly necessary in order to create more profound changes in habit and practice that are sustainable. The deliberate creation of a 'community of Intensive Interactors', or joining an already established 'community of Intensive Interactors', is one way to share responsibility for developing Intensive Interaction practice into the longer term. Self-supporting and self-sustaining communities are generally more successful at avoiding individual burnout and also reducing the potential impact of 'initiative decay' (Buchanan et al., 1999).

Sustainability and 'initiative decay'

As covered in Chapter 9, a concept that is useful to keep in mind when attempting to introduce Intensive Interaction as a novel approach is that of 'initiative decay'. This is defined as a decline over time of the impact of an initiative designed to change working or care practices. Initiative decay is most likely when change is attempted via a short-term fix, such as a one-off training event or short training course. Such short-term fixes tend to ignore the organizational culture and established practices which may well 'swallow' change strategies that do not directly address them. It is therefore important when attempting to implement any change to acknowledge and address such issues as current working cultures; formal and informal hierarchies; the management and leadership of staff teams; organizational routines; the availability of appropriate resources; personal priorities; and ingrained or unreflective practice.

We believe that sustainable change only results from getting staff or carers 'on board' with the process, and this will initially involve genuinely listening to people who question proposed changes and subsequently taking their views into account. Once some genuine debate has been opened up, we can formulate a way to introduce or model changes in a fashion that is more meaningful to those people who we wish to work in a different way. We should always look for ways of answering their questions and addressing any worries that they have, before moving on to the process of actually implementing change.

When we look to achieve sustainable change we should be looking to enhance not only the knowledge and skill development of individual practitioners, but also at how we can set in motion an ongoing process of continual collaborative reflection and support.

Anyone setting up Intensive Interaction interventions would be well advised to explicitly prepare and plan for sustainable practice change, and this will require the creation of longer-term support mechanisms. These may include:

- regular training opportunities at appropriate intervals (these should be flexible since some staff may need more frequent training than others)

- regular opportunities for positive and constructive peer support and advice

- transparency in service planning and development that includes the opinions of service users (whenever possible), direct carers, support workers and/or family members

- the regular availability of enthusiastic and engaging leadership, management and supervision (including hands-on modelling of appropriate Intensive Interaction techniques)

- access to research evidence and relevant literature

- access to a supportive Intensive Interaction network (within the organization and/or externally).

However, no matter how well we plan ahead, or how well we support people to take on Intensive Interaction, we may have to accept the fact that we may not always convince everyone to change in ways we would wish. For some people, using Intensive Interaction can be too challenging for a variety of individual reasons. For some people in some circumstances it can be too emotionally demanding; for other people it is too challenging of their personal inhibitions. Sometimes despite all the evidence and explanation, to some people it can still seem somehow 'inappropriate', and unfortunately for some people, if we are being honest, it can just be too much effort. (Some of these issues, of course, can be referred to the person's line management for appropriate action.)

Interestingly, some people may say all the right things, profess to accept the approach and practise it regularly, but if observed seem to fall some way short of achieving the necessary intensity or mutuality required to call what they are doing *Intensive* Interaction. These people present a particular difficulty as they do not perceive any need to change their practice, although to an outside observer this might seem an obvious necessity. Such situations require particularly sensitive handling, and there is often no easy or quick fix. The best way to approach such situations is to work collaboratively with staff or carers, and endeavour to move everyone in the direction of the required practice change through longer-term input and support.

Using supportive video analysis of sessions of Intensive Interaction can also be helpful in such a situation to assist in giving practitioners 'constructive, concise and informative feedback' (Barber, 2007, p.125). This can incorporate a structured 'Intensive Interaction reflection tool' (for an example see Barber, 2007, p.125) which outlines specific times for showing video for peer mentors to analyse and give feedback on. Williamson recommended a structure that initially required three points of 'warm' or affirmative feedback to be given, followed by up to three points of 'cool' or constructive feedback. Such a structured feedback process was highlighted as nurturing 'an increasingly sustainable culture of Intensive Interaction and valuable discourse among all staff members' (Barber, 2007, p.129) and would be a useful process for all practitioners to consider.

Supportive networking

Probably the best way to introduce and sustain Intensive Interaction is to do so with the support and encouragement of a wide group of sympathetic people who share the same perspective and goals, and understand the ups and downs of working in this way. Such a group of people can be mutually supportive. A supportive network can act as a sounding-board for people to talk through any difficulties associated with using Intensive Interaction and, equally importantly, they can also be people with whom to share achievements and successes. Access to a supportive network also allows people to seek out advice from others who may have encountered and worked through similar scenarios. This process of support should be genuinely mutual, with all the members of the network benefiting from the input of all the other members. It should be as much about giving support (which has its own beneficial effects) as about receiving it.

Such a network should also help to distribute any feelings of individual responsibility for the success, or otherwise, of introducing and supporting an Intensive Interaction intervention. This feeling of shared responsibility should not be underestimated, as feeling isolated and solely responsible for an Intensive Interaction intervention can become quite onerous.

The idea of a supportive community of Intensive Interactors also acknowledges the requirement that, at times outside of the actual interactive sessions or episodes, there can still be important work for practitioners to do. This might well require practitioners to spend time reflecting on their current practice, and to continue to develop their own knowledge of Intensive Interaction and their skills in practically applying the approach, and this is a process best achieved with the help and support of well-informed and encouraging peers. Such a supportive network looks very like a 'community of practice' described by educational theorists Lave and Wenger (1991), and indeed a community of practice (CoP) has been specifically defined as a group of people 'who share a concern, a set of problems, or a passion about a topic, and who deepen their understanding and knowledge of this area by interacting on an on-going basis' (Wenger, 1998, p.4). The establishment of Intensive Interaction Regional Support Groups now provides a forum for just this sort of sharing.

Induction and training issues

One issue that should, and we are sure will, be addressed in the future, is the requirement for an increase in the quantity and breadth of high quality learning resources available to Intensive Interaction advocates and practitioners. Although the central tenets and techniques of the approach have already been set out in the works of Nind and Hewett, a continuous stream of supportive and differentiated explanatory material can only help drive forward Intensive Interaction as an approach useful for an increasingly wide range of people from many different personal and professional backgrounds.

We also feel that the Intensive Interaction community will benefit from the arrival of a new generation of people who can carry this process forward, people who may have different skills and may use different ways of disseminating knowledge and supporting the practice of others, possibly using the latest technological advances.

New resource materials that are more discipline specific might prove useful to practitioners who are studying for more advanced qualifications such as teaching in special education, clinical psychology, speech and language therapy, specialist social work, occupational therapy and possibly even physiotherapy.

At present, some people who are studying to become clinical psychologists get training on Intensive Interaction and some do not. Provision of such training depends on there being a local practitioner with sufficient expertise and will to deliver the training. Leeds University, for example, runs a Doctorate in Clinical Psychology course and Graham provides the students with an introduction to Intensive Interaction. We hope that these are the beginnings of a virtuous cycle – that today's trainee clinical psychologists will take up the approach in greater numbers and so become (some of) the trainers of tomorrow.

Specific Intensive Interaction materials might also be usefully developed to address specific aspects of skill development – for example, 'induction' resources that help people who are new to working with people with severe or profound and multiple learning difficulties or autism. Such induction materials need to address what in some cases can be a complete lack of experience and knowledge about learning disability itself, as well as providing information on Intensive Interaction as a tool to communicate and engage such people in sociable activity.

Training at all levels (novice or expert practitioner, professional or non-professional) can only be enhanced through agreement about what a practitioner needs to be doing for their practice to be accurately labelled as 'Intensive Interaction'. Other therapies have checklists of component skills that can be used to assess whether a therapist is delivering the therapy competently. Development of a similar checklist for Intensive Interaction would likewise allow practitioners' competence to be assessed and could be a useful tool for developing practice through either self- or other-directed learning. There would also be benefits for research – applying the checklist to people delivering Intensive Interaction interventions would give more confidence in the fidelity of what they were offering (that is, researchers and research consumers would have greater confidence that what was being delivered was actually Intensive Interaction).

It could well be that the internet might also be harnessed to help develop and disseminate Intensive Interaction. Social networking sites are increasingly being used as a means for people to exchange ideas in areas of shared interest. Indeed the social networking site Facebook already hosts an Intensive Interaction Users site which is used to share ideas, seek answers to particular problems and post relevant information. Such a way of connecting with other like-minded people seems likely to expand as more and more people come to use such technology.

Valuing People Now (VPN)

According to the strategy document *Valuing People Now: 'Making it Happen for Everyone'* (DoH, 2009), the UK government's vision is that all people with learning disabilities 'are supported to become empowered citizens' (p.38). In this document, a follow-up to the original *Valuing People* document (DoH, 2001), no less than six Secretaries of State (with accompanying impressive photographs!) restate their '...commitment to leading change to transform people's lives and opportunities' (p.2). After further encouraging words from two Ministers of State and the National Director for Learning Disabilities, the document goes on to state explicitly that, for people with complex needs, where social inclusion is concerned:

> 1.6 Addressing the issues for people with complex needs is really about embedding the principles of personalization within all aspects of planning, commissioning and delivery of support services. It is also about recognizing that the very particular support needs of an individual will mean very individualized support packages, including systems for facilitating meaningful two-way communication. (DoH, 2009, p.37)

Page 38 of the document is then completely given over to an exposition of Intensive Interaction, with some historical background, comments on the strategies involved, and a brief passage on the possible beneficial outcomes. It goes on to state that people with learning disabilities should be enabled and supported to 'develop and use appropriate communication systems where people have little or no verbal communication' (p.39).

Such explicit advocacy in the government's strategy document is, we believe, of considerable importance in positioning Intensive Interaction as a mainstream approach that should be made available to everyone with a learning disability who might benefit. The existing, bottom-up and practitioner-led strategy of approach dissemination will need some consideration if we truly wish to achieve the level of training, support and supervision required to fulfil the government's vision successfully. How this comes about, and who takes on the bulk of the work will be interesting to observe, especially in a health and social care policy environment that is deliberately and increasingly configured to favour a 'marketplace' built around competition rather than collaboration between providers of goods and services.

Quality of Intensive Interaction, and how to support it into the future

As Intensive Interaction takes on a less elective and a more central role in '...facilitating meaningful two-way communication' (DoH, 2009, p.37) for people with a social or communicative impairment, the more there may be the potential for tension between the issues of the capacity to train and support carers, staff and concerned professionals, and the quality of any training and support that is given (or more likely purchased from 'specialist' providers). As Intensive Interaction becomes increasingly adopted by services and organizations, both in the UK and abroad, the currently available systems (and 'expert' individuals) that have so far played the leading role in disseminating Intensive Interaction will increasingly become stretched, and quite possibly new organizations will take up the opportunities to get involved in this (and possibly look to make a profit from it). This position, with a requirement for increased capacity, will undoubtedly challenge the previous 'bottom-up' or 'practitioner-led' method of dissemination and support. Planning how to manage such a change may well present some difficulties. The most pressing issue that will present itself will be the requirement of an increasing number of services and organizations wishing to explicitly promote, develop and supervise Intensive Interaction practice within their workforce. They may also wish to recruit experienced staff who can demonstrate some desired level of competence in their Intensive Interaction practice (see comments in Chapter 10, section on *Staff Selection* about how such competency might be measured).

Taken to its logical conclusion this argument could lead to a desire for a system of accreditation or certification to verify competence in Intensive Interaction practice. This would certainly be challenging for those of us who have already developed their Intensive Interaction practice before any thought was given to such a position. Any move to a more structured and formal system of practice certification would need a great deal of thought and open discussion, but it seems likely that this will happen in some form.

If there is to be a move to a more structured and formal dissemination and development strategy then the people who have already come to use Intensive Interaction, and have already succeeded in developing it within their own working or care environments, will somehow have to be included in such a process. Any system will need to make use of the talents and energy of those people who have already brought the approach so far, and they should be enabled to play a central role in the future dissemination and development of Intensive Interaction.

Structure – to be or not to be?

When we begin to compare the popularity and sustainability of approaches like Makaton (now so mainstream that it regularly features in *Something Special* on CBeebies TV), PECS (Picture Exchange Communication) and TEACCH (Treatment and Education of Autistic and Related Communication-Handicapped Children) within learning disability and/or autism services with the popularity and sustainability of Intensive Interaction, it would appear that Intensive Interaction is not so widely known of, and used less consistently. Those readers who are familiar with the training and structure of the organizations who promote the above mentioned approaches may recognize that their training structures are designed to ensure increasingly good practice and accountability. Employers know what their staff will achieve and have clear expectations of the responsibilities of the staff who have attended training. People attending the training know that the trainers have been accredited by the organization so they will be receiving 'what is on the tin'.

In comparison, Intensive Interaction has always been disseminated freely with no restrictions about who can or cannot use it. For the price of a copy of *Access to Communication* (Nind and Hewett, 1994) anyone could implement the approach. This has always been one of the beauties of Intensive Interaction and has resulted in a variety of professions implementing, supporting and promoting the approach.

However, when Intensive Interaction was first publicly aired in 1987 at the Westhill College Conference there was a general ethos of action research and open sharing of innovative practice. More recently there appears to be an ethos of packaging and selling innovative practice that is perhaps driven by the market economy in services where practitioners are encouraged to think about income generation alongside their day-to-day work. As a result of this, the question needs to be asked: Do organizations have more faith in something that they pay for, something that has structure, and something that has a system of accountability? A young friend of Cath's is fascinated by Intensive Interaction and so applied for a job as a teaching assistant in a special school where he has now worked for three years. In all six of his staff evaluations/supervisions he has requested Intensive Interaction training and is still waiting to have this provided. Yet PECS, TEACCH and Makaton, along with various other training opportunities, were available within the first year. We suspect this is not specific to this one school or organization. Established and structured approaches may possibly be easier to ring-fence in terms of funding as there is a large amount of predictability in training needs of staff.

Intensive Interaction training is still largely dependant on both the professional interests and confidence of members of local teams or visiting 'experts'. The dissemination of the approaches discussed above have benefited from de-centralized and local training opportunities – with built-in standards of practice and standards of training. However, decentralization of training opportunities for Intensive Interaction leads us to another potential problem. In the market-driven ethos that typifies services and organizations now, anyone could set themselves up as an Intensive Interaction trainer. But how do organizations know that what is being offered is actually Intensive Interaction? The approach as disseminated by Melanie Nind and Dave Hewett is a strategy to support development of skills over time and includes record keeping, reflection and evaluation, yet people who have attended courses sometimes talk about the approach as if it is just 'imitating' or 'having a brief chat' with someone. How would organizations know that the training offered would result in implementation of good quality Intensive Interaction?

The formation of an Intensive Interaction Institute happened because practitioners were pressing for some clarity and support. The first move towards establishing some support was the creation of Regional Support Groups. At an Intensive Interaction Practitioners weekend workshop in the autumn of 2008, the issue of introducing some structure and standards into the dissemination of the approach was discussed and many people attending thought that organizations would take Intensive Interaction more seriously if there was some predictability in the outcomes of training and some established support mechanisms. However, anybody beginning a programme of formal de-centralization of training and support would have to respect and value the people who have been using and teaching Intensive Interaction before this process could begin.

There are as yet many questions to be answered before any structure could be introduced into the dissemination of Intensive Interaction. Questions like:

- Is there a general agreement that what is widely known as Intensive Interaction reflects what was developed at Harperbury School?

- Would any potential structure contradict the free-flowing nature of Intensive Interaction?

- Who would organize any such structure and who would 'accredit' already existing practitioners and trainers?

- Who would accredit the accreditors?

- Who would finance the necessary work?

We believe that the Regional Support Groups will be instrumental in these ongoing discussions and in the gentle forming of a community of practitioners who can contribute to the exciting future of Intensive Interaction, especially so now that we have person-centred planning and a whole page in a government White Paper, *Valuing People Now* (DoH, 2009).

Accreditation of practitioners or coordinators

This issue of the possible accreditation of individuals who can demonstrate a level of competence in Intensive Interaction practice, or who engage in some structured programme of study on the approach, will need to be addressed with some care. As Intensive Interaction becomes more central to learning disability service provision, there will almost certainly be an increasing desire on the part of organizations and services to assess or demonstrate staff competences in this area. It is highly plausible that organizations will wish to identify potential staff members who are already competent and knowledgeable in Intensive Interaction. Ideally someone who can reliably demonstrate good Intensive Interaction practice should have an advantage over other staff members who cannot, as this should translate into improved quality of care for anyone with a social or communicative impairment.

However, there are two sides to this argument concerning the necessity, or even the desirability of making some kind of external judgements on the competences of individual Intensive Interaction practitioners. There are also far-reaching discussions to be had on the practical difficulty of enacting such a process. Those on one side of this argument will justifiably point out that Intensive Interaction is not something that can be easily measured, and that Intensive Interaction is supposed to be a 'naturalistic' approach that employs interactional skills that are common to all human beings. Advocates of such a position will equally contend that Intensive Interaction is something that should be an expression of a moral standpoint, a personal wish to work in such a person-centred way, rather than it being done to pass an examination, gain personal advancement or fulfil an organizational or even governmental policy directive.

However, from the other perspective, if services and organizations are to provide regular and high quality Intensive Interaction, other methods will have to be considered to meet and manage successfully what could be a vastly increasing demand for competent Intensive Interaction practitioners. The difficult thing is deciding how this can be done, and harder still, who should and could be entrusted to do this. Resolution of the difficult issues of certification and the authority to certificate will, we believe, be central to the next stage of Intensive Interaction development and dissemination.

Finally, where the approach might go next

One possible outcome of the future development of Intensive Interaction could be that there is some differentiation amongst the range of practitioners and advocates of the approach, leading to greater specialism within the Intensive Interaction community. We can conceptualize different forms of Intensive Interaction (such as educational, therapeutic and companionable) which may become increasingly distinct. Alongside this possible differentiation, Intensive Interaction may come to be seen to have a role in the support of a wider section of people within society. Indeed, to some extent this is already starting to happen as briefly described in the section in this chapter *Research evidence for the effectiveness of Intensive Interaction* where new developments have included the use of Intensive Interaction with a person with late stage dementia (Ellis and Astell, 2008).

Issues associated with competency are likely to become increasingly important. Being able to answer the question of 'what are the skills, knowledge and attitudes that need to be demonstrated to call somebody's practice "Intensive Interaction"?' will open the way for more robust research, targeted recruitment strategies, and accrediting practice.

As with all attempts to look too far into the future, however, trying to predict what is yet to come is a certain way to be proved wrong and look foolish. Unquestionably the future of Intensive Interaction belongs to those people who are now starting to use the approach in much greater numbers than previously. Those people who come next will undoubtedly build on the vital work that has already been done in providing people with a social or communicative impairment with a way to enjoy social interactivity. Intensive Interaction has also provided many people with a clear rationale and an accessible methodology that has truly transformed the way we work with, support and even perceive people who had previously seemed so separate from us.

Whatever comes next in the story of Intensive Interaction it will be fascinating to observe, and indeed to be a part of.

References

Achenbach, T.M., Howell, C.T., Aoki, M.F. and Rauh, V.A. (1993) 'Nine-year outcome of the Vermont Intervention Program for low birth weight infants.' *Pediatrics 91*, 45–55.

Ainsworth, M.D. (1967) *Infancy in Uganda: Infant Care and the Growth of Love.* Baltimore, MD: Johns Hopkins Press.

Ainsworth, M.D. and Wittig, B.A. (1969) 'Attachment and exploratory behaviour of one-year-olds in a strange situation.' In B.M. Foss (ed.) *Determinants of Infant Behaviour*, Vol. 4. London: Methuen.

Aitken, S. and Buultjens, M. (1992) *Vision for Doing.* Edingburgh: Moray House Publications.

Anderson, C.M. and Freeman, K.A. (2000) 'Positive behaviour support: Expanding the application of Applied Behavior Analysis.' *The Behavior Analyst 23*, 85–94.

Arthur, A.R. (2003) 'The emotional lives of people with a learning disability.' *British Journal of Learning Disabilities 31*, 25–30.

Bank-Mikklesen, N. (1980) Denmark. In R.J. Flynn and K.E. Nitsch (eds) *Normalisation, Social Integration and Community Services.* Austin, TX: Pro-Ed.

Barber, M. (2000) 'Skills, Rules, Knowledge and Three Mile Island. Accounting for failure to learn among individuals with profound and multiple learning disabilities.' Unpublished PhD Thesis, Manchester Metropolitan University, accessed on 04.01.2010 at www.drmarkbarber.co.uk/theteacherwhomistook.pdf.

Barber, M (2007) 'Imitation, interaction and dialogue using Intensive Interaction: Tea party rules.' *Support for Learning 22*, 3, 124–130.

Barkham, M., Leach, C., Shapiro, D., Hardy, G., Lucock, M. and Rees, A. (2005) 'Rewiring efficacy studies to increase their relevance to routine practice.' *Mental Health and Learning Disabilities Research and Practice 3*, 1, 53–58.

Baylis, N.V.K. (2005) *Learning from Wonderful Lives.* Cambridge: Cambridge Well-Being Books Ltd.

Beck, A.T. (1963) 'Thinking and depression.' *Archives of General Psychiatry 9*, 324–333.

Bender, M. (1993) 'The unoffered chair: The history of therapeutic disdain towards people with a learning difficulty.' *Clinical Psychology Forum 54*, 7–12.

Berne, E. (1964) *Games People Play. The psychology of human relationships.* Reading: Penguin Books.

Bicknell, J. (1983) 'The psychopathology of handicap.' *British Journal of Medical Psychology 56*, 167–168.

BILD, Intensive Interaction Factsheet, accessed on 26.09.2006 at www.bild.org.uk/docs/05faqs/ii.doc

Bohart, A.C. (1993) 'Experiencing: The basis of psychotherapy.' *Journal of Psychotherapy Integration 3*, 1, 51–67.

Bowlby, J. (1953) *Child Care and the Growth of Love*. London and Tonbridge: Penguin Books.

Bowlby, J. (1988) *A Secure Base: Clinical Implications of Attachment Theory*. London: Routledge.

Brady, A. and Raines, D. (2009) 'Dynamic hierarchies: A control system paradigm for exposure therapy.' *The Cognitive Behaviour Therapist 2*, 51–62.

Bredo, E. (1999) 'Reconstructing educational psychology.' In P. Murphy (ed.) *Learners, Learning and Assessment*. London: Paul Chapman Publishing.

Brown, E. (1996) *Religious Education for All*. London: David Fulton.

Brown, G.W. and Harris, T. (1978) *Social Origins of Depression: A Study of Psychiatric Disorder in Women*. London: Tavistock.

Bruner, J.S. (1975) 'The ontogenesis of speech acts.' *Journal of Child Language 2*, 1–40.

Bruner, J.S. (1999a) 'Culture, mind and education.' In B. Moon and P. Murphy (eds) *Curriculum in Context*. London: Chapman Publishing.

Bruner, J.S. (1999b) 'Folk pedagogies.' In J. Leach and B. Moon (eds) *Learners and Pedagogy*. London: Paul Chapman Publishing.

Buchanan, D., Claydon, T. and Doyle, M. (1999) 'Organisation development and change: The legacy of the nineties.' In *No Going Back: A Review of the Literature on Sustaining Strategic Change*. Leicester: NHS Modernisation Agency.

Caldwell, P. (1996) *Getting in Touch: Ways of Working with People with Severe Learning Disabilities and Extensive Support Needs*. Brighton: Pavilion Publishing, Joseph Rowntree Foundation.

Caldwell, P. (2002) *Learning the Language*. Brighton: Pavilion Publishing. (Video)

Caldwell, P. (2006) *Finding You, Finding Me*. London: Jessica Kingsley Publishers.

Cameron, L. and Bell, D. (2001) 'Enhanced interaction training.' *Working with People who have a Learning Disability 18*, 3, 8–15.

Carr, E.G. and Durand, V.M. (1985) 'Reducing behavior problems through functional communication training.' *Journal of Applied Behavior Analysis 18*, 111–126.

Coia, P. and Handley, A.J. (2008) 'Developing relationships with people with profound disabilities through intensive interaction.' In S. Zeedyk (ed.) *Promoting Social Interaction for Individuals with Communicative Impairments*. London: Jessica Kingsley Publishers.

Crabbe, M. and Firth, G. (2007) 'The Intensive Interaction Research Project... and Beyond.' *College of Speech and Language Therapists Bulletin 664*. 12–13.

Csíkszentmihályi, M. (1990) *Flow: The Psychology of Optimal Experience*. New York: Harper and Row.

Culham, A. (2004) 'Getting in touch with our feminine sides? Men's difficulties and concerns with Intensive Interaction.' *British Journal of Special Education 31*, 2, 81–88.

Davis, C., Zeedyk, M., Wallis, S., Betts, N. and Parry, S. (2008) 'Using imitation to establish chanels of communication with institutionalised children in Romania: Bridging the gap.' In S.M. Zeedyk (ed.) *Promoting Social Interaction for Individuals with Communicative Impairments*. London: Jessica Kingsley Publishers.

de Boer, B. (2005) 'Infant directed speech and the evolution of language.' In Tallerman, M. (ed.) *Evolutionary Prerequisites for Language*. Oxford: Oxford University Press.

Department of Health (2001) *Valuing People: A New Strategy for Learning Disability for the 21st Century*. London: HMSO.

Department of Health (2009) *Valuing People Now: 'Making it Happen for Everyone.'* London: HMSO.

Department of Health and Home Office (2000) *No Secrets: Guidance on developing and implementing multi-agency policies and procedures to protect vulnerable adults from abuse*. London: TSO (The Stationery Office).

Elgie, S. and Maguire, N. (2001) 'Intensive interaction with a woman with multiple and profound disabilities: A case study.' *Tizard Learning Disability Review 6*, 3, 18–24.

Ellis, M. and Astell, A. (2008) 'A new approach to communicating with people with advanced dementia: A case study of adaptive interaction.' In M.S. Zeedyk (ed.) *Promoting Social Interaction for Individuals with Communicative Impairments: 'Making Contact'*. London: Jessica Kingsley Publishers.

Emerson, E., Cummings, R., Barrett, S., Hughes, H., McCool, C. and Toogood, A. (1988) Challenging behaviour and community services: 2. Who are the people who challenge services? *Mental Handicap 16*, 16–19.

Emerson, E. and Hatton, C. (1994) *Moving Out: Relocation from Hospital to Community*. London: TSO (The Stationery Office).

Ephraim, G. (1982) 'Developmental Process in mental handicap: A Generative Structure Approach.' Unpublished PhD Thesis, Brunel University.

Ephraim, G. (1986) *A Brief Introduction to Augmented Mothering*. London: Playtrack/Save the Children (unpublished manuscript).

Ephraim, G. (1998) 'Exotic communication, conversations, and scripts – or tales of the pained, the unheard and the unloved.' In D. Hewett (ed.) *Challenging Behaviour. Principles and Practice.* London: David Fulton.

Field, T.M. (1977) 'Effects of early separation, interactive deficits, and experimental manipulations on infant–mother face-to-face interaction.' *Child Development 48*, 3, 763–771.

Firth, G. (2008) 'A dual aspect process model of Intensive Interaction.' *British Journal of Learning Disabilities 37*, 43–49.

Fraiberg, S. (1975) 'The development of human attachments in infants blind from birth.' *Merrill-Palmer Quarterly 21*, 315–334.

Fuller, P.R. (1949) 'Operant conditioning of a vegetative human organism.' *American Journal of Psychology 62*, 587–590.

Gardner, H. (1993) *Frames of Mind: The Theory of Multiple Intelligences.* New York: Basic Books.

Georgiades, N. and Phillimore, L. (1969) 'The Myth of the Hero-Innovator and Alternative Strategies for Organisational Change.' Reprinted in P. Easen (1985) *Making School Centred INSET Work.* London: Routledge.

Glenn, S. (1987) 'Interactive Approaches to Working with Children with Profound and Multiple Learning Difficulties.' In B. Smith (ed.) *Interactive Approaches to the Education of Children with Severe Learning Difficulties.* Birmingham: Westhill College.

Goffman, E. (1981) *Forms of Talk.* Oxford: Blackwell.

Goleman, D. (1995) *Emotional Intelligence: Why it can Matter More than IQ.* New York: Bantam Books.

Goren, C.C., Sarty, M. and Wu, P.Y.K. (1975) 'Visual following and pattern discrimination of face-like stimuli by newborn infants.' *Pediatrics 56*, 544–549.

Granlund, M., Ternby, J., and Olsson, C. (1992) 'Creating communication opportunities through a combined in-service training and supervision package.' *European Journal of Special Needs Education 7*, 3, 229–252.

Hagen, S. (1997) *Buddhism Plain and Simple.* London: Penguin.

Hall, L. and Lloyd, S. (1993) *Surviving Child Sexual Abuse: A Handbook for Helping Women Challenge their Past.* London: Routledge.

Hanks, W. (1991) Introduction. In J. Lave and E. Wenger (eds) *Legitimate Peripheral Participation.* Cambridge: Cambridge University Press.

Harris, R. (2006) *Integrationist Notes and Papers 2003–2005.* Crediton: Tree Tongue.

Harris, R. (2008) *Mindboggling: Preliminaries to a Science of the Mind.* Luton: Pantaneto Press.

Hastings, R.P. and Brown, T. (2002) 'Coping strategies and the impact of challenging behaviours on special educators' burnout.' *Mental Retardation 40*, 2, 148–156.

Hatton, C., Emerson, E., Robertson, J., Henderson, D. and Cooper, J. (1995) *An Evaluation of the Quality and Costs of Services for Adults with Severe Learning Disabilities and Sensory Impairments.* Manchester: Hester Adrian Research Centre.

Heider, F. (1958) *The Psychology of Interpersonal Relations.* New York: Wiley.

Hewett, D. (1994) 'Understanding and writing a methodology of Intensive Interaction – teaching pre-speech communication abilities to learners with severe learning difficulties: A naturalistic inquiry using qualitative evaluation methods.' PhD Thesis, Cambridge Institute of Education.

Hewett, D. (1996) 'How to start doing Intensive Interaction.' In M. Collis and P. Lacey (eds) *Interactive Approaches to Teaching: A Framework for Inset.* London: David Fulton.

Hewett, D. (ed.) (1998) *Challenging Behaviour: Principles and Practice.* London: David Fulton Publishers.

Hewett, D. (2007) 'Do touch: Physical contact and people who have severe, profound and multiple learning difficulties.' *Support for Learning 22*, 3, 116.

Hewett, D. and Nind, M. (1998) 'Commentary One: Practice and progress.' In D. Hewett and M. Nind (eds) *Interaction in Action, Reflections on the Use of Intensive Interaction.* London: David Fulton.

HM Government (1970) *The Education (Handicapped Children) Act 1970.* London: HMSO.

Irvine, C. (1998) 'Addressing the Needs of Adults with Profound and Multiple Learning Disabilities in Social Services Provision.' In M. Nind and D. Hewett (eds) *Interaction in Action.* London: David Fulton.

Irvine, C. (2001) 'Interaction reaction: Keeping Intensive Interaction going'. *PMLD Link 39*, 13–15.

Iwata, B.A., Dorsey, M.F., Slifer, K.J. Bauman, K.E. and Richman, G.S. (1994) 'Toward a functional analysis of self-injury.' *Journal of Applied Behavior Analysis 27*, 197–209 (Reprinted from *Analysis and Intervention in Developmental Disabilities 2*, 3–20, 1982).

Johnson, M.H., Dziurawiec, S., Ellis, H.D. and Morton, J. (1991) Newborns' preferential tracking of faces and its subsequent decline. *Cognition 40*, 1–20.

Johnson, M.H. and Morton, J. (1991) *Biology and Cognitive Development: The Case of Face Recognition.* Oxford: Blackwell.

Jones, R.S.P., Miller, B., Williams, H. and Goldthorp, J. (1997) 'Theoretical and practical issues in cognitive-behavioural approaches for people with learning disabilities.' In B.S. Kroese, D. Dagnan and K. Loumidis (eds) *Cognitive-Behaviour Therapy for People with Learning Disabilities.* London and New York: Routledge.

Kabat-Zinn, J., Massion, A.O., Kristeller, J., Peterson, L.G., Fletcher, K., Pbert, L., Linderking, W. and Santorelli, S.F. (1992) 'Effectiveness of a meditation-based stress reduction program in the treatment of anxiety disorders.' *American Journal of Psychiatry 149,* 936–943.

Kellett, M. (2000) 'Sam's story: Evaluating Intensive Interaction in terms of its effect on the social and communicative ability of a young child with severe learning difficulties.' *Support for Learning 15,* 4, 165–171.

Kellett, M. (2003) 'Jacob's journey: Developing sociability and communication in a young boy with severe and complex learning disabilities using the Intensive Interaction teaching approach.' *Journal of Research in Special Educational Needs 3,* 1, 18–24.

Kellett, M. (2004) 'Intensive Interaction in the inclusive classroom: Using interactive pedagogy to connect with students who are hardest to reach.' *Westminster Studies in Education 27,* 175–188.

Kellett, M. (2005) 'Catherine's legacy: Social communication development for individuals with profound learning difficulties and fragile life expectancies.' *British Journal of Special Education 32,* 3, 116–121.

Kennedy, A. (2001) 'Intensive Interaction.' *Learning Disability Practice 4,* 3, 14–15.

Kirschenbaum, H. and Henderson, V.L. (eds) (1989) *The Carl Rogers Reader.* London: Constable.

Koegel, L.K., Koegel, R.L. and Dunlap, G. (1996) *Positive Behavioral Support: Including People with Difficult Behavior in the Community.* Baltimore, MD: Paul H. Brookes.

Kuyken, W., Padesky, C.A. and Dudley, R. (2009) *Collaborative Case Conceptualisation.* New York: Guilford Press.

Lave, J. and Wenger, E. (1991) *Situated Learning: Legitimate Peripheral Participation.* Cambridge: Cambridge University Press.

Lave, J. and Wenger E. (1999) 'Learning and pedagogy in communities of practice.' In J. Leach and B. Moon (eds) *Learners and Pedagogy.* London: Paul Chapman Publishing.

Leaning, B. and Watson, T. (2006) 'From the inside looking out – an Intensive Interaction group for people with profound and multiple learning disabilities.' *British Journal of Learning Disabilities 34,* 103–109.

Leeds Partnerships NHS Foundation Trust (2007) *Strengths and Needs Analysis and Planning.* Leeds: NHS.

Lovell, D., Jones, S. and Ephraim, G. (1998) 'The effect of Intensive Interaction on the sociability of a man with severe intellectual disabilities.' *International Journal of Practical Approaches to Disability 22,* 2/3, 3–8.

MacDonald, J. (2003) 'Communication staircase.' Leeds PFT Training Course Handout.

Main, M., Kaplan, N. and Cassidy, J. (1985) 'Security in infancy, childhood and adulthood: A move to the level of representation.' In I. Bretherton and E. Waters (eds) *Growing Points in Attachment: Theory and Research.* Monographs for the Society of Research in Child Development Serial 209: 66–104. Chicago, IL: University of Chicago Press.

Maslow, A.H. (1943) 'A theory of human motivation.' *Psychological Review 50,* 4, 370–396.

McInnes, J.M. and Treffry, J.A. (1982) *Deaf-Blind Infants and Children.* Toronto: University of Toronto Press.

McConkey, R. (1981) 'Education without understanding?' *Special Education: Forward Trends 8,* 3, 8–10.

McLeod, J. (1996) 'The humanistic paradigm.' In R. Woolfe and W. Dryden (eds) *Handbook of Counselling Psychology.* London: Sage, pp. 133–155.

Merry, T. (2002) *Learning and Being in Person-Centred Counselling* (Second edition). Ross-on-Wye: PCCS Books.

Money, D. and Thurman, S. (1994) 'Talkabout communication.' *College of Speech and Language Therapists Bulletin 504,* 12–13.

NHS Modernisation Agency (2003) *No Going Back: A Review of the Literature on Sustaining Strategic Change,* accessed at www.modern.nhs.uk/researchinto practice.

Nind, M. and Hewett, D. (1988) 'Interaction as curriculum.' *British Journal of Special Education 15,* 2, 55–57.

Nind, M. and Hewett, D. (1994/2005) *'Access to Communication: Developing the Basics of Communication in People with Severe Learning Disabilities Through Intensive Interaction.'* London: David Fulton.

Nind, M. (1993) 'Access to Communication: Efficacy of Intensive Interaction Teaching for people with severe developmental disabilities who demonstrate ritualistic behaviours.' PhD Thesis, Cambridge Institute of Education.

Nind, M. (1996) 'Efficacy of Intensive Interaction: Developing sociability and communication in people with severe and complex learning difficulties using an approach based on caregiver–infant interaction.' *European Journal of Special Educational Needs 11,* 1, 48–66.

Nind, M. (1997) *Intensive Interaction,* a multi-disciplinary training day for Oxfordshire Learning Disability NHS Trust.

Nind, M. and Hewett, D. (2001) *A Practical Guide to Intensive Interaction*. Kidderminster: British Institute of Learning Disabilities.

Nirje, B. (1969) 'The normalisation principle and its human management implications.' In R. Kugel and W. Wolfensberger (eds) *Changing Patterns in Residential Services for the Mentally Retarded*. Washington, DC: Presidential Committee on Mental Retardation.

Nirje, B. (1980) 'The Normalisation principle.' In R. Flynn and K. Nitsch (eds) *Normalisation, Integration and Community Service*. Baltimore, MD: UPP.

O'Brien, J. (1980) 'The principle of normalization: A foundation for effective services.' In J.F. Gardner, L. Long, R. Nichols and D.M. Lagulli (eds) *Program Issues in Developmental Disabilities: A Resource Manual for Surveyors and Reviewers*. Baltimore, MD: Paul H. Brookes.

O'Brien, J. (1987) 'A guide to personal futures planning.' In B. Wilcox and G.T. Bellamy (eds) *The Activities Catalog: An Alternative Curriculum for Youth and Adolescents with Severe Disabilities*. Baltimore, MD: Paul H. Brookes.

O'Connor, H. (2001) 'Will we grow out of it? A psychotherapy group for people with learning disabilities.' *Psychodynamic Counselling 7*, 3, 297–314.

Ouvry, C. (1991) *Strategies to Meet the Needs of People with Profound and Multiple Learning Disabilities*. School of Education, The University of Birmingham in association with The British Institute of Learning Disabilities.

Parke, R.D. and Tinsley, B.J. (1987) 'Family interaction in infancy.' In J.D. Osofsky (ed.) *Handbook of Infant Development* (Second edition). New York: John Wiley, pp. 579–641.

Perrin, B. and Nirje, B. (1985) 'Setting the record straight: A critique of some frequent misconceptions of the normalisation principle.' *Australian and New Zealand Journal of Developmental Disabilities 11*, 69–74.

Piaget, J. (1955) *Genetic Epistemology, a series of lectures delivered by Piaget at Columbia University*. Irvington, NY: Columbia University Press.

PMLD Network (2008) *PMLD Network Response to Valuing People Now*, accessed on 18.11.2009 at www.mencap.org.uk/document.asp?id=2396

Rogers, C.R. (1957) 'The necessary and sufficient conditions of therapeutic personality change.' *Journal of Consulting Psychology 21*, 2, 95–103.

Rogoff, B. (1990) *Apprenticeship in Thinking: Cognitive Development in Social Context*. Oxford: OUP.

Rogoff, B. (1999) 'Cognitive development through social interaction: Vygotsky and Piaget.' In P. Murphy (ed.) *Learners, Learning and Assessment*. London: Paul Chapman Publishing.

Roth, W-M. (1999) 'Authentic School Science: Intellectual traditions.' In R. McCormick and C. Paechter (eds) *Learning and Knowledge*. London: Paul Chapman Publishing.

Rotter, J.B. (1954) *Social Learning and Clinical Psychology*. New York: Prentice-Hall.

Rousseau, J.J. (1762a) *Émile: or, On Education* (original publication – London: Dent).

Rousseau, J.J. (1762b) *The Social Contract, or Principles of Political Right* (original publication – London: Dent).

Royal College of Psychiatrists, British Psychological Society and Royal College of Speech and Language Therapists (2007) *Challenging Behaviour: A Unified Approach*. Clinical and service guidelines for supporting people with learning disabilities who are at risk of receiving abusive or restrictive practices. London: British Psychological Society.

Sacks, H. (1992) *Lectures on Conversation, Volumes I and II*. Edited by G. Jefferson with an Introduction by E.A. Schegloff. Oxford: Blackwell.

Salovey, P. and Mayer, J.D. (1990) 'Emotional intelligence.' *Imagination, Cognition, and Personality 9*, 185–211.

Samuel, J. and Maggs, J. (1998) 'Introducing intensive interaction for people with profound learning disabilities living in small staffed houses in the community.' In D. Hewett and M. Nind (eds) *Interaction in Action, Reflections on the Use of Intensive Interaction*. London: David Fulton.

Samuel, J., Nind, M., Volans, A. and Scriven, I. (2008) 'An evaluation of Intensive Interaction in community living settings for adults with profound intellectual disabilities.' *Journal of Intellectual Disabilities 12*, 111–126.

Schwartz, B. (1989) *Psychology of Learning and Behavior* (Third edition). New York and London: W.W. Norton.

Scottish Executive (2000) *The Same as You? A review of services for people with learning disabilities*. Edinburgh: Scottish Executive.

Seligman, M.E.P. (1975) *Helplessness: On Depression, Development, and Death*. San Francisco: W.H. Freeman.

Seligman, M.E.P. (1998) *Learned Optimism*. New York: Free Press.

Shainberg, D. (1993) 'Teaching therapists how to be with their clients.' In J. Welwood (ed.) *Awakening the Heart: East/West Approaches to Psychotherapy and the Healing Relationship*. Boston, MA: Shambhala Publications.

Shannon, C. and Weaver, W. (1949) *A Mathematical Theory of Communication*. Urbana, IL: University of Illinois Press.

Sharrock, R., Day, A., Qazi, F. and Brewin, C. (1990) 'Explanations by professional care staff. Optimism and helping behaviour: An application of attribution theory.' *Psychological Medicine 20*, 849–855.

Sinason, V. (1992) *Mental Handicap and the Human Condition: New Approaches from the Tavistock.* London: Free
Association Books.

Snow, C.E. (1972) 'Mothers' speech to children learning language.' *Child Development 43*, 549–565.

Sroufe, L.A. (1985) 'Attachment-classification from the perspective of infant–caregiver relationships and infant
temperament.' *Child Development 56*, 1–14.

Stern, D.N. (2000) *The Interpersonal World of the Infant.* A view from psychoanalysis and developmental psychology. New York: Basic Books.

Stevens, M. (1968) *Observe then Teach: An Observational Approach to Teaching Mentally Handicapped Children.* London:
Edward Arnold.

Stone, J. (1996) *Developmentalism: An Obscure but Pervasive Restriction on Educational Improvement.* East Tennessee
State University, accessed on 17.11.2009 at htpp://epaa.asu.edu/epaa/v4n8.html

Sweeney, C. and Sanderson, M. (2002) *BILD Factsheet – Person-Centred Planning.* Kidderminster: BILD.

Thorndike, E.L. (1920) 'Intelligence and its uses.' *Harper's Magazine 140*, 227–235

Trevarthen, C. (1977) 'Descriptive analyses of infant communicative behaviour.' In H.R. Schaffer (ed.) *Studies in
Mother–Infant Interaction.* New York: Academic Press.

Turk, J. and Brown, H. (1993) 'The sexual abuse of adults with learning disabilities: Results of a two year inci-
dence survey.' *Mental Handicap Research 6*, 193–216.

von Glasersfeld, E. (1996) 'Radical Constructivism: A way of knowing and learning.' In *Studies in Mathematics
Education Series 6.* London: Falmer Press.

Vygotsky, L.S. (1978) *Mind in Society: The Development of Higher Psychological Processes.* Cambridge, MA: Harvard
University Press.

Ware, J. (1996) *Creating a Responsive Environment for People with Profound and Multiple Learning Disabilities.* London:
David Fulton.

Ware, J. (2003) 'Communication.' *Eye Contact 37*, Autumn.

Wason, P.C. (1968) 'Reasoning about a rule.' *Quarterly Journal of Experimental Psychology 20*, 273–281.

Watson, J. and Fisher, A. (1997) 'Evaluating the effectiveness of Intensive Interaction: Teaching with pupils with
profound and complex learning disabilities.' *British Journal of Special Education 24*, 2, 80–87.

Watson, J. and Knight, C. (1991) 'An evaluation of intensive interactive teaching with pupils with very severe
learning difficulties.' *Child Language Teaching and Therapy 7*, 3, 310–25.

Wechsler, D. (1940) Non-intellective factors in general intelligence. *Psychological Bulletin 37*, 444–445.

Wechsler, D. (1949) *Manual for the Wechsler Intelligence Scale for Children.* New York: The Psychological
Corporation.

Wechsler, D. (1955) *Manual for the Wechsler Adult Intelligence Scale.* New York: The Psychological Corporation.

Wenger, E. (1998) *Communities of Practice: Learning, Meaning, and Identity.* Cambridge: Cambridge University
Press.

Whittington, A. and Burns, B. (2005) 'The dilemmas of residential care staff working with the challenging behaviour of people with learning disabilities.' *The British Journal of Clinical Psychology 44*, 59–76.

Williams, C.D. (1959) 'The elimination of tantrum behaviour by extinction procedures.' *Journal of Abnormal and
Social Psychology 59*, 269.

Williamson, J. (2006) Reflective tool for Intensive Interaction. unpublished document, Red Hill Special School,
Brisbane, Australia. In Barber, M. (2007) 'Imitation, interaction and dialogue using Intensive Interaction:
Tea party rules.' *Support for Learning 22*, 3, 124–130.

Wolf, M.M., Risley, T. and Mees, H. (1964) 'Application of operant conditioning procedures to the behaviour
problems of an autistic child.' *Behavior Research and Therapy 1*, 305–312.

Wolfensberger, W. (1972) *The Principle of Normalisation in Human Services.* Toronto: National Institute on Mental
Retardation.

Wolfensberger, W. (1983) 'Social Role Valorisation: A proposed new term for the principle of normalisation.'
Mental Retardation 21, 234–239.

Zeedyk, M.S. (2008) 'Introduction: Bridging a spectrum of communicative impairments.' In S.M. Zeedyk
(ed.) *Promoting Social Interaction for Individuals with Communicative Impairments.* London: Jessica Kingsley
Publishers.

Zeedyk, M.S., Davies, C.E., Parry, S., and Caldwell, P. (2009) 'Fostering social engagement in Romanian children
with communicative impairments: The experiences of newly trained practitioners of Intensive Interaction.'
British Journal of Learning Disabilities 37, 186–196.

Further Reading

Books

Bowlby, J. (1998) *A Secure Base. Clinical Applications of Attachment Theory.* London: Routledge. A collection of lectures given by John Bowlby – a good introduction to the area of attachment theory, research and therapy.

Geddes, H. (2006) *Attachment in the Classroom. The Links Between Children's Early Experience, Emotional Well-Being and Performance in School.* Bath: Worth Publishing. A really practical book about applying attachment theory to understanding children in educational setting – the insights are also applicable to adults in other contexts.

Kabat-Zinn, J., Segal, Z.V.J., Williams, M.G., Teasdale, J.D. (2002) *Mindfulness-Based Cognitive Therapy for Depression: A New Approach to Preventing Relapse.* New York: Guilford Press.

Leeds Partnerships NHS Foundation Trust (2009) *A Framework for Recognising Attainment in Intensive Interaction,* Leeds, NHS.

Merry, T. (2002) *Learning and Being in Person-Centred Counselling* (Second edition). Ross-on-Wye: PCCS Books. An accessible, engaging and stimulating book about person-centred therapy.

Sinason, V. (1992) *Mental Handicap and the Human Condition: New Approaches from the Tavistock.* London: Free Association Books. A classic book, written from a psychoanalytic perspective, which gives a profound insight into the emotional lives of people with a learning disability and which we have kept coming back to over the years.

Ware, J. (1996) *Creating a Responsive Environment for People with Profound and Multiple Learning Disabilities.* London: David Fulton. A really useful and comprehensive book for anyone who wants to enhance the social environment for service users.

Woolfe, R. and Dryden, W. (eds) (1996) *Handbook of Counselling Psychology.* London: Sage. A really comprehensive and accessible book that covers many psychotherapeutic paradigms.

Research papers

Child participants

Some of the most informative and influential research papers with child participants are as follows:

Kellett, M. (2000) 'Sam's story: Evaluating Intensive Interaction in terms of its effect on the social and communicative ability of a young child with severe learning difficulties.' *Support for Learning 15*, 4, 165–171.

Kellett, M. (2005) 'Catherine's legacy: Social communication development for individuals with profound learning difficulties and fragile life expectancies.' *British Journal of Special Education 32*, 3, 116–121.

Watson, J. and Fisher, A. (1997) 'Evaluating the effectiveness of Intensive Interaction: Teaching with pupils with profound and complex learning disabilities.' *British Journal of Special Education 24*, 2, 80–87.

Watson, J. and Knight, C. (1991) 'An evaluation of intensive interactive teaching with pupils with very severe learning difficulties.' *Child Language Teaching and Therapy 7*, 3, 310–325.

Adult participants

Some of the most informative and influential research papers with adult participants are as follows:

Elgie, S. and Maguire, N. (2001) 'Intensive Interaction with a Woman with Multiple and Profound Disabilities: A case study.' *Tizard Learning Disability Review 6*, 3, 18–24.

Leaning, B. and Watson, T. (2006) 'From the inside looking out – an Intensive Interaction group for people with profound and multiple learning disabilities.' *British Journal of Learning Disabilities 34*, 103–109.

Lovell, D., Jones, S. and Ephraim, G. (1998) 'The effect of Intensive Interaction on the sociability of a man with severe intellectual disabilities.' *International Journal of Practical Approaches to Disability 22*, 2/3, 3–8.

Nind, M. (1996) 'Efficacy of Intensive Interaction: Developing sociability and communication in people with severe and complex learning difficulties using an approach based on caregiver–infant interaction.' *European Journal of Special Educational Needs 11*, 1, 48–66.

Samuel, J., Nind, M., Volans, A. and Scriven, I. (2008) 'An evaluation of Intensive Interaction in community living settings for adults with profound intellectual disabilities.' *Journal of Intellectual Disabilities 12*, 111–126.

Wolfensberger, W. (1983) 'Social Role Valorisation: A proposed new term for the principle of normalisation.' *Mental Retardation 21*, 234–239.

Significant position papers

Without including the early ground-breaking papers of Hewett and Nind that set out the theoretical rationale of the approach, some of the most interesting or significant position papers include the following:

Barber, M. (2007) Imitation, interaction and dialogue using Intensive Interaction: Tea party rules. *Support for Learning 22*, 3, 124–130.

Firth, G. (2008) 'A dual aspect process model of Intensive Interaction.' *British Journal of Learning Disabilities 37*, 43–49.

Irvine, C. (2001) 'On the floor and playing…'. *Royal College of Speech and Language Therapy Bulletin*, November, 9–11.

Kennedy, A. (2001) 'Intensive Interaction.' *Learning Disability Practice 4*, 3, 14–15.

Nind, M. (2000) 'Teachers' understanding of interactive approaches in special education.' *International Journal of Disability, Development and Education 47*, 2, 184–199.

Nind, M. and Powell, S. (2000) 'Intensive Interaction and autism: Some theoretical concerns.' *Children and Society 14*, 2, 98–109.

Nind, M. and Thomas, G. (2005) 'Reinstating the value of teachers' tacit knowledge for the benefit of learners: Using 'Intensive Interaction'. *Journal of Research in Special Educational Needs 5*, 3, 97–100.

Samuel, J. (2001) 'Intensive Interaction.' *Clinical Psychology Forum 148*, 22–25.

Useful websites

BILD, *Intensive Interaction Factsheet*
www.bild.org.uk/docs/05faqs/ii.doc

Changing Places
www.changing-places.org

Integrationists
www.integrationists.com

Makaton
www.makaton.org

National Autistic Society
www.nas.org.uk

PECS
www.pecs.org.uk

Qualifications and Curriculum Development Agency, General guidelines: Recognising progress and achievement
www.qcda.gov.uk/qca_1834.aspx

Qualifications and Curriculum Development Agency, learning difficulties
www.qcda.gov.uk

RNIB Eye Contact Magazine Issue 37 – Communication
www.onlineshop.rnib.org.uk/display_item.asp?n=11&c=462&sc=7&id=566&it=2&l=3

Subject

Index

Author Index